THE WORKS

Of the REVEREND

WILLIAM LAW, M.A.,

Sometime Fellow of *Emmanuel* College, *Cambridge*.

In Nine Volumes.

Volume VI.

CONTAINING

I. An Earnest and Serious Answer to Dr. TRAPP'S Discourse of the Folly, Sin, and Danger of being Righteous over-much.

II. An Appeal to all that doubt, or disbelieve the Truths of the Gospel.

Wipf & Stock
PUBLISHERS
Eugene, Oregon

Wipf and Stock Publishers
199 West 8th Avenue, Suite 3
Eugene, Oregon 97401

An Earnest and Serious Answer to Dr. Trapp's Discourse; An Appeal to all who
Doubt the Truths of the Gospel, Volume 6
By Law, William
ISBN: 1-57910-620-X
Publication date 3/12/2001
Previously published by G. Moreton, Setley, 1892

AN EARNEST AND SERIOUS ANSWER

TO

Dr. TRAPP'S DISCOURSE

OF THE

FOLLY, SIN AND DANGER

OF BEING

RIGHTEOUS OVER-MUCH.

By *WILLIAM LAW*, M.A.

An Earnest and Serious ANSWER TO Dr. *Trapp's* Discourse, &c.

MIGHT I follow the *Bent* of my own Mind, my *Pen*, such as it is, should be wholly employed in setting forth the infinite Love of God to Mankind in Christ Jesus, and in endeavouring to draw all Men to the Belief and Acknowledgment of it. This *one great Mercy* of God, which makes the *one only* Happiness of all Mankind, so justly deserves all our Thoughts and Meditations, so highly enlightens, and improves every Mind that is attentive to it, so removes all the Evils of this present World, so sweetens every State of Life, so inflames the Heart with the Love of every Divine and human Virtue, that he is no small Loser, whose Mind is, either by *Writing* or *Reading*, detained from the View and Contemplation of it.

When this Mystery of Divine Love was first manifested to the World, it produced its proper Effects, it put an End to all *Selfishness* and *Division*; for *all that believed were of one heart, and one spirit, and had all things common.** And indeed under the real Influence, and full Belief of this great Mystery of Divine Love, there seems to be no Room left for anything else amongst Christians, but Returns of Love to God, and Flowings out of Love towards one another.

But now it is so difficult to enter into Controversy without being, or at least *seeming* in some Degree unkind to the Person that one opposes, that it is with great Reluctance that I have entered upon my present Undertaking; having nothing more deeply riveted in my Heart, than an universal Love and Kindness for all Mankind, and more especially for those whom God has called to be my Fellow-Labourers in promoting the Salvation of Mankind. But however unwilling, yet I find myself obliged

---

* Acts ii.

to consider, and lay open many grievous Faults in the Doctor's Discourse; and to show to all Christians, that the dearest Interests of their Souls are much endangered by it.

And this I must do with great Plainness and Sincerity, in the Love of Truth, and under the Direction of Charity, saying nothing in the Spirit of an *Adversary*, sparing nothing through *Respect of Persons*, sacrificing nothing to the *Taste* or *Temper* of the World, but setting forth every Thing in that naked Light, in which the Spirit of God represents it to my own Mind.

The Doctor undertakes to stir up, and alarm Mankind with the *Sin, Folly, and Danger, of being righteous over-much*. The Text from which he has the *Title* of his Discourse is very unhappily chosen, and must be looked upon rather as a *severe Reproach*, than any kind of Justification of it. The Text is indeed in the Writings of *Solomon*, and as it stands there, has no Hurt in it; because as the Royal Preacher sometimes introduces *Fools*, and sometimes *Infidels*, making their Speeches, so there is a Necessity of supposing that to be the Case in the Doctor's Text; not only from the Context, which plainly shows there are Two Persons introduced, the one *for*, the other *against* Righteousness; but because the Words, unless stripped of all their proper Meaning, cannot be taken in a Sense that is tolerable, or consistent with the common *Notions* of Piety.

Is it not therefore strange, that the Doctor should choose to have a *Discourse* and *Title* to it, conformable to a Text of *this kind*? For if his Discourse is of a Piece with his Text, must not all sensible People find it as hard to reconcile his Discourse, as to reconcile the Text with the *common Notions* of Piety? Is it not strange, that he should think it right and just, to limit, explain, and model, both the Letter and Spirit of the Gospel by such a Saying in the Writings of *Solomon*, as must be ascribed to the Spirit and Mouth of an Infidel? Is it not still stranger, that such a Text, so offensive to Piety, should have not only been so long dwelt upon in the Doctor's Three Churches, but sent abroad into the Christian World, as a proper *Key* to all the practical Sayings, Parables, and Doctrines, of Jesus Christ?

Supported by this Text, the Doctor endeavours to deter and frighten Christians from the *Sin, Folly*, and *Danger*, of being righteous over-much, and from what he calls the *baneful Plague* of Enthusiasm. But then it is Matter of just Complaint, that he does all this, without ever showing in any Part of his Discourse, wherein true Righteousness, or the right and sober Spirit of Piety consists. If he supposed his Readers to be already well acquainted with the Nature and Extent of Christian Holiness, and to have just and distinct Ideas of Religion, what it is in itself, what Change, Purification, and Perfection, it aims at in human Nature, how, and by what Means, a Man may make himself a full Partaker of all that Benefit, Change, and Perfection, that is intended by it, there would then have been little Occasion for his present Undertaking.

For if they may be supposed thus to know what is right in Religion, they would by such Knowledge be in the best State of Security against that which is wrong.

But the Doctor overlooks this important Matter. He neither supposes them to have this Knowledge, nor endeavours to help them to it; but in a Flow of Zeal, in a loose, declamatory Style, reflects at large upon all Attempts towards a Piety, that is not *modern, common,* and according to the present Power and Fashion of Religion in the World. Thus, you everywhere find hard and severe Reflections cast upon *Pretenders* to Piety, *pretended Spiritualists,* and *Righteous over-much;* great Accusation of *Excesses, Extraordinaries,* and *By-paths;* but nowhere a *Word*, or a *Hint*, in Favour of those, who would only be so *excessive*, so *extraordinary*, and so much out of the *common Paths*, as the blessed Saints, and Martyrs of the Primitive Church were; nowhere are *such People* told, that he wishes them *God speed*, that *their Zeal* is much wanted both amongst *Clergy* and *Laity*, and that the Gospel suffers, because we know not where to find *living Examples* of its Purity and Perfection. Nowhere are such People told, that he writes not *against* them, that He *loves* their Spirit, and should be glad to *add* new Fervours to it; nowhere are they told, what *Christian Perfection* is, what a Holiness of Body, Soul and Spirit it requires, and what Blessedness of Life it gives; how powerfully all are called to it; how earnestly all ought to aspire after it; and how sadly they are mistaken, what Enemies to themselves, who for the Sake of any, or all the Things in the World, die less purified and perfect, than they might have been.

If we had to do only with *one single* Person, sincerely good, yet seeming to carry Matters too high in some Parts of his Duty, if we intended *privately* to dissuade him from such Heights; yet even *this*, thus *privately* done, and to a Person of *Piety*, would be exceeding *dangerous*, and very *unjustifiable;* unless we took the utmost Care at the same Time, *to keep up* the pious Zeal of his Mind, to show him wherein the *true Point* of Perfection consisted, and to encourage his utmost Endeavours after it.

But if this Caution, Instruction, and Encouragement, cannot be omitted without great Hurt to Religion, when we speak only to a Person of *Piety*, and in *private*, about any religious *Extremes*, what must be said of the Doctor's Conduct? who to the World *dead* in *Trespasses and Sin,* preaches up the *Sin, Folly,* and *Danger,* of being Righteous over-much. To the World *Eating and Drinking,* and *rising up to Play,* he harangues upon the Madness, Danger, and Folly, of too much Temperance, Abstinence, Mortification, and Severity of Life. To the World *asleep, insensible,* and *careless,* not only of the Purity and Perfection, but of the First Principles of the Gospel, he *boldly, rashly* reproaches all Appearances of Holiness, that are *uncommon* and *extraordinary.* To *no Part* of the World does he represent or propose the *Perfection* of the Gospel, or recommend it as that, which deserves all that they can do, *or* suffer for Sake of it.

This, therefore, I am obliged to point out, as a *fundamental Defect* in the Doctor's Discourse, and such as renders it an evil *Temptation,* a dangerous *Snare,* and fatal *Delusion,* to all those, who do not read it with a full and thorough Dislike.

Coldness, Indifference, and a lifeless outward Compliance with all the Duties of Religion; a Slavery to Ease, Softness, and sensible Pleasures; a criminal Conformity to the Spirit, Fashions, and Corruptions, of the World; unmortified Passions; a conniving at favourite Sins; deep roots of Pride, Partiality, and Self-Love; an unawakened Conscience; an Insensibility of their corrupt, unreformed, unregenerate State; a Proneness to be content and satisfied with poor Beginnings, Names and Appearances of Virtue; is perhaps the State of more than *Two-thirds* of those that are looked upon to be the Religious amongst us.

Now the Doctor's Discourse has a direct and natural Fitness to lull all these People asleep, to suppress all Stirrings and Intentions of Amendment, to keep up and nourish every Disorder of their Hearts, to increase their Blindness, and awaken nothing in them, but a *hurtful Zeal* to censure and condemn all those, that are endeavouring to practise the *uncommon* Piety of the Gospel.

There is scarce a Reader amongst *this Number* of People, whether he be *Layman* or *Clergyman,* but will find this Effect from the Doctor's Instructions; he will begin to take *fresh Comfort* in his State, to think himself *happy* for having had no *aspirings* after high Improvements in Piety; he will not only be *content* with his Corruptions, but be *fixed,* and hardened against all *inward* and *outward* Calls to a solid Piety; he will approve of the *Deadness* and *Insensibility* of his own Heart, and acquiesce in it, as his true and just *Security,* from the *Sin* and *Folly* and *Danger* of being Righteous over-much.

Again, others there are, I make no doubt, in all Parts of this Kingdom, both amongst Clergy and Laity, Men and Women, rich and poor, whose Consciences are greatly awakened, who see the *general Apostacy* from the Religion of the Gospel, whose Souls are wanting, and wishing nothing so much, as to know how, all that they *are*, all that they *have*, and all that they *do*, may be one continual Sacrifice, and Service of Love unto God; to know how, and in what Manner, and to what Extent, and by what Means, they may and ought to 'be perfect, even as their 'Father which is in Heaven is perfect.'

Now who can help looking with *Love*, *Pity*, and *Compassion*, upon these poor Souls, longing for that, which has been so long *lost;* asking after that, which scarce anyone will tell them anything of, and wanting to enter upon Paths, where there are few or no Footsteps to be seen, nor any Travellers in Motion!

Now had these awakened Souls lived in the First Ages of the Church, nay, I may say in almost any till these very last Ages of it, their Zeal had not been in vain; they could have been at no Loss to know *how* they were to proceed in their heavenly Purpose; because they could have always been immediately directed to some *living Examples* of the perfect Spirit of the Gospel, who were publicly known and acknowledged by all to be such, and who had the same *undisputed Right* to point out every Degree of Christian Perfection, as *John the Baptist* had to preach up *Mortification* and *Self-denial*. Every *Age*, and every *Sex,* consecrated *Virgins*, holy *Widows*, *Converts*, and *Penitents*, Priests and People of *all Conditions*, had their open, known and public Standards to resort to, where everyone was sure to be guided and directed, assisted and encouraged to live up to that Height of Holiness and Perfection, which was proper to their State and Condition.

But now how does the Doctor deal with this Sort of People? What *Love, Instruction, Assistance,* and *Encouragement,* does he reach out to them? Why, truly, he considers them as a deluded, *weak,* or *hypocritical,* or *half-thinking* People, that disturb the Christian Church with their Projects about Perfection, who are to be set right by returning to the Instruction of *common Sense*. He ridicules and exposes every Step they must take in their intended Progress, by adding Absurdities of his own Invention to it. There is nothing for such People throughout his whole Discourse, but Reproaches, Ridicule, and Discouragement.

Are they desirous of all that *Self-denial,* all that *Mortification* of bodily Appetites and sensual Passions, as may *best fit* them to be Temples of the Holy Spirit, he ridicules them as holding the Sinfulness of *smelling a Rose?**

---

* Page 16.

Do they begin to discover the *deep Corruption* of their Nature, the *Superficialness* and *Weakness* of their Virtues, and to fear they have as yet scarce *come up* to the Righteousness of the *Scribes* and *Pharisees*? He tells them, 'The great Enemy of 'Souls adapts his Temptations to all Sorts of Tempers and Dis- 'positions.—Those who are disposed to be good and virtuous, if 'he cannot prevail with them to be vicious, commonly so-called, 'he labours to make them over-virtuous, that is vicious, though 'not commonly so-called; and so involves them in Dangers and 'Mischiefs.'*

Are they such as are only desirous of reforming their *own Lives*, by bringing all their Actions to the Standard of the Gospel, and wholly intent upon their own Advancement in merely *practical Piety*?

To these he shows, that they are in the *very Paths* that lead, and always did lead, to *Fanatic Madness*. Thus, says he, 'To 'what a Height of *Fanatic Madness* in *Doctrine*, as well as 'Practice are some advanced, who set out at first with an 'Appearance of more than ordinary Sanctity in *Practice only*?' And again, 'I do say, that in all Ages Enthusiasts have been '*Righteous over-much;* they began with the last mentioned, and 'ended with the other. And is it not so now?'†

Further, Are there others, who begin to feel the *Mystery* of their Redemption discovered in their own Souls, so that they hunger and thirst after the Manifestation of the Divine Life in them, desiring that Christ may be wholly *formed* and *revealed* in them, that they may *put on* Christ, *be* in him *new Creatures*, led by his Spirit, *growing* in him as Branches in the Vine, hearing the Word of God *written* and *spoken* in their Hearts, in his Light *seeing Light*, and tasting in the inward Man the Powers of the World to come.

For such as these, the Doctor has this Instruction: 'That 'there is,' says he, 'such a Thing as the Operation and Influence 'of the Holy Spirit upon our Souls, though we cannot distin- 'guish it from the Operations of our own Minds, is not only 'granted, but insisted upon, by all sincere and sober Christians. 'But what *Reason*, what *Scripture*, is there for this inward *See- 'ing, Hearing, Feeling*?'‡

According therefore to the Doctor's Divinity, both Reason and Scripture *require*, that the true Christian be *inwardly blind*, inwardly *deaf*, and void of all inward *Feeling*. For if neither Scripture nor Reason will allow of any *inward Senses*, then they must both of them require an *inward Insensibility*. But Scripture, from *Genesis* to the *Revelation*, is full of Proof of these

---

* Page 36.   † Page 39.   ‡ Page 43.

Answer to Dr. Trapp.

inward Senses. I shall not now produce them. I shall here only observe, that *Hardness of Heart* is a common and well-known Phrase of Scripture, and everywhere signifies some Degree of *Blindness, Deafness,* and Loss of *Feeling.** I suppose it will not be said, that it signifies Blindness, or Loss of *outward Eyes* and *Ears,* or *Feeling:* Neither does it signify a Want of *human Reason,* or natural *Sagacity;* for *learned, polite,* and *ingenious* Men are full as subject as others are, to this *Hardness of Heart.* Therefore the Scripture is as *open,* as *plain* and *express,* in declaring *for inward Senses,* as it is in declaring *against* such a Thing as *Hardness of Heart.*

Hardness of Heart is *that* to the *inward* Senses which a *deep,* or, as we call it, a *dead Sleep,* is to the *outward.* It keeps our inward Eyes and Ears closed and stopped, just as Sleep does our outward Eyes, and Ears, and Feeling. A *broken* and a *contrite* Heart unlocks all our inward Senses, and makes us see, and hear, and feel the Things, which could no more be seen, heard, or felt before, than a Man in a deep Sleep can hear, and see, and feel the Things that are said and done about him.

Water violently frozen into a *Rock of Ice,* is very different from the *same Water* melted, rarified, warmed, and moving under the Influences of the *Sun* and the *Air.* Now if this *Water* was a *sensible Being,* we might well suppose, that when it was a *soft, yielding, transparent, flowing* Substance, full of *Light* and *Air,* that it had *certain Senses* in that State; which Senses were *lost,* and *locked up,* as soon as it became a hard, rough, thick, dark, immovable *Rock of Ice,* made so by *Coldness,* or for the Want of the Motion of *Light* and *Air* in it. And that the *Ice* must of all Necessity be *first melted,* before *these Senses* could be found again.

Now this Difference between Water *flowing* full of *Light* and *Air,* and the *same Water* frozen into a dark hard *Rock* of Ice, is but a small Resemblance of the Difference between a *hardened* Heart, and the *same Heart* become *broken.* And a *Lump* of Ice would be as well qualified to deny that *sweet Sensibility* of Water flowing full of *Light* and *Air,* as the natural Man is to dispute those *Senses,* which arise in the Heart, that is broken and penetrated by the *Light,* and *Spirit* of God in it.

But no more of this at present. I now return to the Doctor. His further Instruction to this Sort of People stands thus: They are told by him, that their high Notions of Spiritual Improvements have this Effect: On the one Hand, they lead to *Presumption;* on the other, to *Desperation.* 'He has been told,' he says, 'that some have been actually thrown into Despair. They have been made stark mad, and received into Bedlam, as such.'

---

* Matt.

And then he cries out, 'Was the Religion of Jesus Christ intended 'to make People mad? Is this for the Honour of Christianity?'*
I shall not here question the Doctor's Information. I shall only observe, that when our Saviour was upon Earth, there were Two Sorts of *mad* People about him. The *one Sort* ran about in Disorder, tore their Clothes, and cut their own Flesh; the *other Sort* raved in Malice, threw Dust into the Air, stopped their Ears, and cried out, *Crucify him, crucify him.*

Now it may be asked, which of these Two Sorts of People were in the most *disordered* and *distempered* State? Whose *Madness* was the most *shocking*, that of the *Lunatics*, or that of the *High Priests, Scribes,* and *Pharisees?* Those who only mangled their own Bodies, or those that *thirsted* after the Blood of Christ, and would have no Rest, till they saw his Body nailed to the Cross? To me the *Lunatics* seem to be in a *less Degree* of Disorder; and the Reason is this; because I see that our Saviour could heal them, but not the Priests, Scribes, and Pharisees.

Now is it reasonable, on the account of the *Madness* of these Priests, Scribes, and Doctors of the Law, to say, 'Is this for the 'Honour of the Jewish Law? Was the Law and the Prophets 'intended to make People mad?' Now if the Doctor knows how to excuse the *Law* and the *Prophets,* though these great Students of them were in such a desperate State of *Frenzy* and *Madness*, then Christianity may be blameless; though here and there a Christian may be fit for *Bedlam.*

Again, there are others, who desire to bring the whole Form of their Lives under Rules of Religion, to let the Spirit of the Gospel give Laws to the most ordinary, indifferent, innocent and lawful Things and Enjoyments, so that as the Apostle speaks, 'whether they eat or drink, or whatever they do, they may do all 'to the Glory of God.'

These People are told by the Doctor, That 'wholly abstaining 'from Things indifferent and innocent in themselves, as forbidden 'and unlawful, is a signal Instance of being Righteous over-much; 'and so, on the other hand, is making Things indifferent to be 'necessary, and Matters of Duty.'†

What is here said has some Truth in it, and might be useful in its proper Place, and under right Limitations. But as it here stands in the Discourse, it is a grievous *Snare* and *Deceit* to the Reader. For it is to signify to him, that *wholly abstaining from* Things in themselves *indifferent* and *innocent* cannot be made a *Matter* of true religious Advancement; but is a blamable

---

* Page 37.   † Page 8.

Instance of a Piety in Excess. If the Doctor had meant only to teach, that we should not wholly abstain from Things indifferent and innocent, as if they were *in themselves unlawful*, he should have told his Readers that he meant no more; he should have told them, that such Things might be abstained from *justly*, and *piously* upon a better Principle, and so become very *expedient* and *edifying;* and that he did not condemn the abstaining wholly from such Things, when it was done upon a *Motive* of Piety, for the *better* fulfilling any Duty; but *only* when it was done from a superstitious Notion, of the Things being in *themselves sinful*.

Had he done this, he had prevented the *Snare* and *Deceit* that is now in his Assertion; but then he would, at the same time, have made it useless and insignificant to the Design of his Discourse, and would have left a Door open for such Advances of Piety as he is here opposing.

It might easily be shown, if this was the Place for it, that no one can *truly* fulfil, or live up to the Two First and greatest of all Laws, that of loving God with all our Heart, all our Strength, and all our Mind; and that of loving our Neighbour as ourselves; unless he be willing and glad, in many Instances, *wholly* to *abstain* from Things in themselves indifferent and innocent; and also to make Things that in themselves are indifferent, to be Matters of Duty.

St. *Paul's* Doctrine is this: 'All Things are lawful for me, but 'all Things are not expedient.' This sets the Matter right on both Sides. It leaves Things in their own State of Indifference and Lawfulness, and yet carries us to a higher Rule of acting. It directs us wholly to abstain from some Things innocent in themselves, and to do some Things to which the Law calls us not, because they are *expedient;* because by so doing, we show a higher Love of God, and a greater Desire of doing everything to his Honour and Glory; because we thereby attain a greater Purity and Perfection of Heart, a greater Conquest over all our inward and outward Enemies, and in a greater Degree help forward the Edification of our Neighbour.

Let us look at St. *Paul's* Doctrine and Example in the Two following remarkable Instances. *First*, where he declares it to be *lawful* for those that preach the Gospel to live by the Gospel, and yet makes it Matter of the greatest *Comfort* and *Joy* to himself, that he had wholly abstained from this *lawful* Thing. And declares, it were better for him to die, than that *this Rejoicing* should be taken from him. He appeals to his daily and nightly labouring with his own Hands, that so he might preach the Gospel freely, and not be chargeable to those that heard him. And this he said he did, not for want of Authority to do otherwise, but that he might make himself an Ensample unto them to follow him.

What fine and awakening Instructions are here given to us of the *Clergy*, in a practical Matter of the greatest Moment! How ought everyone to be frightened at the *Thought* of desiring or seeking a *Second Living*, or of rejoicing at *great Pay* where there is but *little Duty*, when the Apostle's Rejoicing consisted in this, that he had passed through all the Fatigues and Perils of preaching the Gospel without any Pay at all! How *cautious*, nay, how *fearful* ought we to be, of going so *far* as the *secular* Laws permit us, when the Apostle thought it more desirable to lose his Life, than to go so far as the very Laws of the Gospel would have suffered him!

It is lawful to receive *more* for doing the Work of the Ministry in any *Parish*, and to spend more upon ourselves than our bare Subsistence requires.—It is *looked upon* as *lawful* to get several *Preferments*, and to make a Gain of the Gospel, by hiring others to do Duty for us at a lower Rate.—It is *looked* upon as *lawful* to quit a *Cure* of Souls of a small Income, for *no other* Reason but because we can get another of a greater.—It is looked upon as lawful for a Clergyman to take the Revenue of the Church, which he serves, to his *own Use*, though he has more than a sufficient Competency of *his own*, and much more than the Apostle could get by his Labour.—It is looked upon as lawful for the Clergy to live in State and Equipage, to buy Purple and fine Linen, out of the Revenues of the Church.—It is looked upon as lawful for Clergymen to enrich their Families, and bring up their Children in the fashionable Vanities, and corrupting Methods of a worldly and expensive Life, by Money got by preaching the Gospel of Jesus Christ.

But now *supposing* all this to be *lawful*, what *Comfort* and *Joy* might we treasure up for ourselves, what Glory and Honour might we bring to Religion, what Force and Power might we give to the Gospel, what Benefit and Edification should we do to our Neighbour, if we *wholly abstained* from all these Things, not by working Day and Night with our own Hands, as the great Apostle did, but by limiting our Wants and Desires according to the plain Demands of Nature, and a religious Self-Denial?

The other Instance of the Apostle's, I appeal to, is that, where he says, it is good neither to eat 'flesh, nor to drink wine, nor 'anything whereby thy Brother stumbleth and is offended.'*
And again, 'If meat make my Brother to offend, I will eat no 'flesh while the world standeth, that I may not offend my

---

* Rom. xiv. 23.

'Brother.'* Hence it appears, that to abstain from Things indifferent, as if they were in themselves sinful, is wrong; but *wholly to abstain* from them upon other Motives, may be the *highest Piety*, and oftentimes Matter of necessary Duty and Edification. But since the Doctor has not looked at this Matter in this twofold View, in which it can only be justly apprehended, he can't well be excused from that *Half-Thinking*, which he so much reproaches in others.

But I must further observe, that there is yet more of *Snare* and *Deception*, in what the Doctor has here said of this Matter. For the Reader may thereby be easily brought into a Belief, that Things in themselves indifferent and innocent, *&c.*, are not the *proper Subjects* of Religion, or *Means* of advancing in Piety, and that he need not bring himself under *any Laws* of Religion concerning such Things. Whereas nothing can be more contrary to Truth, or more hurtful to his Piety, than such a Belief.

Eating, Drinking, Sleeping, Dressing, Resting, Labour, Conversation, Trade, Diversion, and *Money*, are in themselves indifferent, innocent, and useful. But it is in the religious, or irreligious Use of these Things, that some People *live* up to the Spirit of the Gospel, and others *wholly die* to it. And it is from *strict Laws* of Religion made concerning these *indifferent* and *innocent* Things, that the spiritual Life of everyone is to be built up.

And it is for want of religious Laws in the Use of innocent and lawful Things that the Spirit of the Gospel cannot get Possession of our Hearts. For our Souls may receive an infinite Hurt, and be rendered incapable of all true Virtue, merely by the Use of innocent and lawful Things.

What is more innocent than *Rest* and *Retirement?* And yet what more dangerous than Sloth and Idleness? How lawful and praiseworthy is the Care of a Family? And yet how certainly are many People rendered incapable of all Virtue, and dead to all the Calls of God, by a worldly solicitous Temper? How lawful and beneficial is it to us, to eat and drink in such Quantity and Quality, as may render the Body healthful, subservient and useful to the Soul? And yet, what Danger is there in eating and drinking, if we are not under *this strict Law* of Religion, to seek *only* Health, and not the Pleasure of various Tastes in our Food. What *Sensuality* of Discourse shall we not *every Day* fall into, unless it be a fixed Law to us, to speak of no other Joy in our Food, but that which is expressed by our *Grace* before and after our Meals.

---

* 1 Cor. viii. 13.

How indifferent a Thing, and innocent in itself, is *Dress*. And yet what more hurtful and abounding with Sin? It reaches and infects the Heart and Soul, both of the Wearer and Beholder. Its Evils are innumerable. It has destroyed, and does destroy, like a Pestilence.

If the lustful Eye is in the Scripture deemed to be an Adultery, we may see plainly the Reason why the Apostle requires Women to be *covered*, not to beautify their outward Person with costly Ornaments of Dress, or curled Hair, but to be adorned with *Shamefacedness* and *Modesty*. For it is only saying, in other Words, that it becomes not the Piety of Christian Women, to carry and hold out *Snares* and *Temptations* to the unwary Eye, that can so easily be betrayed into so great a Sin.

Now how can all these Evils, which arise from the Use of these Things indifferent and lawful in themselves, be avoided, but by making every Thing in our *common* and *ordinary* Life to be Matter of Conscience; which is, to have its *Rule*, and *Measure*, and *End*, from the Spirit of Religion. And indeed what other End or Intent is there in Religion, but to govern every Motion and Desire of our Hearts, to make all the Actions of our *common Life* pure and holy, by being done in strict Conformity to the Will of God, and under the Light and Guidance of his Holy Spirit? So that every outward *Form* of our Lives, and the *whole Manner* of our living in the World, whether in *Estates, Titles, Shops,* or *Farms,* whether in *Eating, Drinking, Dressing, &c.,* may make it known to all the World, that we do everything in the *Name* of Jesus Christ, suitably to that high Vocation wherewith we are called.

The Apostle directs *Servants* to this Degree of Piety; that is, ' to be obedient to their masters, in singleness of heart, as unto ' Christ. Not with eye-service, as men-pleasers, but as the ' servants of Christ, doing the will of God from the heart. With ' goodwill doing service, as unto the Lord, and not to men.'*
Surely, if poor Slaves, by reason of their Christian Profession, are not to comply with their Business, as *Men-pleasers,* if they are to look wholly unto God in *all their Actions,* and serve in *Singleness of Heart,* as unto the Lord, surely all Christians of other *Employments* and *Conditions,* must be as much obliged to go through their Business with the *same Singleness* of Heart, not as pleasing the Vanity of their own Minds, not as gratifying their own selfish, worldly Passions, but as the Servants of God, that are to live *wholly* unto him in *everything* that they do. It

---

* Eph. vi. 5; Col. iii. 22.

is therefore absolutely certain, that no Christian is to enter *any further* into Business, nor seek any worldly Profit, nor do anything in any other *Measure*, nor for any *other End*, than such as he can in *Singleness* of Heart do unto God, as a reasonable Service.

No Folly of Life whatever can be rightly removed, but by being thus *wholly* cut up by the Roots, by making *everything* subject to the Spirit of Religion. That which is to direct our *Prayers*, and govern us at *Church*, must, with the *same Strictness*, direct our *Conversation*, and govern our Dealings in common Life. We must *Dress* with the same Spirit that we give *Alms*, or go to *Prayers ;* that is, we must no more Dress to be *seen* and *admired* by others, than we must give *Alms*, or make *Prayers* for the same Reasons. And when Religion has its Seat in our Hearts, and is the Work of God's Spirit in us, this acting according to its Direction in *all Things*, will be so far from seeming to be a hard Lesson, that it would be a Pain to act otherwise. It is no Hardship to a *Miser*, to do *every* thing suitable to the greedy Desires of his Heart. The ambitious Man is not troubled with acting always agreeably to his Ambition. If these Persons are in Trouble or Distress, or under any Dejection, you can *only* comfort the one with Honour and Power, and the other with filthy Lucre and Gain.

Yet the Doctor complains of the *Treatise upon Christian Perfection*, because Christians in *Sickness, Distress,* and *Dejection* of Spirit, are there *solely* directed to seek for Comfort and Refreshment in God *alone*. Our Blessed Lord is very short, and yet very full, upon this Article; he only says, 'Be of good 'Comfort, I have overcome the World.' And the Doctor might as well be angry at the *Gospel* for having made no mention of *worldly Amusements* proper for *sick* and *distressed* Christians, as at the *Treatise of Christian Perfection*, for not having done the same.

If I should see a *sick* Man smelling a *Rose*, eating an *agreeable Fruit*, or *diverting* himself with a Child, I should not call him from such sinful Indulgences. But if he wanted Comfort in his State, I would no more direct him to *anything*, but the great and solid Comforts, that are to be found in the Love and Goodness of God, than I would direct him to *another* Saviour than Jesus Christ.

For to tell Christians, that in *some kinds* of Trouble, they might justly seek for Relief, by reading a *Play*, or wanton *Bucolic*, instead of the *Gospel*, would be the same Absurdity, as to have told People in our Saviour's Time, that, in *some Sorts* of Distress, they might justly have Recourse to *Simon Magus*, instead of Jesus Christ.

But now to look back a little. I have considered the Bulk of those Christians that are the most likely to be the Doctor's Readers, under Two Characters. The one, as living some Way or other in a partial, false, superficial, or half State of Piety; the other as an awakened People, called by the Spirit of God to come out of the common Corruptions of the Times. I have shown, that the Doctor's Discourse (where it is not disliked) must do great Hurt, and have dreadful Effects upon those Two Sorts of People; the one Sort it seals up in a false Security, sleeping in the Chambers of Death, without any Oil in their Vessels; the other it frightens, and discourages from their pious Intentions of trimming their Lamps with all Diligence, and living upon the *Watch* for the midnight Call of the Bridegroom's Voice.

That I may therefore do all the Good that I can to both these Sorts of People, that I may awaken the one from their false Security in their half Form of Godliness, and assist and encourage the other to proceed wth all Earnestness, after every Degree of Christian Holiness; I shall, before I proceed any further, lay down a short, but plain Account of the *whole Nature* and *Ground* of the Christian Religion, that everyone may clearly see, why we want the Christian Religion to save us: What it is to do for us; and how it is done. By this Means everyone will best judge of the Importance of this Enquiry, and how he ought to be affected with what is said on either Side of the Matter.

(1.) Man was created a living, real, perfect Image of the Holy Trinity, Father, Son, and Holy Ghost. This I have largely explained, and proved elsewhere.*

(2.) This whole visible World, as far as the Stars and Elements, or any corporeal Being reaches, stands in the *Place*, or takes up that *Extent* of Space, where *Lucifer* and his Angels, before their Fall, had their glorious Kingdom. So far as this visible Frame of Nature extends itself, so far was the Extent of their Kingdom.

(3.) That the *Place* or *Extent* of this World, was the Place or Extent of their Kingdom, is plain, from the Two following Reasons: *First*, Because the Place of this World is *now* their Habitation. For we must by no Means suppose, that God brought them from some other Region into this World only to tempt Man, and make his Life dangerous; but they are here *now*, because they were created to dwell *here*. For fallen Angels

---

* *Grounds and Reasons of Christian Regeneration, &c.*

cannot *possibly* leave the *Place* of their Sin and Fall, they must live in the *Defilements* and *Disorders* of their spoiled Kingdom; and in that Place they must find their Hell and Torment, where thy extinguished their Light and Joy.   Secondly, Because the whole Extent of this World, everything in it, *Sun, Moon, Stars, Fire, Air, Water,* and *Earth, Stones, Minerals,* must all be *dissolved,* and pass through a *purifying Fire.*   Therefore all these Things are polluted, and have in them some Grossness and Disorder from the Fall of the Angels.   Therefore we may see *where* they have lived, and *how far* the Place of their Kingdom extended, by the Extent of those Things that are to be *dissolved* and *purified.*

(4.) When the Angels had, by their Rebellion against God, lost the Divine Life *within* themselves, and brought their *whole outward* Kingdom into Darkness, Grossness, Wrath, and Disorder, so that, as *Moses* speaketh, 'Darkness was upon the Face 'of the Deep,' that is, the whole Deep, or Extent of the Place of this World; then, at the *Fall* of the Angels, and in the *Place* where they were fallen, and out of the *Materials* of their ruined angelical Kingdom, did God begin the *Creation* of this present, material, temporary, visible World.

(5.) 'In the beginning,' saith *Moses,* 'God created the Heaven 'and the Earth'; here, at this *Instant,* ended the Devil's Power over the Place or Kingdom in which he was created: As soon as the whole of his outward, disordered Kingdom was thus *divided* into a *created Heaven* and *Earth,* all was taken out of his Hands, he was *shut out* of everything, and he and all his Hosts became only *poor Prisoners* in their lost Kingdom, that could only *wander* about in Chains of Darkness, looking with impotent Rage and Anger at the *created Heaven* and *Earth,* which was sprung up in their own Place of Habitation, and which they could not *rule* over, because their Nature had *no Communion* with this new created Heaven and Earth.

(6.) Thus was this *outward Kingdom,* of the whole Extent of this World, taken out of the Hands of *Lucifer* and his Angels; all its *Wrath, Darkness, Grossness, Disharmony, Fire,* and *Disorder,* was, by the *Six Days' Creation,* changed into a *temporary* State, restored to a certain, but low Resemblance of its first State, and put into that Form and Order of Sun, Stars, Fire, Air, Light, Water, and Earth, in which we now see it.

(7.) Into this World, thus created out of the *Ruins* of the Kingdom of the fallen Angels, and made *paradisaical,* by the Goodness of God, was Man introduced on the *Sixth* Day of the Creation, to take his Place, as *Lord* and *Prince* of it, to have Power over all outward Things, to discover and manifest the

Wonders of this new created World, and to bring forth such an *holy Offspring*, as might fill up the Places of the fallen Angels. And when that was done, and certain Periods of Time had produced these great Effects, then this *whole Frame* of Things was, by the last *purifying Fire*, to have been raised from its paradisaical State, into which it was put at the Creation, into that *first heavenly* Brightness, and high Degree of Glory, in which it stood before the Fall of *Lucifer*.

(8.) But the first Man, thus created to be a *Prince* and *Father*, of a new angelical Kingdom, stood not out his Trial for this glorious State.

(9.) He came into this World in that *same glorious* Body, in which, after the Resurrection, he shall *be like* the *Angels in Heaven*. For no other Body, but that which was at *first* created, and *died* in *Adam's* Sin, shall rise in Jesus Christ. He only saves and restores that which was lost. The Resurrection will only take away what *Sin*, and *Death*, and *Earth*, had added to the *first created* Body.

(10.) In this Body, which shall rise Triumphant over Death and Hell, did the first created Man stand in this World, *incapable* of receiving any Hurt, or *knowing* Evil from outward Nature. The *Holy Ghost* was the *Breath* of his Life, and the *Son of God* was the *Light*, that illuminated all both within and without him.

(11.) Had he *fixed* his Will to be *absolutely* and *eternally* what he was, had he desired only to eat of the Tree of Life, to live by the Word of God, he had been established, and confirmed to be an eternal Angel, or Divine Man.

(12.) But his Imagination wandered after the Secrets of this outward World, after the Fruit and Knowledge of such Good and Evil, as wrought an entire Change in his Nature. For *everything* must have the Nature of that which it chooses for its *Food*.

His own *strong Will* (a Spark of the Divine Omnipotence) was to be his *Maker;* for he could not be an Angel of Light with less Freedom. What he desired, that he had: as his Imagination worked, so he became to be. He turned from the Tree and Light of Life, and took in the Fruit and Darkness of the *earthly Nature*. And so he fell from his *Height* of Glory as deep into an *earthly Life*, and the Miseries of the Earth, as the Devil fell into a *hellish Life*, and the Miseries of Hell.

(13.) Imagine a most precious *Pearl*, infinitely more bright, infinitely more transparent, infinitely more illuminated, than any that mortal Eyes ever saw. Imagine this Pearl to be in a Moment penetrated, thickened, darkened, deformed in every Part, and through every Pore, with something as hard as *Iron*, as heavy as *Lead*, as rough as *Earth*, as dark as *Soot*, and then you have but a Shadow of that which happened only to the *Body of Adam*, when, by desiring and eating the earthly Fruit, he drew in the earthly Nature of this World into his pearly, paradisaical Body. And here, by-the-by, we may see as in a Glass, what it is that earthly Desires *now do* to every Son of *Adam;* they do *all that* which they did to the first Man, they carry on, keep up, and continue, that *same Death* in us, which he died in Paradise.

(14.) Here it was that his eternal Soul, the *immortal Fire* of Life in him, being swallowed up, and smothered by an *earthly dark* Body, lost the *Light* of the Son of God, and the *Breath* of the Holy Spirit. And this was the *great* and *immediate Death* that he died in Paradise, before he became the Father of Mankind, a Death much more grievous than that which is to bring us all to our Graves. It was a Death that extinguished all that was Divine and Holy in the Human Nature, just as the Sin of Angels had turned them into Devils. Now in looking at *this Death*, or the Extinction of this *first Divine Life*, we have the clearest, fullest View, of what we are to understand by our *Regeneration* by the *Second Adam*. For what can it possibly be, but the Restoration of that *same Divine Life* which was lost in *Adam* the *First*, and to which he *absolutely* died in Paradise? Must not that which is re-generated in the Human Nature, be *something* that has been generated in it *before?* If we want to be redeemed, or regenerated *only*, because *Adam died* in Paradise, and lost the *First Birth* of Human Nature, must not Regeneration be *only* and *solely* the bringing forth again that *First Birth* in the Human Nature? Or will anyone say, that Christ is not in as high a Degree the *Restorer* of our First Birth, as *Adam* was the *Destroyer* of it? Now, though this great Truth, seated in the very Heart of the Christian Religion, speaks at once the *whole Nature* of Regeneration, and leaves no room to mistake about it; yet many learned Men, either not *seeing*, or not *loving*, or being afraid to *own* it, have been forced, not only to mistake, but wholly to sink the most solid, substantial, edifying, and glorious Article of the Christian Faith; and, instead of telling us the *Height* and *Depth* of the Benefit and Blessing of having the *Nature* and *Life* of Christ derived into, or regenerated in us, they can only teach us, what *Kind* of *Word* Regeneration is—that it is a *Figurative Expression*—and that our Saviour may be justified for having made use of it. What learned Pains do some People take to root up the Belief of our having a *Life* and *Birth* from Jesus Christ, in the *same Truth and Reality*, that we had lost a *Life* and

2—2

Birth in *Adam?* They run from *Book* to *Book*, from *Language* to *Language*, they call upon every *Disputant*, consult all *Critics*, search all *Lexicons*, to show us, that according to Scripture, and Antiquity, and the Rules of true Criticism, Regeneration need *signify* no more, than what is meant by the *federal* Rite of Baptism. Nay, what is still worse, they appeal to the *poor Notions* of the blind, infatuated *Jews;* they produce the *Opinions* which they had of a Regeneration talked of, and a Baptism used amongst them, when they rejected and crucified our Saviour, to teach us, *what* we are to understand by our *Divine Birth* in Christ Jesus. But if this be the Use of Learning amongst ourselves, we need not look at *Rome* or *Geneva*, or the ancient Rabbis of the *Jewish Sanhedrim*, to see what miserable Work Learning can make with the Holy Scriptures. For it must be said, that the true Messiah is not *rightly owned*, the Christian Religion is not *truly known*, nor its Benefits rightly *sought*, till the Soul is all Love, and Faith, and Hunger, and Thirst, after this new *Life, Birth,* and *real Formation* of Jesus Christ in it, till without Fear of *Enthusiasm* it seeks and expects all its Redemption from it. But to return.

(15.) Man, thus dead to the Divine Life, thus destitute of the *Son*, and *Holy Spirit* of God, thus fallen into an *earthly Nature*, under the Dominion of an earthly World, which would afford him for a while a miserable Life, and then leave him to a more miserable Death, thus fallen, he could do no more to replace himself in Paradise, or to regain his first Nature, than the Devil could do, to restore to himself his lost Glory.

(16.) But in this State the *infinite Mercy* of God met him. That Love which at the *first breathed*, or *spoke* out of the Mouth of God, a living, holy and Divine Soul and Spirit into him, now again *breathed*, or *inspoke* a Spark, or Seed, or Ray of Divine Light into him, in the Declaration of a *Serpent-Treader;* which Seed or Spark of Life should in Time do *all that*, which *Adam* should have done; that is, should raise up and bring forth a *Generation* of Men, that should become *Sons of God*, and take Possession of that Kingdom from which the Angels had fallen.

(17.) Here now began the merciful Mystery of Man's Redemption; for this *Seed* of a Divine Life, or *inspoken Word* of Grace, or *Treader* of the Serpent, was the Holy Jesus, the *Second Adam*, who from that Time, stood in the Place of the First Man, and became the Father and Regenerator of *Adam* himself, and all his Posterity. And from that Time it may be said in a certain and true Sense, that the *Incarnation* of the Son of God began; because he was from *that Time* entered again into the human Nature, as a *Seed*, or *Beginning* of its Salvation, hidden under the *Veil* of the Law, and not made manifest, till he was born in the Holy, and highly Blessed Virgin *Mary*. And in this Sense it is, that our Blessed Lord said of himself, that *he was the Light of the World*, as *Adam* might have said of himself, that he was the Sin and Death of the World ; because, as Sin and Death came *wholly* from him upon *all Men*, so the Light of Life came as wholly and universally from Jesus Christ. And in this Sense also St. *John* says of him, ' that he was the true Light ' which lighteth every Man that cometh into the World.' Because every Man, wherever born, has from him this Light of Life, this inward Saviour, or Seed of his Salvation, in the Birth of his own Life, which is to overcome the Darkness, resist the Evil, and bruise the Serpent that is in his fallen Nature. This Beginning of the Divine Birth in our Souls, if it is not stifled and suppressed by us, but inwardly reverenced, and attended to, as the Voice and Call of God *within* us, is our certain Guide and Leader to Christ, born in the Fulness of Time, and sacrificed for us upon the Cross.

(18.) What we want from Jesus Christ, as our Redeemer, is manifest by that which he offers and gives to us, namely, a Birth from *Himself*, a Birth from the *Holy Spirit*, a Redemption from the *Hell* that is in our Souls, and from the *Death* and *Corruption* that is in our Bodies.

(19.) We were no more created to be in the Sorrows, Burdens, and Anguish, of an *earthly Life*, than the Angels were created to be in the *Wrath* and *Darkness* of Hell. It is as contrary to the *Will* and *Goodness* of God towards us, that we are *out* of Paradise, as it is contrary to the Designs and Goodness of God towards the Angels, that some of them are *out* of Heaven, Prisoners of Darkness.

The Grossness, Impurity, Sickness, Pain and Corruption of our Bodies, is brought upon us by ourselves in the same Manner as the dark, hideous serpentine Forms of the Devils are brought upon them. How absurd, and even blasphemous, would it be, to say with the Scripture and the Church, that we are by *Nature Children of Wrath, and born in Sin*, if we had that Nature which God at first gave us? What a Reproach upon God to say, that this World is a *Valley of Misery*, a *Shadow of Death*, an Habitation of *Disorders*, *Snares*, *Evils*, and *Temptations*, if this was an *original* Creation, or that State of Things for which God created us? Is it not as consistent with the Goodness and Perfections of God, to speak of the *Misery* and *Disorder* that holy Angels find *above*, and of the Vanity, Emptiness and Sorrow of the *heavenly State*, as to speak of the Misery of *Men*, and the Sorrows of *this World*, if Men and the World were in *that Order* in which God at first had placed them ? If God could make *any* Place *poor*, and *vain*, and miserable, or create any Beings into a State of *Vanity and Vexation of Spirit*, he might do so in *all Places*, and to *all Beings*.

(20.) But by the Mercy of God in Christ Jesus, this Prison of an earthly Life is turned into a State of *Purification*, it is made a *Time* and *Place* of putting off our *filthy* and *defiled* Garments, and of *slaying* and *sacrificing* that corrupt old Man of Sin that is hid under them. And God suffers the *Sun* to shine upon us, and the *Elements* to afford us Nourishment, for *no other* End, but that we may all have *Time* and *Opportunity* to hear the *Call* of the Son of God, to embrace a second *Adam*, to be *born again* of him, to be renewed by the *Holy Spirit*, and be made capable of that Kingdom from which *Lucifer* and his Angels fell.

(21.) Look at our Saviour's Sermon on the *Mount*, and indeed at all his Instructions, and you will find them pointing at nothing else on *our Side*, but a *Denial* of ourselves, and a *Renunciation* of the World. And indeed how could it be otherwise ? For if we are ourselves *something* which we were not created to be, and if this is our Misery, that we have raised and awakened a *Nature* and *Life* in us, which is not our *first*, that we had from God ; must not the First Step towards our Salvation be, a denying and departing with *our whole Will* and *Inclination* from that which we have made ourselves to be, from that Life which we have awakened in us ? If *Self* is our Misery and Captivity, must not our Deliverance require a total, continual Self-denial ? If we want a Redeemer, *only* because we have *wandered* out of Paradise, and could not get *back* to it ourselves ; if we are overcome by this World, only because the *Will* and *Desire* of our first Father *sought* after it, what Wonder is it that he who is to *replace* us in Paradise should call us to a *Renunciation* of the World ? If this World has got its Dominion over us, *merely* because the *Will* and *Desire* of Man turned itself towards the Earth ; how can its Dominion over us be *destroyed*, but by our *turning* our whole *Will* and *Desire* towards Heaven ?

(22.) Vain Man, taken with the *Sound* of heavenly Things, and *Prospects* of future Glory, yet at the same Time a *fast Friend* to all the Interests and Passions of Flesh and Blood, would fain compound Matters between God and Mammon. He is very willing to acknowledge a *Saviour*, that died on the Cross to save him ; he is ready to receive outward *Ordinances*, and *Forms* of Divine Worship, and to contend with Zeal for the Observance of them. He likes Heaven, and future Glory, on these Conditions. He is also ready to put on an *outward Morality* of Behaviour, to let Religion polish his Manners, that he may have the Credit and Ornament of a *prudential Piety*, *well-ordered Passions*, and a *Decency* of outward Life; this gives no Hurt, or at least no *Death's-Blow* to the old Man. But to lay the Axe to the *whole Root* of our Disease, to cut all those *silken Cords* asunder, which tie us to the World, and the World to us, to deny every Temper and Passion that cannot be made Holy, Wise, and Heavenly; to die to every Gratification which keeps up, and strengthens the Folly, Vanity, Pride and Blindness of our *fallen Nature ;* to leave no *little Morsels* of Sensuality, Avarice and Ambition, for the *old Man* to feed upon, however well *covered* under his Mantle; this, though it be the very Essence of Religion on *our Part*, is what he flies from with as much Aversion as from *Heresy* and *Schism*. Here he makes learned Appeals to *Reason* and *Common Sense* to judge betwixt him and the Gospel; which is just as wise, as to ask the learned *Greek*, and the worldly *Jew*, whether the *Cross* of Christ be not *Foolishness*, and a just Rock of Offence; or to appeal to *Flesh* and *Blood* about the narrow Way to that *Kingdom of Heaven*, into which itself cannot possibly have any Entrance.

(23.) To seek for anything in Religion, but a *new Nature* fitted for a new World, is knowing neither it, nor ourselves. *To be born* again, is to be fit for Paradise, in whatever Part of the Universe we live. *Not to be born again*, is continuing *where* the Sin and Death of *Adam left* us, whatever *Church*, or *Sect* of Religion we have Fellowship with. All *Ways* and *Opinions*, all *Forms* and *Modes* of Divine Worship, stand on the *Outside* of Religion. They may be, and certainly are, great and desirable *Helps* to the Kingdom of God, when we consider them only as the *Gate*, or *Guide* to that *inward Life*, which wants to be raised, and brought forth in us. But this is unquestionably true, that our *Salvation* consists *wholly* and *solely* in the *Birth* of the Son of God, and the *Renewal* of the Holy Ghost, in our Souls. When *this* begins, our Salvation *begins ;* as this goes on, our Salvation *goes on ;* when this is finished, our Salvation is *finished*. This alone *saves* the Soul; because this alone restores the First Paradisaical, Divine Nature, which is the true Image of God, and which alone can enter into the Kingdom of Heaven.

(24.) If we had only a *notional Knowledge* that our First Father had *sinned*, and knew no more of his *sinful Condition* than History tells us of it; if we had only certain *instituted Types* and *Figures* to keep up the Remembrance of it in our Minds, we should never be the worse for his Sins; we should have no Hurt by *owning* ourselves to be Children of a sinful Father, if his *Nature*, *Life* and *Spirit* was not propagated in us: So, if we have only a *notional Belief* that Jesus is become the

Second Adam, to redeem or *regenerate* the fallen Nature ; if we know this only in the *Notion* and *History* kept up in our Minds by *outward Figures* and *Ordinances,* though we contend ever so much for this Belief of a Saviour, and write *Volumes* in Defence of it ; yet he is not *our Saviour,* till his *Nature, Life,* and *Spirit,* be born in us. If there be any Man in the World, in whom the *Nature* of *Adam* is not, he has *no Sin* from *Adam.* If there be any Man, in whom the *Life* of Jesus is not, he has *no Righteousness* from him. We must have Life and Righteousness in the same *Truth and Reality* in us from the Second *Adam,* as we have Sin and Death in us from the First.

(25.) The Whole of the Matter is this : This World is our *Curse* and *Separation* from God; by the Mystery of our Redemption it is turned into a short State of *Purification,* and can only be made so, by our going with our *whole Will* and *Desire* out of it, and away from it, as *Adam* by *his Will* and *Desire* sought after, and fell into it. The Second *Adam* must take us out, as the First *Adam* brought us into this World. Our Bodies are our Burdens which Sin has laid upon us : Our *stinging, wounding* Passions are the *Nails* which must fasten our Hands and Feet to the *Cross* on which we are to die, and commend our Spirit into the Hands of God, as our Lord did. But yet, all this Turning with our *whole Will,* and *Desire* towards God, and Paradise, all this *Bearing* our Cross, and passing through the *fiery Trials* of this Life, is still but *preparatory* to our Salvation, which wholly consists in the *Incarnation* of the Son of God in the Soul, or Life of Man. *That* must be *done,* and *born* in us, which was done, and born in the Virgin *Mary.* As our Sin and Death is, *Adam in us,* so our Life and Salvation is, *Christ in us,* This is it alone that *saves* us, that *delivers* us from the *Fall,* that *restores* all that was lost in *Adam ;* by this alone what died in *Adam,* is brought to Life again in us ; by this alone we can be taken out of an earthly *Life, Nature,* and *World,* and translated into a heavenly *Life,* Nature, and World.

(26.) Christ, by the overshadowing of the Holy Spirit, became in the Body of the holy Virgin *Mary,* of the same Nature with that *First Man,* which was created in Paradise, who, according to the *Purpose* of God, was to have been the *Father* of an holy, paradisaical *Race* of Men. Now the *First Purpose* of God must *stand,* and that which God designed must *come to pass.* But seeing the First *Adam* failed in this *Design* of God, and was not the *Generator* of such a Race of Men, therefore the Wisdom of God provided a *Second Adam,* who was born of the Virgin *Mary* in the *same Degree* of Perfection, in which the first Man was *created.* To this holy, paradisaical, human Nature, the *Son of*

God was *personally* united; and thus Christ, the Second *Adam*, took the *Place* of the First, and stands as the Regenerator, Redeemer, Second Father of all the Sons of *Adam*. Now as we are *earthly, corrupt*, and *worldly* Men, by having the *Nature* and *Life* of the First *Adam* propagated in us, so we must become *holy, paradisaical*, and *heavenly* Men, by having the *Life* and *Nature* of the Second *Adam* derived into, or regenerated in us; or, as the Scripture speaks, by being *born again* of him. Therefore if we are to have the *Nature* of Christ regenerated in us, as the Life of *Adam* is *born* in us; if we are to be *like him* in Nature, as we are like to *Adam* in Nature; if we are to be the heavenly Sons of the one, as we are the earthly Sons of the other, then there is an *absolute Necessity*, that *That* which was *done* and *born* in the Virgin *Mary*, be also by the *same Power* of the Holy Ghost *done* and *born* in us, by a *Seed* of Life derived into us from Christ our Regenerator. The *Mystery* of Christ's Birth must be the Mystery of *our Birth;* we cannot be his Sons, but by having the *Birth of his Life* derived into us; for the *new* paradisaical Man must be brought forth in the *same manner* in every individual Person; *that* which brought forth this holy Birth in the *First Adam* at his Creation, and in the *Second Adam* in the Virgin *Mary, that alone* can bring it forth in any one of their Offspring. Jesus Christ therefore stands as our *Regenerator*, to help us by a *Second Birth* from him, to such an *holy, pure, and undefiled* Nature, as he himself received in the *Blessed Virgin*, and which we should have received in Paradise from our *First Father*.

From the Time of the Fall of *Adam*, the *incorruptible Seed* of Christ is in us all, in the whole human Nature; he has Power, as the Son of God, to quicken and raise it up, till it comes to be that First holy Image of the Blessed Trinity. And when a Divine Faith arises in this *Seed of Life*, by which it lays hold on Christ as the Author, Preserver, and Finisher of its Life, as the Atonement, Saviour and Deliverer from the Death and Hell that surrounds it, then it grows up into a *new, inward* Man, of the same Nature with *that* which *appeared* in Paradise, and with *that* which was *born* in the Virgin *Mary*. Then the Birth of the Son of God, the Birth of the Spirit, and that *First holy Humanity* which *Adam* lost, are all restored to us, but in a *Mystery* in the inward Man *hid* in God, till the Resurrection shall separate everything that is *earthly, dark*, and *corruptible*, from it. Thus by Faith in Christ we *put on Christ*, he becomes *formed in us*, we eat *his Flesh*, and drink *his Blood*, and have *his Nature* and *Life in us;* that is, we have a Flesh and Blood, a holy Humanity, derived into us from Christ, in the *same Reality* as we have Flesh and Blood, a corrupt Humanity from *Adam*, our First Father. Thus we are real Members, living Branches, and new-born Children, of Christ, our Regenerator; he is our Father, and as such, as certainly brings us into the Kingdom of Heaven, Heirs of all his Glory, as *Adam* brought us into the Prison of this World, Heirs of all his Sin and Misery. This is the Whole of the Christian Redemption. Let us look where we will, and talk of what we will, there is no Possibility of Salvation for any one Son of *Adam*, but in this *Divine Birth*, nor can this Birth be had any other way. And to this great Truth all the Writings of the New Testament bear undeniable Witness. For the further and full View of this important Matter, I refer the Reader to another *little Book*,* which, if I could afford it, should be sent *gratis* into all Parts of the Kingdom. Look now at *yourselves*, at the *World*, at *Religion*, in this true Light, and surely you must enough see and feel the desirable Nature of every Virtue, and every Degree of it, which the Gospel sets before you. Surely you must awaken into a strong Abhorrence of everything, that the *Fall* has brought upon you, whether it be in your *Souls*, your *Bodies*, or the *State* of the World into which you are fallen. To renounce the poor Interests of a worldly Life, to be content with a *Pilgrim's Fare* in it, to live looking and longing after that which you have lost ; to have no more of Covetousness, of Pride, of Vanity, and Ambition, than *John the Baptist* had ; to live unto God in your *Shops*, your *Employments* and *Estates*, with such Thoughts and Desires of going to your heavenly Father, as the *lost Son* had when he saw his poor Condition, eating *Husks* among *Swine*, is only a Proof that you are, like him, *come to yourselves*, that you begin to see *what*, and *how*, and *where* you are. Surely you can need no Exhortations to hasten and run to your Redeemer, to ask and beseech him in Faith and Love to do everything in you and for you, that your darkened corrupted Heart, and polluted Body, stands in need of. He now stands as near you, as full of Love over you, as he did to *Lazarus* when he raised him from the Dead. He is no further from your Call, than he was from the Call of blind *Bartimæus*, whose Eyes he immediately opened. Surely it should now be more needless to exhort you to look earnestly and diligently after every Means of recovering your first glorious State, than to exhort the Blind to receive their Sight, the Sick to accept of Health, or the Captive to suffer his Chains to be taken off. For when you thus see your *Misery* and your *Redemption* in this strong Light, both of them so exceeding

---

* *Grounds and Reasons of Christian Regeneration, &c.*

great, you see *something* that must needs penetrate and awaken the inmost Depth of your Soul, that leaves you no room to *doubt* about the Nature of any Virtue, no Liberty to indulge *one vain* Passion, or to think it any Hardship that the Gospel calls you to be *perfect*. For in *this Light* every Virtue of the Gospel stands known and recommended to us, just as *Health, Purity* and *Sight*, stand recommended to a *sickly, noisome, blind Leper*, who was shut up in a *Place* that continually increased all his Evils. It strips us of nothing but the *Uncleanness* of Leprosies, the *Miseries* of Sores, Pains, and Blindness. It takes nothing from the World which is about us, but its Poison and Power of infecting us. So that to be called to the Height of all Virtue attainable in this Life, however excessive it may seem to the *Reasonings* of Flesh and Blood, is only being called *away* from every *Misery* and *Evil* that can be avoided by us. Jesus Christ is become our Regenerator, that we may again be made like unto God, have the *Purity* and *Perfection* of an angelic Nature, and be made capable of enjoying the infinite Riches and Treasures of the Divine Nature to all Eternity. No Virtue therefore has any *blamable Extreme* in it, till it *contradicts* this general End of Religion, till it *hinders* the Restoration of the Divine Image in us, or make us *less fit* to appear amongst the Inhabitants of Heaven. *Abstinence, Temperance, Mortification* of the Senses and Passions, can have *no Excess* till they hinder the *Purification* of the Soul, and make the Body less useful and subservient to it. *Charity* can have *no Excess* till it *contradicts* that Love which we are to have in Heaven, till it is *more* than that which would *lay down* its Life even for an *Enemy*, till it *exceeds* that which the first Christians practised, when they had *all things common ;* till it exceeds *that* of St. *John,* who requires him that has *Two Coats,* to give to him that has none, and he that *has Meat* to do likewise ; till it is loving our poor Brethren *more* than Christ has loved us ; till it goes *beyond* the Command of loving our Neighbour as we love ourselves ; till it forgets that our own Life is to be preserved.

See now how the Doctor instructs and enlightens his Readers on these Two great Articles, Christian *Temperance,* and *Charity.* To remove the Restraints of the First, he says, ' Our Blessed ' Saviour came eating and drinking, was present at Weddings, ' and other Entertainments ; nay, at one of them worked a ' Miracle to make Wine, when it is plain, there had been more ' drank than was absolutely necessary for the Support of Nature, ' and consequently something had been indulged to Pleasure ' and Cheerfulness.'*

---

* Page 17.

O Holy Jesus, that thy Divine Life should, by a Preacher of thy Gospel, be made a *Plea* for Liberties of Indulgence! The Doctor's Argument lies in this; that our Saviour worked a *Miracle to help them to more Wine*, when they had already *drank to the Indulgence of Pleasure* and *Cheerfulness,* therefore he could be *no Enemy* to such pleasant Indulgences; therefore it is *lawful* for us Christians to delight in them. Now if this Lawfulness is well proved, the Doctor may go on and prove these Indulgences to be *good* and *pious;* because what our Saviour worked a *Miracle to promote*, must needs be esteemed to be so. And so the adding another Bottle, when Friends are rejoicing, may be made to be a *Christian Duty.* But the Doctor should have remembered, that the *Wine* here spoken of, was not *common Wine*, and therefore has not the *least Relation* to our *common Drinking*—that it was not Wine from the *Juice* of the Grape—that it had nothing in it, but what came from a heavenly Hand—that it must have in it the *Purity* and *Virtue* of him that made it—that it had as good *Qualities* in it, and was fitted to have the *same Effects* upon *some* that drank it, as the *Clay,* which he moistened with *his Spittle*, had upon the Eyes of the *Blind.* He should have remembered, that it was *Water*, only *so altered*, and endued with *such Qualities,* as he pleased to *put into* it; and therefore we may be sure, it was Water as *highly blessed* for their Use, as they were *capable* of; we may be sure it was fitter to allay the Heat and Disorder of their Drinking, than if it had been *Water unaltered* by our Saviour. How suitable was this Miracle to a Feast! How worthy of so Divine a Person! To make them *cooler,* by giving them Water made fitter for that Purpose, and to raise their *Faith* by its miraculously seeming to be turned into the best of Wine. Well might it be said of this Miracle, that he thereby *manifested forth his Glory*, *and his Disciples believed on him.* But according to the Doctor's horrid Account of this Miracle, it must be said, that he thereby showed his Approbation of *continuing* such Pleasures of Drinking, and has left us a Proof, that we may do the same. But I must further vindicate the Life and Example of our Blessed Lord from the Indignity and Irreverence done to it by the Doctor. Our Blessed Lord came indeed, as he says of himself, *eating and drinking.* But how, or in what Manner, or in what Sense, did he say this of himself? Why, it was in Opposition to, and Distinction from, *John the Baptist*, who came eating only *one Sort* of Food. And it was to show the *Jews* their great Guilt in this respect, that *nothing* could do them any good. For the *Mortification* of the Baptist they condemned, as coming from the Devil; and the *Condescension* of the Holy

Jesus in coming to their Tables, they accused as *Gluttony* and *Wine-bibbing.* Now the Doctor is plainly doing what our Lord accused the *Jews* of; he with them condemns the *Mortification* of the Baptist, as coming from the Devil. But he differs from the *Jews* in this, that he does not condemn, but *approves* of our Lord, as a *Friend* to Feasts, and merry Meetings.

Our Saviour, suitable to his gracious Love, in coming into the World, sought the Conversation of Sinners and Publicans; because he came to *save that which was lost,* and because he knew that some amongst such Sinners were more movable, than the proud Sanctity of the learned Pharisees. But may we thence conclude, that the *Lives* of such Sinners were not blamable in his Sight? Is not this as well, as to imagine he *favoured* the Indulgences of Feasting and good Fellowship, because he was found there? The Holy Jesus conversed *more freely,* spoke of himself, and of the Kingdom of God, *more divinely* to a *wicked Woman of Samaria,* than he appears to have done to his Disciples. May we thence conclude, that he *approved* of a Woman of that Character, or that he thereby set his *Seal* to the Goodness and Lawfulness of her Way of living? Is not this as well, as to make his *Presence* at a Wedding, an *Approbation* of the Freedom and Indulgences of such Feasts?

O Holy Jesus, thou didst nothing of thyself, thou soughtest only the Glory of thy Father, from the Beginning to the End of thy Life; thou spentest whole Nights in Prayer in Mountains and Desert Places; thou hadst not where to lay thy Head; thy common poor Fare with thy Disciples was *barely Bread* and *dried Fish;* thy miraculous Power never helped thee to any Dainties of Refreshment, though ever so much fatigued, and fainted with Labour. But yet, because this Holy Jesus came into the World to save *all Sorts* of Sinners, and to show that every Kind and Degree of Sin could be taken away, and forgiven by him, therefore he came into *all Places,* and entered into *all Sorts* of Companies. He did not, as the Baptist, tie himself to *one Sort* of Food, but he came eating and drinking. But why did he so? It was, that he might reprove and convert Sinners at their own Tables. He came, not to indulge himself, or to find such Gratifications as the Baptist abstained from, but to *work Miracles,* to awaken and astonish Sinners in the *Midst* of their Indulgences.

It is said, that wherever the *King* is, there is the *Court.* But with much more Reason may it be said, that wherever our Saviour came, *there* was the *Temple,* or the *Church.* He came to *Feasts* and *Entertainments* with the same Spirit, for the same End and in the same Divine Power, as he went to raise a *dead*

Corpse; namely, to show forth the Glory of God. Wherever he came, it was in the *Spirit* and *Power* of the Redeemer of Mankind; everything he did, was only to destroy the Works of the Devil, to deliver Men from his Power, raise the *Dead,* and give *Sight* to the Blind, and *Ears* to the Deaf; it made no Difference to him, whether he did this in the *Temple,* or in the *Streets,* at a *Feast,* or at a *Funeral.* As he was everywhere God, so every Place became Holy to him. *Lastly,* If our Saviour came *Eating* and *Drinking,* and was present, as is pretended, at cheerful Entertainments, to show his *Approbation* of such Indulgences, and to leave us a *Proof,* that we may do so too; how came *John the Baptist,* that severe Master of Mortification, to be a fit Preparer of the Way to the Kingdom of Heaven? Surely his *Voice* must *cry wrong,* if such Mortification was not *right.* And if our Saviour disapproved of the *Severity* of his Life and Manners, how came he to point him out to the *Jews,* as a *burning* and *shining Light?* Thus much may serve to vindicate our Saviour's holy Life and Example from the shocking Misapplication the Doctor has made of it.

Let us now see how he treats and instructs the charitable Christian in these Words: 'What! says the *Half-Thinker,* is 'not Charity to the Poor, a most excellent Thing? And can I 'be too charitable? Can I therefore bestow too much upon the 'Poor? I answer, Would you consider the other Side, you 'would perceive, that though you cannot be too charitable, yet 'you may bestow too much upon the Poor, to the Ruin of your 'Wife and Children, which is not Charity, but *Madness,* and a 'great and *most grievous Sin.* Did you never hear, that '*Charity begins at Home?* Did you never read that of St. '*Paul?* If any provide not for his own, and especially those 'of his own House; he hath denied the Faith, and is worse 'than an Infidel.'*

The Doctor's Proverb I shall leave to himself. But the Text of St. *Paul,* which he has as grossly mistaken and misapplied, as he did our Saviour's Miracle, I must take out of his Hands. St. *Paul's* Words are quoted to prove, that it is *Madness, a great and grievous Sin,* for anyone, through Charity to the Poor, to render himself unable to provide for his *Wife* and *Children.* Now the Apostle in this Place speaks no more about *this Sin,* than he speaks against the Sin of *Watching* and *Prayer.* Nay, what is more, there is not in all his Writings, or in the whole New Testament, the *least Supposition* or *Hint* that such a Sin ever was, or would be committed by any charitable

---

* Page 60.

Man. The Apostle was singly speaking of *such Women* as were to be taken into the Order of *Widows*, for the Service of the Church, and to be *maintained* by it.* Verse 4, he says, that such Widows as had *Children* or *Nephews* that could support them, such were not to be maintained by the Church. And to such *Sons* and *Nephews* who have *Mothers* and *Aunts* that thus want their Assistance, he says, ' If anyone provide not for his ' own, especially for those of his own House,' *i.e.* If any *Sons* or *Nephews*, having Mothers or Aunts become *desolate Widows*, and take not care to assist them, especially if they live with them, such have renounced the Piety of the Gospel, and have not so much Humanity as *Infidels*. This alone is the Plain Doctrine of the Apostle, which the Doctor has grossly perverted, to the condemning of that which he never thought of, either there, or in any Part of Scripture. On the contrary, the Scripture abounds with Passages that might persuade us, that no *Family* could ever be ruined by the *Alms* and *Charity* of its Father. 'I have been young, and now am old,' saith the Psalmist, 'yet never saw I the Righteous forsaken, or their Seed ' begging their Bread. The liberal Soul shall be made fat, and ' he that watereth, shall be watered again.' They that cannot believe this, want the Faith of Christians. Had anyone in the Apostle's Time reduced his Wife and Children to *Want*, by his *great Charity* to the Poor, the Apostle would have been so far from rebuking him, as a *half-thinking Fool*, or exposing him to others, as guilty of *Madness*, and *grievous Sin*, that he would have told them, that he had consecrated *himself* and *Family* to the Church, that he and they were thereby become the dear Objects of the Church's *Care* and *Love*, since their present Distress was brought upon them by a boundless Love and Compassion for the Poor. I will now suppose that the Apostle had condemned a *Charity* in a *Father* that was to the Detriment of his *Wife* and *Children ;* I will put the following *Case* in as high Terms as the Doctor can well desire. Let it be supposed that some good *Bishop*, possessed of as rich a *Bishopric* as that of *Winchester*, should through his extensive Love and Charity for the Poor throughout his whole Diocese, be forced to use the *utmost Frugality* in Family Expense, and to bring up his Children in *Employments* of Labour, to help themselves to *Food* and *Raiment ;* one a *Carpenter*, in which Business our Saviour is said to have laboured in his Youth ; another a *Maker of Tents*, the *Trade* of the great Apostle ; and the rest in the like manner. Let it be supposed, that when he died, he left only

---

1 Tim. v. 5, 8.

Twenty Pounds a Year amongst them, not to be *possessed* by any one of them, but only to be *used* by everyone, as *Sickness* or *Age* made them stand in need of it, with this Injunction, that it should be given to other *sick* and *helpless* People, when there was *no such* amongst themselves. Let it be supposed that by his Life and Conversation, he had filled his Wife and Children with the *true* and *perfect* Spirit of the Gospel, that they *loved* and *rejoiced* in his Memory for all the Good that he had done to them, desiring nothing but to go through the World in that same *Humility*, *Piety*, *Charity*, *Love* of God, and *Renunciation* of the World, as he had done. Will the Doctor say, that this *Bishop* had *ruined* his Wife and Children? that *half-thinking* had betrayed him into a *most grievous* Sin, that he had by this Life *denied the Faith*, and become *worse* than an *Infidel?* I will venture to say, that if such a Bishop should ever appear in this Kingdom, he would bid fair to put an End to *Infidelity* through all his Diocese, though it were the largest in the Nation. Now if the Doctor does not *know* of anyone, either amongst the *Laity* or *Clergy*, who is *ruining* his Wife and Children by a *greater* and *more blamable* Charity than that of this Bishop, it must be said, that he has been in too much Haste; that his *Zeal* has not proceeded from *Knowledge;* and that he has been throwing *cold Water* upon Charity, before there was any *Flame* in it.

I now proceed to show in a more general Way, the blamable Nature and Design of the Doctor's Discourse. The whole Christian World, from the Time of our Saviour to this Day, has been praying, 'Thy Kingdom come, thy Will be done on Earth 'as it is in Heaven.' Sacraments, Divine Worship, and the Order of the Clergy, are appointed as ministerial Helps for this End, to raise, set up, and establish, this Kingdom of God on Earth. The *Fall* of Man brought *forth* the Kingdom of this World; Sin in all Shapes is nothing else but the *Will* of Man driving on in a State of *Self-Motion*, and *Self-Government*, following the Workings of a Nature *broken off* from its Dependency upon, and Union with, the Divine Will. All the Evil and Misery in the Creation arises *only* and *solely* from this one Cause. There is not the smallest Degree of Distraction, Pain, or Punishment, either within us, or without us, but what is owing to this, *viz.*, that Man stands *out of* his Place, is not *in*, and *under*, and *united* to God as he should be, as the Nature of Things require. God created everything to partake of his *own Nature*, to have some Degree and Share of his *own Life* and *Happiness*. Nothing can be good or evil, happy or unhappy, but as it does or does not stand in the same Degree of *Divine*

Life in which it was created, receiving in God, and from God, all that Good that it is capable of, and co-operating with, and under him, according to the Nature of its Powers and Perfections. As soon as it turns *to itself*, and would, as it were, have a *Sound* of its *own*, it breaks off from the *Divine Harmony*, and falls into the Misery of its own *Discord;* and all its Workings then are only so many Sorts of Torment, or Ways of feeling its own Poverty. The Redemption of Mankind can then only be effected, the Harmony of the Creation can only then be restored, when the Will of God is the Will of every Creature. For this Reason our Blessed Lord having taken upon him a created Nature, so continually declares against the doing anything of himself and always appeals to the Will of God, as the only *Motive* and *End* of everything he did, saying, that it was his *Meat* and *Drink to do the Will* of him that sent him.

What now can be so desirable to a sober, sensible Man, as to have the *vain, disorderly* Passions of his own corrupted Heart *removed* from him, to be filled with such *Unity, Love,* and *Concord,* as flows from God, to stand *united* to, and *co-operating* with the Divine Goodness, willing nothing, but what God wills, loving nothing, but what God loves, and doing all the Good that he can to every Creature, from a Principle of *Love* and *Conformity* to God. Then the Kingdom of God is come, and his Will is done in that Soul, as it is done in Heaven. Then Heaven itself is in the Soul, and the Life, and Conversation of the Soul is in Heaven. From such a Man the Curse of this World is removed; he walks upon consecrated Ground, and everything he meets, everything that happens to him, helps forward his *Union,* and *Communion* with God. For it is the *State* of our *Will,* that makes the *State* of our *Life;* when we receive everything *from* God, and do everything *for* God, everything does us the *same Good,* and helps us to the same Degree of Happiness. *Sickness* and *Health, Prosperity* and *Adversity,* bless and purify such a Soul in the *same Degree;* as it turns everything *towards* God, so every Thing becomes *Divine* to it. For he that *seeks* God in everything, is sure to *find* God in everything. When we thus live wholly unto God, God is wholly ours, and we are then happy in all the Happiness of God; for by uniting with him in *Heart,* and *Will,* and *Spirit,* we are united to all that he is, and has in himself. This is the Purity and Perfection of Life, that we pray for in the Lord's Prayer, that *God's Kingdom may come,* and *his Will be done* in us, as it is in Heaven. And this we may be sure is not only *necessary,* but *attainable* by us, or our Saviour would not have made it a Part of our daily Prayer. It may now then justly be asked, have we yet obtained that, which we have been so long, and so universally praying for? Can we look upon the Church of this Nation, as drawing *near*, or even *tending* to this State of Perfection? Can we be carried to any one *Parish*, either in *Town* or *Country*, where it can with Truth be said of any one *Pastor* and his *Flock*, that there the Kingdom of God is *coming*, and his Will *begins* to be done on Earth, as it is done in Heaven? Can we therefore find any *one Parish*, where the *Pastor* has not *great Reason* to reject the Doctor's Discourse, and to pray both for himself and his Flock, that they may enter *much further* into the Spirit and Practice of Christianity, than they have yet entered, that the Gospel may have *much greater* Power over them than it hath yet had, and that they all may, with a most awakening Conviction, *see* and *understand* what it is, that has made so *Divine* and *powerful* a Religion, so without its *proper Effect* upon them? For if the Case be thus, if we stand at this amazing Distance from that State of Perfection to which Christ has called us, though we have his infallible Promise to be with us to the End of the World, to assist us with *such Power* and *Strength* from above, as to obtain, and do everything that we pray for, through a *right Faith* in him, and Conformity to his Laws and Example; if the Case be thus, does not *Heaven* and *Earth* seem to call upon *every Minister* of the Gospel, to take *some Share* to himself of this *miserable State* of Things, and to endeavour to convince both *himself* and his *Flock*, that they have not yet been Christians in *true earnest*, that they have professed Christ with the Tempers of *Jews* and *Heathens*, that they have not yet entered into the *narrow Way* that leads to Life; that they have not yet enough *renounced* the World; not enough *denied* themselves; not enough *emptied* their Hearts of Passions hurtful to Piety; not enough *offered* and *devoted* themselves to God; not enough made the Spirit of Religion the Spirit of *their Lives;* not enough sought for Strength and Deliverance from Sin by a *firm* and *living Faith* in Jesus Christ, who is made *Righteousness* and *Sanctification* to every Sinner that turns to God through Faith in him; not enough prayed, and desired that they might be *born again* of God by the awakening and quickening the *incorruptible* Seed of Divine Life in their Souls, so that Christ may be truly said to be *formed* in them; not enough prayed, and desired to be *everywhere,* and on *all Occasions,* under the perpetual Influence and Guidance of the Holy Spirit, that they may think, and say, and do everything by his Holy Inspiration; not enough looked to that *first and great* Commandment, of loving God with our whole Heart and whole Strength; not enough endeavoured to keep the *next,* which is like unto it, that of loving our Neighbour, *as we love* ourselves; not enough renounced such

Fashions, Customs, and Conformities, to the World, as greatly corrupt the Heart, and grieve and separate the Holy Spirit from it. Now which way soever we consider the lamentable State of Religion amongst us, whether they be Evils *within* or *without* the Church, no Evil can be *removed*, nor any *Remedy* be procured by us of the *Clergy*, but in this *one Way*, That every *Individual* of the *Order*, from the highest to the lowest, begin in right Earnest with himself, open the Book of his *own Heart* and Life, and consider seriously in the Presence of God, whether, according to *his Degree* in the Ecclesiastical Function, the World has had its *due* Share of *Salt* and *Light* from him; whether all that is in the World, the *Lust of the Flesh*, the *Lust of the Eyes*, and the *Pride of Life*, have been so *openly*, so *constantly* discouraged and renounced by him, that the *whole Form* of his Life has been one loud, continual Call to all Orders of Christians, to set their Affections on Things above, to mind only the one Thing needful; to have nothing at Heart, but to be in Christ new Creatures, seeking, intending, desiring nothing through the Pilgrimage of this Life, but to *live unspotted from the World*, and to obtain every Height of Holiness, and heavenly Affection, which becomes those who are to be called Sons and Heirs of God with Christ Jesus. If Religion was at this Time in a most flourishing State amongst us, abounding with such Congregations as made up the primitive Church, it would be *great Injustice* to suppose that the Clergy had not, under God, been the *chief Instruments* of building it up to such a State of Perfection, since they are considered by our Saviour himself, as the *Salt* and *Light* of the World, which are to preserve it both from Darkness and Corruption. Seeing then that an *universal Corruption* of Manners is on all hands confessed to have overspread this Christian Nation, and the *true Spirit* of Religion hardly *anywhere* to be seen, nothing can be more *reasonable* in itself, more suitable to the *present State* of Things, than for every *Clergyman*, whereever his *Lot* is fallen, to suspect himself to have, in *some Degree* or other, contributed to this common Calamity, and to be *more* or *less* chargeable with the Guilt of it, and to try to discover his *own State*, by such like Questions as these, laid *home* to his Conscience. If Christianity has not done that to my Flock which is the *only End* and Intent of it, is there nothing of this Failure *chargeable* upon my Conduct over it? Can my righteous Judge lay nothing grievous to my Charge on that Account? Can my own Heart bear me Witness that I did not run in my *own Will*, was not driven by *human Passions*, but stayed and waited till the *Holy Spirit* called me to this Office? Have I not undertaken the *Care* of other's Souls, before I had ever any *true* and *real* Care of my own? Have I not presumed to *convert* and *strengthen* others, before I was converted myself? To preach by *hearsay* of the Grace, and Mercy, and Salvation, of the Gospel, whilst I myself was an *obedient Slave* to Sin? Have I not taken upon me to *explain* and *lay open* the Mysteries of God's Love in Christ Jesus, before they had had their *proper Entrance* into my own Soul? Has my own *Repentance, Compunction,* deep *Sensibility* of the Burden of Sin, and *want* of a Saviour, taught me how to make the Terrors of the Lord known in the Deep of every Man's Heart, and to awaken and pierce the Consciences of Sinners? Has my own *true and living Faith* in Christ my Saviour, my own Experience of the atoning, cleansing, sanctifying Power of his precious Blood, enabled me with great Boldness to tell all Sinners, that to the *Faith which worketh by Love*, Christ always and infallibly saith, what he said in the Gospel, ' Thy Sins are forgiven : thy ' Faith hath saved thee ; go in Peace' ?

Can my own Heart, and God, who is greater than our Hearts, bear me Witness that in my sacred Office I have not sought *myself*, or my *own Things*, but the Things of Jesus Christ? If I have changed one *Flock* or *Station* for another, or added one *Cure* to another, have I done it in *Singleness of Heart, as unto the Lord*, and not for *myself ?* Has all that I have *sought* or *done* of this Kind, been *only* from this *Motive*, and in this *View*, that I might be more truly *faithful* to him that hath called me, and be more and more *spent* and *sacrificed* for the Salvation of Souls? Have I neglected no Means of fitting and preparing myself for the Illuminations of God's Holy Spirit, which alone can enable me in any Measure to speak to, and work upon, the Hearts and Consciences of Men? Have I earnestly longed, and laboured after every Kind and Degree of inward and outward Holiness, and Purity of *Body, Soul,* and *Spirit*, that my *standing* at the *Altar* may be acceptable to God, and my Prayers and Intercessions for my Flock *avail* much before him? Has my own *Self-denial, Renunciation* of the World, and *Love* of the Cross of Christ, enabled me to preach up those Duties in their *full Extent ?* Has my own strictly *pious Use* of the Things of this World, my own Readiness to relieve and assist every Creature to the utmost Extent of my Ability, fitted me to call others to these Things with Power and Authority ? Have all Ages and Conditions of People under my Care had their proper Instruction and Warning from me, so that I have spared no Folly, Vanity, Indulgence, or Conformity to the World, that hurts Men's Souls, and hinders their Progress in Piety ? Have I done all that by my Prayers and Preaching, Life and

Example, which Christ expects from those whom he has enjoined to feed his Sheep? Can my Flock by looking at me see what Virtues they want? Can they by following me, be led to every Kind and Degree of Christian Perfection? Lastly, has the Will of God and the Spirit of the Gospel been the Beginning and End, the Reason and Motive, the Rule and Measure, of my liking or disliking, doing or not doing, everything among those People with whom I have lived as their Minister? These are a few of such Questions as the present State of Religion in this *Island* calls upon every Minister of the Gospel to sift and try himself by. For as the *Order* of the Clergy is instituted for no other End, but for the *preserving* of Religion and true Piety in the World; so when any Age is more than ordinarily sunk in Vice and Impiety, the *whole Order* of the Clergy, and *every Member* of it, have great reason not only to be deeply *afflicted*, but greatly *affrighted* at it, and to suspect and fear their *own Conduct*, since that which is *their particular* Work, has had so *little* Success. They have great reason to apprehend, that it is some Degeneracy of Spirit, some common Misbehaviour, some general Negligence, some want of Example, some Failure in Doctrine, some Defect in Zeal and Care of their particular Flocks, that *too much* contributes to *so general* a Corruption of Manners. This does not suppose, that it is in the Power of our Order to regulate the Manners of People as we please; it only supposes, that of all human Means it has the *greatest Effect;* and that when any Nation or People are either very *good* or very *bad*, the Behaviour of the Clergy may *reasonably* be reckoned to have *greatly* contributed to it. Let us all therefore of the Clergy, who have any *right Sense* of the Nature of our Order, any *true Love* for our Brethren of it, awaken and stir up one another to a faithful Diligence in our Callings, not such as may secure us from public Scandal, and the Laws of the Land, but such a faithful Diligence as the Nature of our Office, the Spirit of the Gospel, and the present Decay of Religion, calls for. Let us beseech and entreat one another deeply to consider the great Need that this poor Nation hath of a *zealous, pious, exemplary, disinterested* and *laborious* Clergy; to consider the *dreadful Judgments* of God, that may justly be expected to fall first upon *our own Heads*, if this *true, only* Relief and Remedy is not procured by *all* of us, according to the *utmost* of our Ability. It is now no time for *Ease, Indulgence*, or worldly *Repose;* all is to be renounced, all is to be sacrificed; and we must in the *Spirit of Martyrdom* awaken the World into a *Faith* and *Love* of the Gospel. Now is the Time that we must *give up* all our worldly Regards, 'forsake all that we have; that we must hate Father

' and Mother, Wife and Children, and Brothers and Sisters, yea,
' and our own Lives also,' or we cannot be faithful Ministers of
Jesus Christ. The same Spirit which first planted the Gospel,
is now required to *recover* and *restore* it amongst us. We must
break off our Chains of *worldly Prudence*, and come forth in the
Spirit and *Power* of the Gospel; so live, and speak, and act,
whether in the Pulpit or out of it, that all who see and hear us
may be forced to confess that God is in us of a Truth, and that
his Holy Spirit hath sent us. A *Ministry* that hath not *this
Power*, that have not *full Proof*, both to themselves and others,
that the Holy Spirit is thus *with them*, opening the Kingdom of
God in their own Souls, and enabling them to preach it to
others with Spirit and Power, are to answer to God for their
Want of it.

To ask whether the Assistance of the Holy Spirit is to be
ordinary or *extraordinary*, is as needless and groundless a Distinction, as to ask whether a *Minister* of the Gospel ought to be
an *ordinary* or *extraordinary* good Man. The Operation of the
Holy Spirit in us since the *Fall*, is a *supernatural* Power, and
therefore in a just Sense *always* extraordinary, because enabling
us to be and do that, which the ordinary Power of fallen Nature
is insufficient for; but it is more or less restored to us, as we are
more or less fitted to receive it. And all that *Assistance* or
Renovation of the Holy Spirit which an Apostle might expect,
for the raising his own personal Holiness to its *greatest Height*,
or for enabling him with *Spirit* and *Power* to move, affect, and
convert the Hearts of Men to the Faith of the Gospel, may be
justly expected now by such Ministers of the Gospel, as do all
that which an Apostle did to obtain and receive it. Our
Religion is *founded* on this Doctrine,—that we are to be *born
again* of the Holy Spirit,—that it is to be the *Breath* and *Life* of
our new-born, inward Man,—that there is no *Sanctificatian* of
the Heart, no *Illumination* of the Mind, no *Knowledge* of Divine
Mysteries, no *Love* of holy Things, *possible* to be had, but in and
by the *Motion* and *Life* of this Holy Spirit *renewed* or *born
again* in us;—that its *Life, Motion,* and *Power*, in us, increaseth
according to our Faith, Prayers, and Desires of it.

Is it not now a *flat Denial* of all this to say, as is said by
some, that the *Establishment* of the Gospel in the World,
together with the Assistances of *human Learning* and *Languages*,
has been the *Occasion* why the Assistance of the Holy Ghost is
abated, and become only such as may be called *ordinary?* For
if we consult either Scripture or Experience, must it not be said,
that *worldly Peace* and *Prosperity* want *as much* to be sanctified
by the Holy Spirit, as *Persecution* and *Distress?* That *human*

Learning and *Knowledge* need as *high Degrees* of Divine Grace and Help, as *human Ignorance?* Is not the Blindness, the Infatuation and Corruption of *Men of Letters*, as notorious as that of *unlearned Men?* Does an *Editor* of *Terence, Horace*, or *Virgil*, receive such Illumination from *Plays* and *Poetry?* Do *Cardinals* and *Pluralists* receive so much *Unction* and *Assistance* from *human Establishments*, as to need *less* to be led and governed by the Holy Spirit of God? Or will we say, that a *critical Study* of divided Languages, and a Religion established in worldly *Ease* and *Peace*, are not only in themselves free from *Danger* and *Corruption*, but have so much of the *Nature of the Holy Spirit* of God in them, that they can be to us in *his Stead*, and make his sanctifying Operations upon us needed in a *less Degree?*

On the Part of God, our *Redemption* in Jesus Christ, and our *Sanctification* by the Holy Ghost, stand always in the *same Degree of Nearness and Fulness* to all of us; there is hardly a Chapter in the New Testament that can be understood, or its Doctrines observed, but upon the Supposition of this great Truth. If Christ is less *formed* in us than he was in the first Saints of the Church, if we come not to the *perfect Man, to the Measure of the Stature of the Fulness of Christ*, it is not because Christ is now become only our Redeemer in an *ordinary Way or Degree*, but it is because we have not *so turned to* him, not so turned *from* ourselves, not so counted all Things but *Dung*, that we might win Christ, and be found in him, as the first Saints did. If the Holy Spirit does not now in *such a Degree* renew, quicken, move, and sanctify our Hearts, and fill us with *such Degrees* of Divine Light and Love, as was done in the first Age of the Church, it is not because this sanctifying Spirit has committed *some Part* of his Work to *human Learning*, and so is become only our Sanctifier in a lesser and *ordinary Degree*, but it is because we ourselves have *forsaken this Fountain of living Waters, and hewed out broken Cisterns* for ourselves; it is because we have *grieved* this holy Spirit, *resisted* his Motions, *quenched* his holy Fire, and under an *outward Profession* of Christ have kept up that *Old Man, with his Deeds*, which cannot be the Temple and Habitation of the Holy Spirit.

If therefore we have any true Sense of the Nature and Weight of our Ecclesiastical Calling, any Desire to do the *full Work* of the Ministry, to satisfy the Wants and Necessities of our Flocks, if we have any Fear of being condemned as *useless, insignificant* Labourers in Christ's Vineyard, it is high time to awake from this Dream of an *ordinary* and *extraordinary* Sanctification of the Holy Spirit; it serves only to keep us *unsanctified*, shut up in *Death*, in the *dead Workings* of our own corrupted Nature, to keep us *learnedly* content with our State, as if we were *rich*, and *increased in Goods*, and *had Need of nothing*,* and hinders us from knowing that we are *wretched, and miserable, and poor, and blind, and naked.*

Several of the Clergy, whose Lot is fallen in this corrupt Age, may be supposed to have taken upon them the sacred Office, and to have lived in it, not enough according to the Nature and Spirit of it, merely through the *Degeneracy* of the Times, and from a Consideration that they are well enough, according to the *Measure* of Religion that now passes in the World. And perhaps there are few, if any, of the Order, however eminent for good Works, whose Virtues have not received *some Abatement* from the same Cause. This therefore may be added as another Reason why all the Clergy of this Land should search into their Lives and Conduct with the utmost Severity, and bring everything to the Test of the Letter and Spirit of the Gospel.

The Christian Religion has not had its proper Effect, nor obtained its intended End, till it has so set up the Kingdom of God amongst us, that 'his Will is done on Earth, as it is done 'in Heaven.' This is the Perfection that every Christian, when advancing forward in the several Degrees of Holiness and Purification, is to *tend* to, and *aspire* after. And if they who are to be taught, are to be thus separated from an earthly Nature, thus emptied of all worldly Passions, thus dead to the Workings of Self-will, and Self-love, that the Spirit of God may be all in all in them, what Manner of Men ought they to be, who are to *teach, promote, advance,* and *lead* the Way to this Purity and Perfection ? What a Distance ought he to be from every *Appearance* of Pride, that is to draw others to love and practise the profound Humility of the Blessed Jesus ? How ought he to deny his Appetites, to humble his Body, and be steady in all Kinds of Self-Denial, who would convince his Flock that *they who sow to the Flesh, shall of the Flesh reap* Destruction ? How heavenly-minded, how devoted to God, how attentive to the one Thing needful, how unspotted from the World ought he to be, who is to persuade others that they cannot possibly *serve God and Mammon?* How empty ought he to be of all *selfish* Cunning, all *worldly* Policy, all Arts and Methods of *Ambition*, who is to fix it deep in the Hearts of his Hearers, that *unless they become as little Children, they cannot see, nor enter into the Kingdom of God?* What open Hands, and open Heart ought he to have, what an Extent of Charity ought to be visible in him,

---

* Rev. iii. 17.

who is to bring his Flock to this Faith, that 'it is more blessed 'to give than to receive?' How remarkably, undeniably plain, open, sincere, undesigning, and faithful, should he be, who is to recommend, plant, and establish sincerity, Plainness, Simplicity, Truth, and Innocence, amongst his Flock? There is such a necessary Fitness in these Things, that the Force and Power of Religion must be much prevented, when its Precepts are recommended to the World by such as excuse themselves from the plain and open Practice of them?

The Office of the Ministry is of the highest Nature; it is a Trust which no Language can sufficiently express; and the unfaithful Discharge of it is, of all Conditions in Life, the most dreadful. To be charged with the *Death* and *Blood* of Souls, by that God who laid down his Life to redeem them, is a Condemnation that will carry more of Guilt and Punishment in it than any other. Would you know the Office of a Christian Pastor, you must look at the Office of Christ; would you know what Manner of Spirit he ought to be of, you must look at the Spirit of Christ. For the Work of the Ministry is only the Work of Christ committed to other Hands, who are to supply his Absence, to be here in his Stead, to be doing the same Things, and with the same Spirit that he did, till the End of the World.

Nothing is so highly *honourable* as to bear a Part in the Priesthood of Christ, and be employed in the Work of the Ministry; but then it should be *well considered*, that it is only honourable in the *same Sense* as it may be said that nothing is more honourable than to suffer as a *Martyr*. It is an Honour that is as different from all worldly Figure and Distinction, as the Glory of Christ upon the Cross is different from the Triumph of an earthly Prince. When therefore we think of the *Honour* and *Dignity* of the Pastoral Function, we should be careful to remember, that it is only the Honour of *dying* a Martyr, an Honour of *humbling, abasing,* and *sacrificing* ourselves with Christ, and continuing the Exercise of his suffering Priesthood for the Salvation of the World. The holy Function is often considered only as an *authoritative Commission* to minister in holy Things; but it is much more than this; it is a Call and Command to act with the Spirit of Christ, to represent his Purity, to continue his Holiness, to bear a Part of his Sacrifice, and devote themselves for the Good of others, as he did. A Priest that has *only* his Ordination to distinguish him, wants as much to make him a true Priest, as *Judas* wanted to make him a true Apostle. For though Holiness gives no Man a *Commission* to exercise the Pastoral Office, yet all who are called to it, are as much ordained and appointed to a *peculiar Holiness* of Life, as to the *Administration* of the Sacraments; and when they cease to be as *Light* and *Salt* to the rest of the World, they sin against the Pastoral Office in as *high a degree* as they that enter upon it without any Authority.

For the sacred Office is God's *Appointment*, to continue through all Ages of the World, the Spirit and Power of Christ, for reconciling Men to God, in the same *Manner*, and by the *same Means* of Holiness, Sacrifice, and Devotion, which Christ exercised when he was upon Earth. We need no other Proof of this, than this one Saying of our Blessed Lord: 'As my Father hath sent 'me, so send I you.' That is, for all the Ends for which I am come into the World, for all the same Ends I send you into it, to be there in my stead, to supply my Absence, to carry on the Work that I have begun, to exercise my Power, to act with my Spirit, to continue the Exercise of my Love, and Labour, and Suffering, for the Salvation of Mankind. To be sent by our Blessed Lord for the same Ends as he was sent into the World, is such an Appointment of us to all Kinds and Degrees of Holiness, as can never be rightly discharged, but by our giving and devoting ourselves wholly and absolutely unto God.

Imagine that you had lived with our Blessed Lord when he was upon Earth, that you had learned the Dignity and Divinity of his Person, that you had seen the Love which he bore to Mankind, that you had entered into the glorious Designs of his Kingdom; which were, to convert the Inhabitants of the Earth, poor Creatures of Flesh and Blood, into Sons of God, and Heirs of eternal Glory.

Imagine that you had seen him after his Resurrection, when he had redeemed the World, conquered Sin, Death, and Hell, and was about to take Possession of his Throne; imagine that then, in that State, you had seen him commission some of his Followers to be *Priests* and *Intercessors* with God on Earth, as he had been, to *feed*, and *nourish*, and *watch* over his Flock, as he had done, to go before them in *such exemplary* Holiness, such Love of God, such Compassion for Sinners, such Contempt of the World, such Poverty of Spirit, such Obedience and Resignation, as they had him for an Ensample; had you been present at all this, how would you then have *heard* and *felt* these Words: 'As my Father hath sent me, so send I you'?

What Sentiments of Piety, what Magnificence of Spirit, what exalted Holiness, would you have expected of those, who were called to succeed so great a Master in so great a Work? Could you think they could be fit for this Office, or were enough like him that had called them to it, unless they had *renounced* and *sacrificed* everything for the Sake of it? Could you think that any Care but that of the Church of God was proper for them? Would you not own that the Conversion of Sinners to God, ought to have been their *one only* Labour and Pains? that they were to seek for no other Happiness in this World, than such as their Lord and Master had done, but consider themselves as called from the common Affairs, Ease and Pleasures of Life, to be in Christ's Stead towards the rest of Mankind, to conduct them safely to eternal Happiness? Now when we consider the Apostles in this Light, as being the first that were entrusted with the *Care of Souls*, and from Christ himself, we can see no *Degree* of Zeal, no Height of Piety, no Compassion for Sinners, no Concern for the Honour of God, no Contempt of Sufferings, no Disregard of worldly Interest, no Watchings or Mortifications, no Fervours of Devotion, to which we of the Clergy are not equally obliged. For the Salvation of Mankind is still the same glorious, great and necessary Work that it was in their Days, is still to be carried on by the same Means, and is now in the Hands of the Clergy, as it was then in theirs. If it was their Happiness and Glory to be faithful to him that called them, to forget the little Interests of Flesh and Blood, and have nothing at Heart, but the Advancement of God's Kingdom, we shall fail both of Happiness and Glory, if we seek it any other way. If an Apostle, considering the Weight of reconciling Souls unto God, is forced to cry out, 'Who is sufficient for these things?' shall we think any Care but that which is the greatest, sufficient to make us stand uncondemned before God? It is a fatal Deception to imagine, that the Life of a Minister of God is ever to be a Life of Ease or worldly Repose. For though the temporal Sword be not always drawn against them, nor they forced to flee from one City to another, yet the World, the Flesh, and the Devil, have perhaps never so much Difficulty to be resisted, as in temporal Prosperity, nor have the Ministers of Christ ever more Occasion to put on all their Armour, than when the World is given up to Ease, and Peace, and Plenty. Swarms of Vice steal upon us in these Seasons, the Spirit and Life of Religion is in danger of being lost, and the Salvation of Souls is made more difficult, than in the most perilous Times. And how is such a State of Temptation to be resisted, such a Torrent of Vice to be opposed, but by the Clergy's showing themselves *visible* and *notorious* Examples of all the contrary Virtues. When Mankind are wallowing in Debauchery, wantoning in Pleasures, and given up to Vanity and Luxury in all Shapes, it is then the Duty of the faithful Minister, by his being crucified to the World, to proclaim himself the Messenger of a crucified Saviour, and to make his own self-denying, mortified, and heavenly Life, a *plain, open,* and *constant* Reproof of all vain Indulgences. For to yield to, or fall in with the Softness, Vanity, Luxury, Indulgence, or Avarice of the World, is the same Infidelity and Breach of Trust in the sacred Office, as to depart from the true Faith, and fall in with some abominable Heresy.

I believe I need not now help the Reader to observe, that the Doctor's Undertaking is further liable to these great Objections against it: *First,* That it calls us from the *Sin* and *Danger* of being *Righteous over-much,* when we are always to own, that we are not yet *Righteous enough.* Secondly, That it proposes to *stir* us up against *this Sin and Danger,* at a time, when this Nation is in Danger of the *severest Judgments* of God upon it, for a *general Irreligion* and Profaneness. *Thirdly,* That it tends to lead the *Clergy* from a *just Sense* of what the Nature of their Office, the Nature of Religion, and the present State of this Nation, requires of them. That it tends to raise an *ill Spirit* in them, not only to be *content* with an ordinary common Degree of Piety in themselves, and their Flocks, but, with a *watchful,* and *jealous* Eye to guard against all the *Beginnings* of an uncommon, or more than ordinary Sanctity of Life, either in themselves or others.

Thus, says he, 'To what a Height of Fanatic Madness in 'Doctrine, as well as Practice, are some advanced, who set out 'at first with an Appearance of *more than ordinary Sanctity in* 'Practice only?'* Is not this calling upon the *Clergy* to beware, how they admit these *Beginnings* of a more than ordinary Sanctity of Life, either in themselves, or those committed to their Care? Is it not plainly telling them, that they must stick *closely* and *steadily* to such Sanctity of Practice, as may be called ordinary, or else they will be in Fanatic Madness? Here is no Force put upon his Words, 'a more than ordinary Sanctity in 'Practice only,' is marked out as the genuine natural Cause of *Fanatic Madness;* and therefore the *Cause* is equally condemned with the *Effect.* Had he meant that his Reader should not have the *same Dislike* of the one, as of the other, or had he been afraid of his doing so, would he not have put in a Word in Favour of a *more than ordinary* Sanctity of Life? would he not have said, that he did not intend to *blame* that, or at least not *so much* as the other? But not a Word of this, a more than ordinary Sanctity in *Practice only,* and Fanatic *Madness,* are considered as *Cause* and *Effect,* and left in the same State of

---

* Page 39.

Condemnation, to be equally guarded against, and avoided by the Reader. So that in a Nation over-run with all manner of Corruption both of Principle and Practice, where the *ordinary State* of Religion has hardly the Form of Godliness, People are in *this State* of Things to content themselves with *such a Sanctity of Life*, as may be deemed to be *ordinary*.

And here I can't help addressing myself with great Affection to all my younger Brethren of the Clergy. According to the Course of Nature, you are likely to have the Care of the Church wholly upon your Hands in a short time; and therefore it is chiefly from you that the Restoration of true Piety is to be expected in this Nation. I beseech you, therefore, for your own Sakes, for the Gospel's Sake, for the Sake of Mankind, to devote yourselves *wholly* to the Love and Service of God. As you are yet but Beginners in this great Office, you have it in your Power to make your Lives the greatest Happiness, both to yourselves, and the whole Nation. You are entered into *Holy Orders* in degenerate Times, where *Trade* and *Traffic* have seized upon all holy Things; and it will be easy for you, without Fear, to swim along with the corrupt Stream, and to look upon him as an Enemy, or *Enthusiast*, that would save you from being lost in it. But think, my dear Brethren, think in time, *what Remorse* you are treasuring up for yourselves, if you live to *look back* upon a loose, negligent, corrupt, disorderly, worldly, unedifying Life, spent amongst those whose Blood will be required at your Hands. Think, on the other Hand, how blessedly your Employment will end, if by your *Voices*, your *Lives*, and *Labours*, you put a Stop to the Overflowings of Iniquity, restore the Spirit of the *Primitive Clergy*, and make all your Flock bless and praise God, for having sent you amongst them. Lay this down as an infallible Principle, that an *entire, absolute Renunciation* of all worldly Interest, is the only *possible Foundation* of that exalted Virtue which your Station requires. Without this, all Attempts after an exemplary Piety are in vain. If you want anything from the World by way of *Figure* and *Exaltation*, you shut the Power of your Redeemer out of your own Souls; and instead of converting, you corrupt the Hearts of those that are about you. Detest therefore, with the *utmost Abhorrence*, all Desires of making your Fortunes, either by *Preferments* or *rich Marriages*, and let it be your only Ambition to stand at the *Top* of every Virtue, as *visible Guides* and *Patterns* to all that aspire after the Perfection of Holiness. Consider yourselves merely as the *Messengers* of God, that are solely sent into the World on *his Errand*, and think it Happiness enough, that you are called to the *same Business*, for which the Son of

God was born into the World. I don't call you from a *sober Use* of human Learning, but I would fain persuade you to think nothing worthy of your Notice in *Books* and *Study*, but that which *directly* applies to the *Amendment* of the Heart, which makes you more *holy*, more *Divine*, more *heavenly*, than you would be without it. You want nothing, but to have the *Corruption* of your natural Birth *removed*, to have the Nature, Life and Spirit of Jesus Christ *derived into* you; as this is *all* that you *want*, so let this be *all* that you *seek* from *Books*, *Study*, or *Men*. This is the *only*, certain Way to become *eminent Divines*, instructed to the Kingdom of Heaven. And above all, let me tell you, that the *Book* of all Books is your *own Heart*, in which are written and engraven the deepest Lessons of Divine Instruction; learn, therefore, to be deeply attentive to the Presence of God in your Hearts, who is always *speaking*, always *instructing*, always *illuminating* that Heart that is attentive to him. Here you will meet the Divine Light in its *proper Place*, in that *Depth* of your Souls, where the *Birth* of the Son of God, and the *Proceeding* of the Holy Ghost, are always ready to spring up in you: And be assured of this, that so much as you have of *inward Attention* to God in your Hearts, of inward *Love* and *Adherence* to his holy *Light* and *Spirit* within you, so much as you have of real, unaffected *Humility* and *Meekness*, so much as you are dead to your *own Will* and *Self-love*, so much as you have of *Purity of Heart*, so much, and *no more*, nor *any further*, do you see and know the Truths of God. These Virtues are the only *Eyes*, and *Ears*, and *Senses*, and *Heart*, by which you will know and understand everything in Scripture, in that *Manner*, and in that Degree, in which God would have it understood, both for your own Good, and the Good of other People. It was owing to this *Purity of Heart*, and *Attendance* upon God, that an *ancient Widow*, named *Anna*,* knew him to be the *true Messiah*, whom the *Rulers*, *Chief Priests*, and *Doctors* of the Law, condemned as an *Impostor*. Had they, instead of their Adherence to *critical Knowledge*, and *rabbinical Learning*, been devoted to God in such Purity of Heart as she was, they had known as much of the Kingdom of God as she did. Place therefore all your Hope and Confidence, all your learned Help and Skill, in the ardent Love and Practice of *these Virtues*, and then, and then only, you will be able Ministers, holy Priests, and Messengers of God; your cleansed Hearts, like so many purified *Mirrors*, will be always penetrated, always illuminated, by the Rays of Divine Light, and you will no more need the *Critics*, to

---

* Luke ii. 36.

tell you what God speaks to you in the Scriptures, than to tell you what God speaks to you in your own Hearts. There are indeed in the Scriptures *Secrets* and *Mysteries*, only fully to be known in God's own Time, and not a *Minute* sooner; but of all Men in the World, the critical Dealers in *Words* and *Particles*, know the *least* of them, and make the *vainest* Attempts to understand them. But Scripture, considered as a Doctrine of *Life*, *Faith*, and *Salvation* in Jesus Christ, is a *sealed* or *unsealed*, an *open* or *shut up* Book to every Heart, in the same Proportion as it stands turned to the World, or turned to God. Nothing understands God, but the Spirit of God; nothing brings the Spirit of God into any Mind, but the renouncing all for it, the turning wholly to it, and the depending wholly upon it. *Human Learning* is by no means to be rejected from Religion; for it is of the *same good* Use and Service, and affords the *same Assistance* to Religion, that the *Alphabet*, *Writing* and *Printing* does. But if it is raised from this *Kind* and *Degree* of Assistance, if it is considered as a Key, or *the Key*, to the Mysteries of our Redemption in Jesus Christ, instead of *opening* to us the Kingdom of God, it *locks* us up in our *own Darkness*. It is a Truth confessed on all Hands, that the Kingdom of *Grace* is the *Beginning* of the Kingdom of *Glory*, and that they differ only in *degree*. Is not this plainly confessing, that the Light of the Kingdom of Grace must be *one* and the *same* with that of the Kingdom of Glory? How else can one be the Beginning of the other? And must not *that*, which is to be our one only Light in Heaven in a *full Degree*, be now our *one only* Light of all heavenly Things in a lower Degree? Therefore all that we see and know of the Kingdom of God *now*, must be by that *same Light* by which we shall see and know the Kingdom of God hereafter. God is an *all-speaking*, *all-working*, *all-illuminating* Essence, possessing the Depth, and bringing forth the Life of every Creature according to its Nature. Our Life is out of this Divine Essence, and is itself a creaturely Similitude of it; and when we turn from all Impediments, this Divine Essence becomes as *certainly* the true Light of our Minds *here*, as it will be *hereafter*. This is not *Enthusiasm*, but the Words of Truth and Soberness; and it is the running away from *this Enthusiasm*, that has made so many great Scholars as useless to the Church as *tinkling Cymbals*, and all *Christendom* a mere *Babel* of learned Confusion. I shall now only add one Word more: A composed Gravity of Life, a suitable Decency of outward Behaviour, is not the Thing that is demanded of you; your Piety must be solid, your Lives exemplary, the Perfection of your Virtues must shine before Men, or you will all of you in your *several Degrees*, stand chargeable with the ill State of Religion, that is about you.

I must now take Notice of an injurious Quotation or two that the Doctor has made from the *Treatise of Christian Perfection*. The Doctor quotes me as affirming, 'That not only the Wicked-'ness and Vanity of this World, but even its most lawful and 'allowed Concerns, render Men unable to enter, and unworthy to 'be received into the true State of Christianity.' And again that 'the Wisdom from above condemns all Labour as equally fruit-'less, but that which labours after everlasting Life.' Then the Doctor affirms thus: 'Here's an utter Condemnation of all 'Trades, and of all Professions, of all Business, and secular 'Concerns whatever.'* Does the Doctor then believe that I bought *Pen, Ink*, and *Paper*, and wrote that Book, to show that no Christian ought to *make, buy* or *sell* Pen, Ink, and Paper? And that I published that Book to prove that it was my Opinion that it was utterly unlawful for a Christian to be a *Printer*, a *Bookbinder*, or a *Bookseller?* Does not the Doctor know, that the *Christian Perfection* in the Two first Pages, to prevent all Mistake, openly *declares* for the *Continuance* of Mankind in their several States and Conditions, openly *declares* against a *Cloister*, or *any singular State of Life*, openly asserts Christian Perfection to consist in the *holy and religious* Conduct of ourselves in *every State* of Life?† Does he not know that in the *Serious Call to a Devout Life, &c.*, which presently followed the other Book, the very *Title* declares solely for a Piety *adapted to the State and Condition of all Orders of Men?* But there is something still more wonderful, more regardless of Right and Wrong in the Doctor's Charge against me; for in this very Passage quoted by him, secular Business is expressly affirmed to be *most lawful and allowed Concerns*. And yet from this Passage affirming the Lawfulness of worldly Business, and proceeding upon it as a certain Truth, the Doctor has extracted the Unlawfulness of all secular Concerns whatever. Again, Does not the Doctor know that he designedly mangled the Words he quoted, and left out that Part which showed the Reason of my so expressing myself? That I was there speaking to that Parable of our Lord's, where all that were bidden to the Feast, refused to come. *The First*, because he had bought a *Piece of Ground;* the other, because he must *try his Oxen;* the Third, because he *had married a Wife*. Then the Master in Anger said, 'None of these Men shall taste of my Supper.' Whence I thus observed 'This Parable teaches us, that not only the

---

* Page 15. † Page 2.

Answer to Dr. Trapp.

'Vices and the Vanity of the World, but its most lawful and
'allowed Concerns, render Men unable to enter, and unworthy to
'be received into the true State of Christianity.' And does not
everyone see this to be the plain, necessary, and inoffensive
Sense of the Parable? Had I not made Nonsense of it, if I had
said, that *lawful Business* could *not* become a *Hindrance* of
Men's Salvation? For are there not here Three *lawful Concerns*
become Three *Hindrances* of their coming to the Feast, and
Three *Reasons* of their being declared unworthy of it? Then
I go on to show, that it is not the Employment itself that is condemned,
but its being made a *Reason*, or *Excuse*, as in the
Parable, for not living wholly unto God, adding these Words,
the 'true Wisdom from above condemns all Labour as equally
'fruitless, but that which labours after everlasting Life.' Let but
Religion *determine the Point,* and *what can it signify, whether
a Man forgets God in his Farm,* or a *Shop,* or at a *Gaming Table?*
Now what is there here condemned, but the *forgetting God?*
Or will anyone say, that a *Shop,* and a *Farm,* are here condemned,
because God is to be *remembered* in them, or because
they are to be made Employments of Piety, that *labour after
everlasting Life?* The Doctor proceeds to charge me with
'positively asserting, that all Christians are, in all Ages, obliged
'to sell all that they have, and give it to the Poor.' I have been
so far from asserting this, that I have with all my Might said,
and proved the direct contrary, that *no Christians of any Age* are
obliged to it. Speaking of the Command of our Saviour's to
the young Man, 'to sell all, and give it to the Poor,' I have
shown, by Variety of Arguments, and Texts of Scripture, that
that Command calls no rich Man to *sell* what he has; that it
calls him only to do that with his Estate, which he is called to,
by the whole Tenour of Scripture, as having Riches, that are
not his own, of which he is only a Steward, and not a Proprietor,
as being obliged to love his Neighbour as himself in the Use of
them. That the Command of *selling all,* implies only such
heavenly Affection, such 'Disregard of Riches, as is expressed,
'by being dead to the World, having our Conversation in
'Heaven, being born again from above, and having overcome the
'World.' From the Beginning to the End of this Matter, I have
utterly rejected *all feeling,* and shown, that it means only a perfect
Charity, a *parting with the Self-Enjoyment of our Estates,
to make them, as far as we are able, the common Support of* those
People whom we are to love, as we love ourselves, and as Christ
has loved us. The Doctor, therefore, in this Accusation, must
be allowed to have stuck closely to his Text; he has not been
Righteous over-much. The Doctor makes now an Inference or

two from this Doctrine of Charity. 'According to this Divinity,' says he, 'it is a Sin to be rich.' Here he is just as wrong as he could possibly be. For, according to the Divinity in the Book of *Christian Perfection*, and the *Serious Call, &c.*, the Blessedness, the Piety, the Happiness arising from the Possession of Riches, is demonstrated from Chapter to Chapter, and visibly painted in a great Variety of Characters. Those Two Books were published chiefly to show to rich Men their exceeding Happiness. And I can consistently say, that I should reckon it a Happiness to myself, to be one of the Number, supported only by this one Saying of our Lord's; that 'it is more blessed 'to give, than to receive.' Another Inference the Doctor makes, is this; that according to this Divinity, 'if a Man sues you for 'your House or Land, without the least Pretence of Right, you 'are bound to recede from your Right, and let him have it, rather 'than defend it.'* There had been as much *Truth*, and more *Wit*, if he had said, when *Thieves have any Design of entering into your House, you are obliged to have no Locks or Bolts upon your Doors.* For I have said no more of the Unlawfulness of appealing to *Courts of Justice*, to secure us in the just Possession of our House and Land, than of the Unlawfulness of going to a *Smith* for Locks and Bolts, when Thieves want to have our Goods. I take it to be as lawful to live under *human Government*, and to enjoy the Benefit of it, as to live under the Light and Benefit of the *Sun*. And I look upon *Courts of Justice*, which are to protect People in the Enjoyment of their Property, to be the first and chief Benefit of Government. And if they were absolutely unlawful, for the same Reason would all *Locks*, and *Doors*, and *Fences* be so too. On the other hand, I have said, that the abstaining from Contentions at Law, choosing to *suffer*, and bear with *Variety of Injuries*, where we might *legally* defend ourselves, and bring *Punishment* upon those that injure us, is a *proper Part* of Christian Self-denial, a just *Conformity* to the Meekness, and suffering Spirit of our Blessed Lord, and highly beneficial to our own spiritual Advancement. And must not everyone, that owns the Gospel, say the same? Has not our Saviour himself first said so? But does it therefore follow, that a Man has no *Rights*, or none that he may *own;* because it may be often, and in *many Cases*, a Matter of great Piety to suffer wrongfully with Patience? The short of the Matter is this : All Things that are lawful, are not expedient, nor edifying. Of Contentions at Law, most of them are very apt to do us great Hurt, many of them are piously to be avoided, through

---

* Page 15.

Patience and Meek-suffering of Wrong; but some may be necessary, even as Parts of our Duty. Is there anything more plain, or self-evident, than this? The Doctor might have observed, that I spoke of *Law-Suits* only under the Article of *Self-denial*, and therefore was only to speak of the Duty, Piety and Benefit, of forbearing from them; that there was great Necessity that this Doctrine of Meekness, and patient Suffering of ill Usage, should be *fully* set forth, both to *Clergy* and *Laity;* that I had no more Reason to tell People that *Courts of Justice* were in themselves lawful, and such as might *justly* be appealed to in some Cases, than to tell them that it was lawful to live in this *Island*, and that they need not seek for a *Country* where there was no Laws nor Government to protect them. The Doctor has something like an excuse for the *Weakness* and *Injustice* of all the foregoing Remarks and Censures; they are to be considered only as *little Dashes* of his Pen upon Books, which he says 'are not considerable enough to be formally ' refuted.'* Something like this I remember was formerly said by the Bishop of *Bangor*, now Lord Bishop of *Winchester*, concerning my Letters to him. But his Lordship had the Prudence and Equity not to make *inconsiderate* Remarks upon Books, that he thought not inconsiderable enough to be formerly refuted by him. Into whose Head could it enter to think of *formally confuting Thomas à Kempis, Taylor's Life of Christ*, or his *Holy Living and Dying?* Or what must we think of his Piety, who should say, that he only forbore such a Work, because the Reasonings in those Books were too inconsiderable to be formally refuted? I desire no Authority for what I have written, but the Gospel, or I could soon show that everything in my Books that offends the Doctor, is again and again to be found, not only in these pious Authors, but in the Writings of the most eminent Saints through all Ages of the Church.

FINIS.

* Page 22.

AN

APPEAL

To all that Doubt, or Disbelieve

The Truths of the GOSPEL,

WHETHER

They be DEISTS, ARIANS, SOCINIANS, Or *Nominal* Christians.

IN WHICH

The true Grounds and Reasons of the whole Christian FAITH and LIFE are plainly and fully demonstrated.

By *WILLIAM LAW*, M. A.

To which are added,
Some Animadversions upon Dr. *Trapp*'s Late REPLY.

LONDON:
Printed for W. INNYS and J. RICHARDSON, in *Pater Noster Row*. 1740.

An Advertisement to the Reader.

I Have Nothing to say by way of Preface or Introduction. I only ask this Favour of the Reader, that he would not pass any Censure upon this Book, from only dipping into this, or that particular Part of it, but give it one fair Perusal in the Order it is written, and then I shall have neither Right, nor Inclination to complain of any Judgment he shall think fit to pass upon it.

An Appeal to all who Doubt the Truths of the Gospel.

Chapter I.

Of Creation in general. Of the Origin of the Soul. Whence Will and Thought are in the Creature. Why the Will is free. The Origin of Evil solely from the Creature. This World not a first, immediate Creation of God. How the World comes to be in its present State. The first Perfection of Man. All Things prove a Trinity in God. Man hath the triune Nature of God in Him. Arianism *and* Deism *confuted by Nature. That Life is uniform through all Creatures. That there is but one kind of Death to be found in all Nature. The fallen Soul hath the Nature of Hell in it. Regeneration is a real Birth of a Divine Life in the Soul. That there is but one Salvation possible in Nature. This Salvation only to be had from Jesus Christ. All the Deist's Faith and Hope proved to be false.*

IT has been an Opinion commonly received, though without any Foundation in the Light of Nature, or Scripture, that God created this whole visible World, and all Things in it, *out of Nothing*. Nay, that the Souls of Men, and the highest Orders of Beings, were created in the same Manner. The Scripture is very decisive against this Original of the Souls of Men. For *Moses* saith, 'God breathed 'into Man (*Spiraculum Vitarum*) the Breath of Lives, and Man 'became a Living Soul.' Here the Notion of a Soul created *out of Nothing*, is in the plainest, strongest Manner rejected, by the first Written Word of God; and no *Jew* or *Christian* can have the least Excuse for falling into such an Error; here the highest and most Divine Original is not darkly, but openly, absolutely, and in the strongest Form of Expression ascribed to the Soul; it came forth as a Breath of Life, or Lives, out from the Mouth of God, and therefore did not come out of the Womb of *Nothing*, but is what it is, and has what it has in itself, from, and out of the first and highest of all Beings.

For to say that God breathed forth into Man the Breath of Lives, by which He became a *Living Soul*, is directly saying, that *That* which was Life, Light, and Spirit in the living God, was breathed forth from Him to become the Life, Light and Spirit of a Creature. The Soul therefore being declared to be an Effluence from God, a *Breath* of God, must have the *Nature* and *Likeness* of God in it, and is, and can be nothing else, but something, or so much of the *Divine Nature*, become creaturely existing, or breathed forth from God, to stand before Him in the *Form* of a Creature.

When the Animals of this World were to be created, it was only said, Let the Earth, the Air, the Water bring forth Creatures after their kinds; but when Man was to be brought forth, it was said, 'Let us make Man in our own Image and 'Likeness.' Is not this directly saying, Let Man have his Beginning and Being out of us, that He may be so related to us in his Soul and Spirit, as the Animals of this World are related to the Elements from which they are produced. Let Him so come forth from us, be so breathed out of us, that our triune, Divine Nature may be manifested in Him, that he may stand before us as a creaturely Image, Likeness, and Representative of that which we are in ourselves.

Now, from this original Doctrine of the Creation of Man, known to all the first Inhabitants of the World, and published in the Front of the first Written Word of God; these great Truths have been more or less declared to all the Nations of the World. *First*, That all Mankind are the *created Offspring* of the One God. *Secondly*, That in all Men there is a Spirit or Breath of Lives, that did not begin to be *out of Nothing*, or was created out of Nothing; but came from the true God into Man, as his *own Breath* of Life breathed into Him. *Thirdly*, That therefore there is in all Men, wherever dispersed over the Earth, a *Divine, immortal, never-ending* Spirit, that can have nothing of Death in it, but *must* live for ever, because it is the Breath of the *ever-*

living God. *Fourthly*, That by this immortal Breath, or Spirit of God in Man, all Mankind stand in the same Nearness of Relation to God, are all equally his Children, are all under the same Necessity of paying the same Homage of Love and Obedience to Him, all fitted to receive the same Blessing and Happiness from Him, all created for the same eternal Enjoyment of his Love and Presence with them, all equally called to worship and adore Him in Spirit and Truth, all equally capable of seeking and finding Him, of having a Blessed Union and Communion with Him.

These great Truths, the first Pillars of all true and Spiritual Religion, on which the Holy and Divine Lives of the ancient Patriarchs was supported, by which they worshipped God in a true and right Faith; these Truths, I say, were most *eminently* and *plainly* declared in the express Letter of the *Mosaic* Writings, here quoted. And no Writer, whether *Jewish* or *Christian*, has so plainly, so fully, so deeply laid open the true Ground, and Necessity of an *Eternal, never-ceasing Relation* between God, and all the Human Nature; no one has so incontestably asserted the *Immortality* of the Soul, or Spirit of Man; or so deeply laid open, and proved the Necessity of *one* Religion, *common* to all Human Nature, as the Legislator of the *Jewish Theocracy* has done. *Life and Immortality are* indeed justly said to be *brought to Light by the Gospel;* not only because they there stand in a new Degree of Light, largely explained, and much appealed to, and absolutely promised by the Son of God Himself, but chiefly because the precious *Means* and *Mysteries* of obtaining a *blessed* Life, and a *blessed* Immortality, were only revealed, or brought to Light by the Gospel.

But the incontestable *Ground* and *Reason* of an immortal Life, and eternal Relation between God, and the whole Human Nature, and which lays all Mankind under the same Obligations to the same true Worship of God, is most fully set forth by *Moses*, who alone tells us the *true Fact; How*, and *Why* Man is immortal in his Nature, *viz.*, because the Beginning of his Life was a Breath, breathed into Him from God; and for this End, that he might be a living Image and Likeness of God, created to partake of the Nature and Immortality of God.

This is the *great Doctrine* of the *Jewish* Legislator, and which justly places Him amongst the *greatest Preachers* of true Religion. St. *Paul* used a very powerful Argument to persuade the *Athenians* to own the true God, and the true Religion, when he told them, 'that God made the World and all Things therein; 'that He giveth Life and Breath, and all Things; that he hath 'made of *one Blood*, all Nations of Men to dwell on the Earth;

'that they should *all seek* the Lord, if haply they might feel 'after, and find Him, seeing He is not far from any of us, *because 'in Him we live, move, and have our Being.*'* And yet this Doctrine, which St. *Paul* preaches to the *Athenians*, is nothing else, but that *same Divine* and *Heavenly* Instruction, which He had learnt from *Moses*, which *Moses* openly and plainly taught all the *Jews*. The *Jewish* Theocracy therefore was by no means an *Intimation* to that People, that they had no Concern with the true God, but as Children of *this World*, under his temporal Protection or Punishment; for their Lawgiver left them *no room* for such a Thought, because He had as plainly taught them their *eternal Nature* and *eternal Relation*, which they had to God in common with all Mankind; as St. *Paul* did to the *Athenians*, who only set before them that *very Doctrine* that *Moses* taught all the *Jews*. The great End of the *Jewish* Theocracy was to show, both to *Jew* and *Gentile*, the absolute, uncontrollable Power of the one God, by such a *Covenanted Interposition* of his Providence, that all the World might know, that the *one God*, from whom both *Jew* and *Gentile* were fallen away, by departing from the Faith and Religion of their First Fathers, was the only God, from whom all Mankind could receive either Blessing or Cursing.

This was the great Thing intended to be proclaimed to all the World by *this Theocracy, viz.*, that only the God of *Israel* had Power to save or destroy, to punish or reward, according to his Pleasure; and that therefore all the Gods of the Heathens, were mere Vanity. If therefore any *Jews*, by *reason* of those extraordinary Temporal Blessings and Cursings which they received under their Theocracy, grew *grossly ignorant*, or dully senseless of their eternal Nature, and eternal Relation to God, and of that *one true Religion*, which by Nature they were obliged to observe in common with all Mankind; if they took God only to be their *local* or *tutelary* Deity, and themselves to be only Animals of this World; such a Grossness of Belief was no more to be charged upon their great Lawgiver, *Moses*, than if they had believed, that a Golden Calf was their true God. But to return to the Creation.

2. It is the same Impossibility for a Thing to be created *out of* Nothing, as to be created *by* Nothing.† It is no more a Part, or Prerogative of God's Omnipotence to create a Being out of Nothing, than to make a Thing to be, without any one *Quality* of Being in it; or to make, that there should be *Three*, where

---

* Acts xvii. 24.
† See *Spirit of Prayer*, Part II., page 58, &c. *Way to Divine Knowledge*, page 247, &c.

there is neither *Two*, nor *One*. Every Creature is nothing else, but *Nature* put into a *certain Form* of Existence ; and therefore a Creature not formed *out of* Nature, is a Contradiction. A *Circle*, or a *Square* cannot be made *out of Nothing*, nor could any Power bring them into Existence, but because there is an *Extension* in Nature, that can be put into the *Form* of a Circle, or a Square : But if dead Figures cannot by any Power be made *out of Nothing*, who sees not the Impossibility of making Living Creatures, Angels, and the Souls of Men out of Nothing ?

3. *Thinking* and *Willing* are Eternal, they never began to be. Nothing can think, or will *now*, in which there was not Will and Thought from *all Eternity*. For it is as possible for Thought *in General* to begin to be, as for *That* which thinks in a particular Creature to *begin* to be of a *Thinking* Nature : therefore the Soul, which is a *Thinking*, *Willing* Being is come forth, or created *out of* That which hath *Willed* and *Thought* in God, from all Eternity. The *created* Soul is a Creature of *Time*, and had its Beginning on the *Sixth* Day of the Creation ; but the *Essences* of the Soul, which were then formed into a Creature, and into a State of Distinction from God, had been in God from all Eternity, or they could not have been *breathed* forth from God into the Form of a living Creature.

And herein lies the true Ground and Depth of the *uncontrollable Freedom* of our Will and Thoughts : They must have a *Self-motion*, and *Self-direction*, because they came out of the *Self-existent* God. They are eternal, Divine Powers, that never began *to be*, and therefore cannot begin to be in Subjection to any Thing. That which *thinks* and *wills* in the Soul, is That *very same* unbeginning Breath which *thought* and *willed* in God, before it was breathed into the Form of an human Soul ; and therefore it is, that Will and Thought cannot be bounded or constrained.

Herein also appears the high Dignity, and never-ceasing Perpetuity of our Nature. The *Essences* of our Souls can never cease to be, because they never began to be : and nothing can live eternally, but that which hath lived from all Eternity. The Essences of our Soul were a Breath in God before they became a Living Soul, they lived in God before they lived in the created Soul, and therefore the Soul is a Partaker of the Eternity of God, and can never cease to be. Here, O Man, behold the great Original, and the high State of thy Birth; Here let all that is within thee praise thy God, who has brought Thee into so high a State of Being, who has given Thee Powers as eternal, and boundless as his own Attributes, that there might be no End or Limits of thy Happiness in Him. Thou begannest as *Time* began, but as Time was in Eternity before it became *Days* and *Years*, so Thou wast in God before Thou wast brought into the Creation: And as Time is neither a *Part* of Eternity, nor *broken* off from it, yet come *out of it;* so thou art not a Part of God, nor broken off from Him, yet born out of Him. Thou shouldst only will that which God willeth, only love that which He loveth, co-operate, and unite with Him in the whole Form of thy Life; because all that Thou art, all that Thou hast, is only a Spark of his own Life and Spirit derived into Thee. If thou desirest, inclinest, and turnest to God, as the *Flowers* of the Field desire, and turn towards the Sun, all the Blessings of the Deity will spring up in Thee; Father, Son, and Holy Ghost, will make their Abode with Thee. If thou turnest in towards thyself, to live to thyself, to be happy in the Workings of an *own Will*, to be rich in the Sharpness and Acuteness of thy *own Reason*, thou choosest to be a *Weed*, and canst only have such a Life, Spirit and Blessing from God, as a *Thistle* has from the *Sun*. But to return.

4. To suppose a *Willing, Understanding* Being, created *out of Nothing*, is a great Absurdity. For as *Thinking* and *Willing* must have *always* been from all Eternity, or they could never have been either in Eternity, or Time; so, wherever they are found in any particular, finite Beings, they must of all Necessity, be direct Communications, or Propagations of *that Thinking and Willing*, which never could begin to be.

The Creation therefore of a Soul, is not the Creation of Thinking and Willing, or the making That to *be*, and to *think*, which before had Nothing of Being, or Thought; but it is the Bringing the *Powers* of Thinking and Willing out of their *Eternal State* in the One God, into a *Beginning State* of a Self-conscious Life, distinct from God. And this is God's omnipotent, creating Ability, that He can make the *Powers* of his *own Nature* become Creatural, Living, Personal Images of what He is in Himself, in a State of *distinct Personality* from Him: So that the Creature is one, in its finite, limited State, as God is one, and yet hath nothing in it, but that which was in God before it came into it: For the Creature, be it what it will, high or low, can be Nothing else, but a limited Participation of the Nature of the Creator. Nothing can be in the Creature, but what came from the Creator, and the Creator can give nothing to the Creature, but that which it hath in itself to give. And if Beings could be created out of Nothing, the Whole Creation could be no more a Proof of the Being of God, than if it had sprung up of itself out of Nothing: For if they are brought into Being out of Nothing, then they can have *Nothing of God* in *them;* and so can bear *no Testimony* of God; but are as good a Proof, that there is no God, as that there is one. But if they have *any Thing* of God in them, then they cannot be said to be created out of Nothing.

5. That the Souls of Men were not created out of Nothing, but are born out of an *Eternal Original,* is plain from hence; from that *Delight* in, and *Desire* of *Eternal Existence,* which is so strong and natural to the Soul of Man. For nothing can delight in, or desire Eternity, or so much as form a *Notion* of it, or *think* upon it, or any way reach after it, but that alone which is generated from it, and come out of it. For it is a Self-evident Truth, that Nothing can look higher, or further back, than into its *own Original;* and therefore, Nothing can look or reach back into Eternity, but that which came out of it. This is as certain, as that a *Line* reaches, and can reach no further back, than to that *Point* from whence it arose.

Our bodily Eyes are born out of the *firmamental Light* of this World, and therefore they can look no further than the *Firmament:* But our Thoughts know no Bounds; therefore they are come out of that which is boundless. The Eyes of our Minds can look as easily backwards into that Eternity which always hath been, as into that which ever shall be; and therefore it is plain, that *That* which *Thinks* and *Wills* in us, which so easily, so delightfully, so naturally penetrates into all Eternity, has always had an Eternal Existence, and is only a Ray or Spark of the Divine Nature, brought out into the Form of a Creature, or a limited, personal Existence, by the Creating Power of God.

6. Again. Every Soul shrinks back, and is frightened at the very Thought of falling into Nothing. Now this undeniably proves, that the Soul was not created *out of* Nothing. For it is an Eternal Truth, spoken by all Nature, that every Thing strongly aspires after, and cannot be easy, till it finds and enjoys that Original out of which it arose. If the Soul therefore was brought forth out of Nothing, all its *Being* would be a *Burden* to it; it would want to be dissolved, and to be delivered from every kind and Degree of *Sensibility;* and nothing could be so sweet and agreeable to it, as to think of falling back into That *Nothingness,* out of which it was called forth by its Creation. Thus is the Eternal, immortal, Divine Nature of the Soul, which the *Schools* prove with so much Difficulty one of the most obvious, self-evident Truths in all Nature. For Nothing but that which is Eternal in its own Nature, can have the least Thought about Eternity.

If a *Beast* had not the *Nature* of the Earth in it, Nothing that is on the Earth, or springs out of it, could be in the least Degree agreeable to it, or desired by it. If the Soul had not the *Nature* of Eternity in it, Nothing that is eternal could give it the *smallest* Pleasure, or be able to make *any kind* of Impression upon it. For as Nothing can taste, or relish, or enter into the agreeable Sensations of this World, but that which hath the *Nature* of this World in it; so Nothing can taste, or relish, or look into Eternity with any kind of Pleasure, but that which hath the *Nature* of Eternity in it.

7. If the Soul was not born, or created *out of* God, it could have no *Happiness* in God, no *Desire*, nor any *Possibility* of enjoying Him. If it had *nothing of God in it*, it must stand in the *utmost Distance* of Contrariety to him, and be utterly incapable of living, moving, and having its Being in God: For every Thing must have the *Nature* of That, out of which it was created, and must live, and have its Being in that *Root* or *Ground* from whence it sprung. If therefore there was nothing of God in the Soul, nothing that is in God could do the Soul any Good, or have *any kind* of Communication with it; but the *Gulf* of Separation between God and the Soul, would be even greater than that which is between Heaven and Hell.

8. But let us rejoice, that our Soul is a *Thinking, Willing* Being, full of Thoughts, Cares, Longings, and Desires of Eternity; for *this* is our *full Proof*, that our Descent is from God Himself, that we are born *out of* Him, breathed forth *from him;* that our Soul is of an Eternal Nature, made a Thinking, Willing, Understanding Creature *out of* That which hath *Willed* and *Thought* in God from all Eternity; and therefore must, for ever and ever, be a Partaker of the Eternity of God.

And here you may behold the sure Ground of the absolute Impossibility of the *Annihilation* of the Soul. Its Essences never began to be, and therefore can never cease to be; they had an *Eternal Reality* before they were in, or became a distinct Soul, and therefore they must have the same Eternal Reality in it. It was the *Eternal Breath* of God before it came into Man, and therefore the Eternity of God must be *inseparable* from it. It is no more a Property of the Divine Omnipotence to be *able* to annihilate a Soul, than to be able to make an *Eternal Truth* become a *Fiction* of Yesterday: And to think it a Lessening of the Power of God, to say, that he cannot annihilate the Soul, is as absurd, as to say, that it is a Lessening of the *Light* of the *Sun*, if it cannot *destroy*, or *darken* its own Rays of Light.

O, dear Reader, stay a while in this important Place, and learn to know thyself: All thy Senses make Thee to know and feel, that thou standest in the *Vanity* of *Time;* but every Motion, Stirring, Imagination, and Thought of thy Mind, whether in *fancying*, *fearing*, or *loving* Everlasting Life, is the same *infallible* Proof, that Thou standest in the *Midst of Eternity*, art an Offspring and Inhabitant of it, and must be for ever inseparable from it. Ask when the *first Thought* sprung up, find out the Birth-Day of Truth, and then thou wilt have found out, when the Essences of thy Soul first began to be. Were not the Essences of thy Soul as old, as *Unbeginning*, as *unchangeable*, as *Everlasting* as Truth itself, Truth would be at the *same Distance* from Thee, as absolutely *unfit* for Thee, as utterly unable to have *any Communion* with Thee, as to be the *Food* of a *Worm*.

The *Ox* could not feed upon the *Grass*, or receive any Delight or Nourishment from it, unless Grass and the Ox had *one and the same* Earthly Nature and Original; Thy Mind could receive no Truth, feel no Delight and Satisfaction in the Certainty, Beauty, and Harmony of it, unless Truth and the Mind stood both in the same Place, had *one and the same* unchangeable Nature, Unbeginning Original. If there will come a Time, when *Thought itself* shall cease, when all the Relations and Connections of Truth shall be *untied;* then, but not till then, shall the Knot, or Band of thy Soul's Life be unloosed. It is a Spark of the Deity, and therefore has the Unbeginning, Unending Life of God in it. It knows nothing of Youth, or Age, because it is born Eternal. It is a Life that must burn for ever, either as a Flame of Light and Love in the Glory of the Divine Majesty, or as a miserable Firebrand in that God, which is a *Consuming Fire*.

9. It is impossible, that this World, in the State and Condition it is now in, should have been an *immediate* and *Original* Creation of God: This is as impossible, as that God should create Evil, either *Natural* or *Moral*. That this World hath Evil in all its Parts; that its Matter is in a corrupt, disordered State, full of Grossness, Disease, Impurity, Wrath, Death and Darkness, is as evident, as that there is Light, Beauty, Order and Harmony everywhere to be found in it. Therefore it is as impossible, that this outward State and Condition of Things, should be a *first* and *immediate* Work of God, as that there should be Good and Evil in God Himself. All Storms and Tempests, every Fierceness of Heat, every Wrath of Cold proves with the *same Certainty*, that outward Nature is not a *first Work of* God, as the *Selfishness*, *Envy*, *Pride*, *Wrath*, and *Malice* of Devils, and Men proves, that they are not in the *first State* of their Creation. As no Kind or Degree of *Moral Evil* could possibly have its Cause in, or from God, so there cannot be the least Shadow of *Imperfection* and *Disorder* in outward

Nature, but what must have sprung up in the *same manner*, and from the *same Causes*, as Sickness and corrupt Flesh is come into the Human Body, namely, from the Sin of the Creature. Storms, Tempests, Gravel, Stone, sour and dead Earth are the *same Things*, the *same Diseases*, the *same Effects* of Sin, produced in the *same manner* in the outward Body of Nature, as corrupt Flesh, *Fevers, Dropsies, Plagues, Gravel, Stone,* and *Gout,* are produced in the outward Body of Man. For That, and That only which produces Stone in the *Body of Man,* did produce Stone in the *outward Nature,* as shall plainly appear by and by. For Nature within, and without Man, is *one* and the *same,* and has but one and the same way of Working; a *Stone* in the Body, and a Stone out of the Body of Man, proceeds from one and the *same Disorder* of Nature.

When therefore you see a *diseased, gouty, leprous, asthmatical, scorbutic* Man, you can with the utmost Certainty say, this is not that Human Body which God *first* created in Paradise; so, when you see the Disorders of *Heat* and *Cold,* the *poisonous Earth, unfruitful Seasons,* and *malignant Qualities* of outward Nature, you can with the same Certainty affirm, this State of Nature is not a *first* Creation of God, but *that same* must have happened to it, which has happened to the Body of Man. For *dark, sour, hard, dead Earth,* can no more be a first, immediate Creation of God, than a *Wrathful Devil,* as such, can be created by Him. For dark, sour, dead Earth is as disordered in its kind, as the Devils are, and has as certainly lost its *first* heavenly Condition and Nature, as the Devils have lost theirs. But now, as in Man, the *little World,* there is Excellency and Perfection enough to prove, that Human Nature is the Work of an all-perfect Being, yet, so much Impurity and Disease of corrupt Flesh and Blood, as undeniably shows, that Sin has almost quite spoiled the Work of God. So, in the *great World,* the Footsteps of an infinite Wisdom in the Order and Harmony of the Whole, sufficiently appears; yet, the Disorders, Tumults, and Evils of Nature, plainly demonstrate, that the present Condition of this World is only the *Remains* or *Ruins,* first, of a *Heaven* spoiled by the Fall of Angels, and then of a *Paradise* lost by the Sin of Man. So that Man, and the World in which He lives, lie both in the *same State* of Disorder and Impurity, have both the *same Marks* of Life and Death in them, both bring forth the same sort of Evils, both want a Redeemer, and have need of the same kind of Death and Resurrection, before they can come to their first State of Purity and Perfection.

10. That this outward World was not created *out of Nothing*, is plainly taught by St. *Paul,* who declares, *Rom.* i. 20, that the

Creation of the World is out of the *Invisible Things of God;* so that the outward Condition and Frame of Visible Nature, is a plain Manifestation of that Spiritual World from whence it is descended. For as every *Outside* necessarily supposes an *Inside,* and as temporal *Light* and Darkness must be the Product of Eternal Light and Darkness, so this outward, visible State of Things necessarily supposes some inward, invisible State, from whence it is come into this Degree of Outwardness. Thus all that is on Earth is only a Change or Alteration of *something* that was in Heaven : And Heaven itself is Nothing else but the *first glorious Out-birth,* the *Majestic Manifestation,* the *beatific Visibility* of the One God in Trinity. And thus we find out, how this temporal Nature is related to God ; it is only a *gross Out-birth* of that which is an *Eternal Nature,* or a *blessed Heaven,* and stands only in such a Degree of Distance from it, as *Water* does to *Air ;* and this is the Reason why the *last Fire* will, and must turn this gross, Temporal Nature into its first, heavenly State. But to suppose the gross Matter of this World to be made *out of* Nothing, or to be a Grossness that has proceeded from Nothing, or compacted Nothing, is more absurd, than to suppose *Ice* that has *congealed* Nothing, a *Yard* that is not made up of *Inches,* or a *Pound* that is not the Product of *Ounces.*

11. And indeed to suppose this, or any other material World to be made out of Nothing, has all the same Absurdities in it, as the supposing *Angels* and Spirits, to be created out of Nothing.

All the Qualities of all Beings are Eternal ; no *real Quality* or *Power* can appear in any Creature, but what has its *eternal Root,* or *generating* Cause in the Creator. If a Quality could *begin* to be in a Creature, which did not *always* exist in the Creator, it would be no Absurdity to say, that a Thing might begin to be, without any Cause either of its Beginning, or Being. All Qualities, Properties, or whatever can be affirmed of God, are *self-existent,* and *necessary existent.* Self and necessary Existence is not a *particular* Attribute of God, but is the *general Nature* of every Thing that can be affirmed of God. All Qualities and Properties are *self-existent* in God : Now, they cannot change their Nature when they are derived, or formed into Creatures, but must have the *same Self-birth,* and necessary Existence in the Creature, which they had in the Creator. The Creature *begins* to be, when, and as it pleased God ; but the *Qualities* which are become *Creaturely,* and which constitute the Creature, are *self-existent,* just as the same Qualities are in God. Thus, *Thinking, Willing,* and *Desire* can have no *outward Maker,* their Maker is *in themselves,* they are self-existent Powers *wherever* they are, whether in God, or in the Creature, and as they form themselves in God, so they form themselves in the Creature. But now, if no Quality can *begin* to be, if all the Qualities and Powers of Creatures must be *eternal* and *necessary* existent in God, before they can have any Existence in any Creature; then it undeniably follows, that every created Thing must have its whole Nature *from,* and *out of* the Divine Nature.

All Qualities are not only good, but *infinitely perfect*, as they are in God; and it is *absolutely* impossible, that they should have any *Evil* or *Defect* in them, as they are in the One God, who is the great and *Universal All*. Because, where *all Properties* are, there must necessarily be an *all possible perfection:* And that which must *always* have *All* in itself, must, by an *absolute* Necessity, be *always all perfect*. But the same Qualities, thus infinitely good and perfect in God, may become *imperfect* and *evil* in the Creature; because in the Creature, being limited and finite, they may be *divided* and *separated* from one another by the Creature itself. Thus *Strength* and *Fire* in the Divine Nature, are Nothing else but the *Strength* and *Flame of Love*, and never can be anything else; but in the Creature, *Strength* and *Fire* may be separated from *Love,* and then they are become an *Evil*, they are Wrath and Darkness, and all Mischief: And thus that same *Strength* and *Quality,* which in Creatures making a right Use of their *own Will,* or *Self-motion*, becomes their *Goodness* and *Perfection*, doth in Creatures making a wrong Use of their Will, become their evil and mischievous Nature: And it is a Truth that deserves well to be considered, that there is *no Goodness* in any Creature, from the highest to the lowest, but in its *continuing* to be such an *Union* of *Qualities* and *Powers,* as God has brought together in its Creation.

In the highest Order of created Beings, this is their standing in their *first Perfection,* this is their *Fulfilling* the whole Will or Law of God, this is their *Piety,* their *Song* of Praise, their *Eternal Adoration* of their great Creator. On the other hand, there is no Evil, no Guilt, no Deformity in any Creature, but in its *dividing* and *separating* itself from something which God had given to be in Union with it. This, and This alone, is the *Whole Nature* of all Good, and all Evil in the Creature, both in the *moral* and *natural* World, in Spiritual and Material Things. For Instance, *dark, fiery Wrath* in the Soul, is not only very like, but it is the very self-same Thing in the Soul which a *Wrathful Poison* is in the Flesh. Now, the Qualities of *Poison* are in themselves, all of them *good Qualities,* and necessary to *every* Life; but they are become a *Poisonous Evil,* because they are *separated* from some other Qualities. Thus also the Qualities of *Fire* and *Strength* that constitute an *Evil Wrath* in the Soul, are in themselves very *good Qualities*, and necessary to every good Life; but they are become an evil Wrath, because separated from some other Qualities with which they should be united.

The Qualities of the *Devil* and all fallen Angels, are good Qualities; they are the *very same* which they received from their infinitely perfect Creator, the very same which *are*, and *must be* in all heavenly Angels; but they are an hellish, abominable Malignity in them *now*, because they have, by their *own Self-motion*, separated them from the *Light* and *Love* which should have kept them glorious Angels.

And here may be seen at once, in the clearest Light, the *true Origin* of all Evil in the Creation, without the least Imputation upon the Creator. God could not *possibly* create a Creature to be an *infinite All*, like Himself: God could not bring any Creature into Existence, but by deriving into it the *self-existent, self-generating, self-moving* Qualities of his own Nature: For the Qualities must be in the Creature, *that* which they were in the Creator, only in a State of Limitation; and therefore, every Creature must be *finite*, and must have a *Self-motion*, and so must be capable of moving right and wrong, of uniting or dividing from what it will, or of falling from that State in which it ought to stand: But as every Quality, in every Creature, both within and without itself, is equally *good*, and equally *necessary* to the Perfection of the Creature, since there is nothing that is evil in it, nor can become evil to the Creature, but *from* itself, by its *separating That* from itself, with which it can, and ought to be united, it plainly follows, that *Evil* can no more be charged upon God, than *Darkness* can be charged upon the *Sun;* because every Quality is *equally good*, every Quality of Fire is as good as every Quality of Light, and only becomes an Evil to that Creature, who, by his *own Self-motion*, has separated Fire from the Light in his own Nature.

12. If a delicious, fragrant *Fruit* had a Power of separating itself from that rich *Spirit*, fine *Taste*, *Smell*, and *Colour* which it receives from the Virtue of the *Sun*, and the Spirit of the *Air;* or if it could in the *Beginning* of its Growth, turn away from the *Sun*, and receive no Virtue from it, then it would stand in its own first Birth of *Wrath*, *Sourness*, *Bitterness*, and *Astringency*, just as the *Devils* do, who have *turned back* into their own dark Root, and rejected the *Light* and *Spirit* of God: So that the hellish Nature of a Devil is Nothing else, but its own *first Forms* of Life, withdrawn, or separated from the heavenly Light and Love; just as the *Sourness*, *Astringency*, and *Bitterness* of a Fruit, are Nothing else but the *first Forms*

of its own vegetable Life before it has reached the Virtue of the *Sun*, and the Spirit of the *Air*.

And as a *Fruit*, if it had a *Sensibility* of itself, would be full of Torment, as soon as it was shut up in the *first Forms* of its Life, in its own *Astringency*, *Sourness*, and Stinging *Bitterness :* So the Angels, when they had *turned back* into these very same *first Forms* of their own Life, and broken off from the Heavenly Light and Love of God, they became their own Hell. No *Hell* was *made* for them, no *new Qualities* came into them, no *Vengeance* or *Pains* from the God of Love fell upon them ; they only stood in that State of *Division* and *Separation* from the Son, and Holy Spirit of God, which, by their own Motion, they had made for themselves. They had nothing in them, but what they had from God, the *first Forms* of an Heavenly Life, Nothing but what the most heavenly Beings have, and must have, to all Eternity ; but they had them in a State of Self-torment, because they *had separated them* from that *Birth* of Light and Love, which alone could make them glorious Sons, and blessed Images of the Holy Trinity.

The same strong *Desire*, fiery *Wrath*, and Stinging *Motion* is in Holy Angels, that is in Devils, just as the same *Sourness*, *Astringency*, and biting *Bitterness* is in a full ripened Fruit, which was there before it received the Riches of the Light and Spirit of the *Air*. In a ripened Fruit, its first Sourness, Astringency, and Bitterness is not *lost*, nor *destroyed*, but becomes the *real Cause* of all its rich *Spirit*, fine *Taste*, fragrant *Smell*, and beautiful *Colour ;* take away the *working, contending* Nature of these *first Qualities*, and you *annihilate* the Spirit, Taste, Smell, and Virtue of the Fruit, and there would be nothing left for the *Sun* and *Spirit* of the Air to enrich.

Just in the same manner, that which in a Devil is an evil *Selfishness*, a wrathful *Fire*, a Stinging *Motion*, is in an Holy Angel, the *everlasting Kindling* of a Divine Life, the *strong Birth* of an Heavenly Love, it is a *real Cause* of an ever-springing, ever-triumphing Joyfulness, an ever-increasing Sensibility of Bliss.

Take away the *working, contending* Nature of these first Qualities, which in a Devil, are only a *Serpentine Selfishness*, *Wrath*, *Fire*, and Stinging *Motion ;* take away these, I say, from Holy Angels, and you leave them neither *Light*, nor *Love*, nor heavenly Glory, Nothing for the Birth of the Son, and Holy Spirit of God to rise up in.

So that here you may see this glorious Truth, that the Love and Goodness of God is as *plain* and *undeniable* in having given to the fallen Angels, those *very Qualities* and Powers which are now *their Hell*, as in giving the first Sourness, Astringency and Bitterness to *Fruits*, which alone makes them capable of their delicious Spirit, Taste, Colour, and Smell.

13. And thus you see the uniform Life of all the Creatures of God; how they are all raised, enriched, and blessed by the *same Life* of God, derived into different Kingdoms of Creatures. For the Beginnings and Progress of a perfect Life in Fruits, and the Beginnings and Progress of a perfect Life in Angels, are not only like to one another, but are the very same Thing, or the working of the very *same Qualities*, only in different Kingdoms. *Astringency* in a *Fruit*, is the very same Quality, and does the same Work in a Fruit, that *attracting Desire* does in a Spiritual Being; it is the same *Beginner, Former*, and *Supporter* of a Creaturely Life in the one, as in the other. No Creature in Heaven, or Earth, can *begin* to be, but by this *Astringency*, or *Desire*, being made the Ground of it: And yet this Astringency kept from the Virtue of the *Sun*, can only produce a *poisonous Fruit*, and this *astringent Desire* in an Angel, turned from the Light of God, can only make a *Devil*. The biting, stinging Bitterness of a Fruit, if you could add *Thought* to it, would be the very *gnawing Envy* of the Devil: And the envious Motion in the Devil's Nature, would be Nothing else but that Stinging Bitterness which is in a Fruit, if you could *take Thought* from the Devil's Motion.

14. From this Attraction, Astringency, or Desire, which is *one* and the *same* Quality in every individual Thing, which is the *first Form* of Being and Life, the very *Ground* of every Creature, from the highest Angel to the lowest Vegetable, we are led by an unerring Thread to the *first Desire*, or that Desire which is in the *Divine Nature*. For as this Attraction, or astringent Desire is in Spiritual and corporeal Things, one and the same Quality, working in the same Manner, so is it *one* and the *same* Quality with that *first, unbeginning Desire*, which is in the Divine Nature.

That there is an attracting Desire in the Divine Nature, is undeniable, because *Attraction* is essential to all Bodies; and *Desire*, which is the same Quality, is absolutely inseparable from all intelligible Beings; therefore, that which is necessarily existent in the Creature, upon the Supposition of its Creation, must necessarily be in the Creator; because no inherent, operative Quality can be in the Creature, unless the same kind of Quality had always been in the Creator: Therefore, Attraction or Desire, which are inseparable from every created Being and Life, are only various *Participations* of the Divine Desire; or *Emanations* from it, formed into different Kingdoms of

Creatures, and working in all of them according to their respective Natures.

In *Vegetables*, it is that Attraction, or Desire, which brings every growing Thing to its highest Perfection : In Angels, it is that blessed Hunger, by which they are filled with the Divine Nature : In Devils, it is turned into that Serpentine Selfishness, or crooked Desire, which makes them a Hell and Torment to themselves.

15. On the other hand, as we thus prove *a posteriori*, from a View of the Creature, that there must be an *attracting* Desire in the Divine Nature ; so we can prove *a priori* also, from a Consideration of God, that there must be an *attracting Desire* in every Thing that ever was, or can be created by God : For nothing can come into Being, but because God *wills* and *desires* it ; therefore the *Desire* of God is the Creator, the Original of every Thing. The Creating *Will*, or *Desire* of God, is not a *distant*, or *separate* Thing, as when a Man wills or desires something to be done, or removed at a Distance from him ; but it is an Omnipresent, working Will and Desire, which is itself, the Beginning and Forming of the Thing desired. Our own Will, and desirous Imagination, when they work and create in us a *settled Aversion*, or *fixed Love* of anything, resemble in some Degree, the Creating Power of God, which makes Things out of itself, or its own working Desire. And our Will, and working Imagination could not have the Power that it has now even after the Fall, but because it is a Product, or Spark of that *first* Divine Will or Desire which is omnipotent.

16. Here therefore we have plainly found the true Original, or *first Source* of all Things. The *Desire* in God is the first *Former, Generator*, and *Creator* of all Things ; they are all the *Births* of this omnipotent, working Desire ; for every Thing that comes into Being, must have the Nature of that Power that formed it, and therefore the Nature of every Creature must stand in an *attractive Desire*, that is, every Thing must be a *Created, attractive Power ;* because it is the *Birth*, or *Product* of a Desire, or attractive Power, and could neither come into, nor continue in Being, but because it was generated not only *by*, but *out of* an attracting Desire. And herein lies the *Band*, or *Knot* of all created Being and Life.

17. *Will* or *Desire* in the Deity, is justly considered as God the *Father*, who from Eternity to Eternity, *wills* or *generates* only the *Son*, from which eternal Generating, the Holy Spirit eternally proceeds : And this is the infinite Perfection or Fulness of Beatitude of the Life of the Triune God.

Now, as the unbeginning, eternal Desire is in God, so is the created Desire in the Creature; it stands in the *same Tendency*, hath the Nature of the Divine Desire, because it is a *Branch* out of it, or created from it. In the Deity, the Eternal Will or Desire, is a *Desiring*, or *Generating* the Son, whence the Holy Spirit proceeds; the Desire that is come out of God into the *Form* of a Creature, has the *same Tendency*, it is a Desire of the Son and Holy Spirit. And every created Thing in Heaven and Earth attains its Perfection, by its Gaining in some Degree, the *Birth* of the Son and Holy Spirit of God in it: For all Attraction and Desire in the Creature, *generates* in them as it did in God; and so the Birth of the Son and Holy Spirit of God arises in *some Degree*, or other, in all Creatures that are in their proper State of Perfection.

18. And here lies the Ground of that plain, and most fundamental Doctrine of Scripture, that the Father is the *Creator*, the Son the *Regenerator*, and the Holy Spirit the *Sanctifier*. For what is this but saying in the plainest manner, that as there are *Three* in God, so there must be *Three* in the Creature, that as the *Three* stand related to one another in God, so must they stand in the same Relation in the Creature. For if a threefold Life of God must have distinct Shares in the Creation, Blessing, and Perfection of Man, is it not a Demonstration, that the Life of Man must stand in the same threefold State, and have such a Trinity in it, as has its true Likeness to that Trinity which is in God?

That which *generates* in God, must generate in the Creature; and that which is *generated* in God, must be generated in the Creature; and that which *proceeds* from this Generation in the Deity, must *proceed* from this Generation in the Creature: And therefore, the same *threefold Life* must be in the Creature in the same manner as it is in God. For a Creature that can only exist, and be blessed by the *distinct Operation* of a Triune God upon it, must have the same Triune Nature that is answerable to it. And herein lies our true, and easy, and sound, and edifying Knowledge and Belief of the Mystery of a Trinity in Unity: And this is all that the Scripture teaches us concerning it. It is not a Doctrine that requires learned or nice Speculations, in order to be rightly apprehended by us. But when with the Scriptures, we believe the Father to be our *Creator*, the Son our *Regenerator*, and the Holy Spirit the *Sanctifier;* then we are learned enough in this Mystery, and begin to know the Triune God in the same Manner in *Time*, that we shall know him in *Eternity*.

And the Reason why this great Mystery of a Trinity in the Deity is thus revealed to us, and the Necessity of a Baptism in the Name of the Father, Son, and Holy Spirit, laid upon us, is this; it is to show us, that the Divine, Triune Life of God is lost in us, and that nothing less than a Birth from the Son and Holy Spirit of God in us, can restore us to our first Likeness to that Triune God, who at first created us. This I have fully shown in the little *Treatise* upon *Regeneration*.

19. When Man was created in his Original Perfection, the Holy Trinity was his *Creator;* the *Breath of Lives*, which *became a Living Soul*, was the Breath of the *Triune* God: But when Man began to *will*, and *desire*, that is, to *generate* contrary to the Deity, then the Life of the Triune God *extinguished* in him.

The *Desire* in Man being turned from God, lost the *Birth* of the Son, and the *Proceeding* of the Holy Spirit; and so fell into, or under the Light and Spirit of this World: That is, of a Paradisaical Man, enjoying Union and Communion with Father, Son, and Holy Ghost, and living on Earth in such Enjoyment of God, as the *Angels* live in Heaven, he became an Earthly Creature, subject to the Dominion of this outward World, capable of all its evil Influences, subject to its Vanity and Mortality; and as to his outward Life, stood only in the highest Rank of *Animals*. This and This alone, is the true *Nature* and *Degree* of the *Fall* of Man; it was neither more nor less than this. It was a Falling out of *one World*, or Kingdom, into *another*, it was changing the Life, Light and Spirit of God, for the Light and Spirit of this World. Thus it was that *Adam* died the very Day of his Transgression, he died to all the Influences and Operations of the Kingdom of God upon him, as we die to the Influences of this World, when the Soul leaves the Body; and, on the other hand, all the Influences, Operations and Powers of the Elements of this Life became opened in him, as they are in every Animal at its Birth into this World.

All other Accounts of that Fall, which *only* suppose the Loss of some Moral Perfection, or Natural Acuteness of his Rational Powers, are not only senseless Fictions, but are an express Denial of the Old and New Testament Account of it; for the Old Testament expressly says, that *Adam* was *to die* the *Day* of his Transgression, and therefore it is certain, that He then did die, and that the Fall was his losing his first Life: And to say that he did not die to that first Life in which he was created, is the same Denial of Scripture, as to say, that he did not eat of the forbidden Tree.

Again, the same Scripture assures us, that after the *Fall*, his *Eyes were opened;* I suppose this is a Proof, that before the *Fall*, they were *shut*. And what is this, but saying in the plainest manner, that before the Fall, the *Life*, *Light* and *Spirit* of this

World, were *shut* out of him? and that the Opening of his Eyes, was only another way of saying, that the Life and Light of this World were opened in him?

If an *Angel*, or any Inhabitant of Heaven, was to be sent of a Message into this World, it must be supposed, that neither the Darkness, nor Light of this World could act according to their Nature upon him; and therefore, though he was here, he must be said not to have the *opened Eyes* of this World: But if this Heavenly Messenger should be taken with our Manner of Life, should be in Doubts about returning to Heaven, and long to have such Flesh and Blood as ours is, as earnestly as *Adam* longed to eat of the earthly Tree; and if by this Longing, he should actually obtain that which he desired; must it not then be said of him, when he had got this new Nature, *his Eyes were opened*, to see *Light* and *Darkness;* and that only for this Reason, because the Heavenly Life was departed from him, and the Earthly Life of this World was opened in Him? And thus it was that *Adam* died, and thus his Eyes were opened.

Again, when his Eyes were thus opened, or the Light and Life of this World thus opened in him, he was immediately ashamed and shocked at the Sight of his own Body, and wanted to *hide* it from himself, and from the Sight of the Sun. Now, how could this have happened to him, if his Body had not undergone some very extraordinary Change, from a State of Glory and Perfection, to a lamentable Degree of Vileness and Impurity?

All the Terror at his fallen State, seems to arise from the sad Condition, in which he saw and felt his outward Body. This made him ashamed of himself; this made him tremble, at hearing the Voice of God; this made him creep behind the Trees, and endeavour to hide and cover his Body with Leaves.

And is not all this the same Thing, as if *Adam* had said, 'All 'my Sin, my Guilt, my Misery, and Shame, is published before 'Heaven and Earth, by this sad State and Condition in which 'my Body now appears.'

But now, what was this sad State and Condition of his Body? What did *Adam* see in the Manner and Form of it that filled him with such Confusion? Why, he only saw that he was fallen from his Paradisaical Glory, to have the same gross Flesh and Blood as the Beasts and Animals of this World have; which was, to bring forth an Offspring in the same earthly Manner, as they did. He could see, and be ashamed of no other Deformity in his Body, but that which he had in common with the Animals of this World; and therefore there was nothing else in his outward Form that He could be ashamed of; and yet it was his *outward Form* that filled him with Confusion. And is not this the greatest of all Proofs, that before his Fall, his Body had not *this Nature* and Condition of the Beasts in it ? Is it not the same Thing, as if he had said, ' this Body which now makes me ' ashamed, and which I want to hide, though it be only with ' thin Leaves, because it brings me down amongst the Animals ' of this World, is not that first Body of Glory into which God at ' first breathed the Breath of Lives, and in which I became a ' Living Soul.'

Again, if *Adam's* Body had been of the same kind of Flesh and Blood as ours is now, only in a better State of Health and Vigour, How could he have been created Immortal ? If he was not created Immortal, how can it be said, that Sin alone brought Mortality, or Death into human Nature ? But if he had Immortality in his first created State, then he must have such a Body as none of the Elements, or Elementary Things of this World could act upon ; for there is no Death in any Creature of this World, but what is brought upon it by that Strife and Destruction which the four Elements bring upon one another. But if Sin alone gave the Elements, and all Elementary Things their first Power of acting upon the Body of *Adam ;* then it is plain, that before his Sin, he had not, could not have a Body of *such Flesh* and *Blood* as we now have, but that he stood, as to the *State, Nature,* and *Condition* of his outward Body, at as great a Distance and Difference from the Animals of this World, as Heaven does from Earth, and was created with Flesh and Blood as much exalted above, and superior to the Nature and Power of all the Elements, as the Beasts of this World are under them.

And herein plainly appears the true Sense of that saying, ' God made not Death,' that is, he made not *That* which is *mortal,* or *dying* in the Human Nature, but Sin alone formed and produced *That* in Man, which could, and must die like the Bodies of Beasts. *Death,* and the *Grave,* and the *Resurrection,* are all three, standing Proofs, that the Body of *bestial* Flesh and Blood, which we now have, at the Sight of which *Adam* was ashamed, which must die, which can rot in the Grave, which must not be seen after the Resurrection, was not that first Body, in which *Adam* appeared before God in Paradise : For if it is an undeniable Truth of Scripture, that this *Flesh and Blood cannot enter into the Kingdom of God;* it must be a Truth of the same Certainty, that *this Flesh* and *Blood* could not by God Himself be brought into Paradise ; but that it must have the *same Original* with every other polluted Thing that is an Abomination in his Sight, or incapable of entering into the Kingdom of God.

20. That the Gospel also plainly shows, that Man was created in the Dignity and glorious Enjoyment of the Triune Life of God, and that his Fall, was a falling into the earthly Life of the Light and Spirit of this World, I have sufficiently proved from the greatest Articles of our Christian Faith, concerning the Necessity, Nature, and Manner of our Redemption, in the Book of *Christian Regeneration.* I have there shown, that Baptism in the Name of the Father, Son, and Holy Ghost, signifies Nothing but our being born again into this Triune Life of God.—That the Necessity of being born again of the *Word* or Son of God, of being born of the *Spirit*, or receiving Him as a Sanctifier of our newly raised Nature, plainly proves that what we lost by the Fall, was this Triune Life of God: He that denies this, denies the whole of the Christian Redemption.*

21. It has been already observed, that when Man was created in his Original Perfection, the Holy Trinity was his Creator; but when Man was fallen, or had lost his first Divine Life, then there began a new Language of a *Redeeming* Religion. Father, Son, and Holy Ghost were now to be considered, not as creating every Man as they created the Frst, but as *differently* concerned in raising the fallen Race of Mankind, to that first Likeness of the Holy Trinity in which their first Father was created: Hence it is, that the Scriptures speak of the Father, as *Drawing*, and *Calling* Men; because the *Desire* which is from the Father's Nature, must be the first Mover, Stirrer, and Beginner. This Desire must be moved and brought into an *anguishing State*, and have the Agitation of a Fire that is *kindling;* and then Men are truly *drawn* by the *Father*.

The Son of God is now considered as the *Regenerator* or Raiser of a new Birth in us; because he enters a second Time into the Life of the Soul, that his own Nature and Likeness may be again generated in it, and that he may be *That* to the Soul in its State, *which* he is to the Father in the Deity.

The Holy Ghost is represented as the *Sanctifier*, or Finisher of the Divine Life restored in us; because as in the Deity, the Holy Ghost proceeds from the Father and the Son, as the amiable, blessed *Finisher* of the Triune Life of God; so the fallen Nature of Man cannot be raised out of its unholy State, cannot be blessed and sanctified with its true Degree of the Divine Life, till the Holy Spirit arises up in it.

Since then the Triune God, or the three Persons in the one God, must have this Difference of Shares, must reach out this

---

* See *Spirit of Prayer*, Part II., page 63, &c., page 91. *Way to Divine Knowledge*, pages 39-53.

different Help to the Raising up of fallen Man, it is undeniable, that the first created Man stood in the Image and *real Likeness* of the one God, not only representing, but *really having* in his Birth and Life, the Birth and Life of the Holy Trinity. God the Father, Son, and Holy Ghost had *such* a Unity in Trinity *in Man*, as they had in the Deity itself: How else could Man be the Image and Likeness of the Holy Trinity, if it was not such a Birth in Man, as it was in itself? Or, how could the Holy Trinity dwell and operate in Man, each Person according to its respective Nature, unless there was the same threefold Life in Man as there is in God? How could the Holy Trinity be an Object of Man's Worship and Adoration, if the Holy Trinity had not produced itself in Man? The Creature is only to own and worship its Creator; therefore Father, Son, and Holy Ghost must have each of them their *Creaturely* Offspring, or *Product* in Man, if Man is to worship Father, Son, and Holy Spirit. If therefore you deny *Angels*, and the Souls of perfect Men to have the triune Nature, or Life of God in them: If you deny that Father, Son, and Holy Spirit, have such Union and Relation in the Soul, as they have out of it, you are guilty of as great Heresy and Apostacy from the Gospel, as if you denied the Father to be the Creator or Him that *calleth* and *draweth*, the Son to be the Redeemer, or Him that regenerateth, and the Holy Spirit to be Him that sanctifieth Human Nature.

22. Again: Consider this great Truth, which will much illustrate this Matter; you can be an *Inhabitant* of no World, or a *Partaker* of its Life, but by its being inwardly the *Birth* of your own Life, or by having the *Nature* and *Condition* of that World *born* in you. As thus, *Hell* must be *inwardly born* in the Soul, it must *arise* up within it, as it does without it, before the Soul can become an Inhabitant of it.

Again: That which is the Life of this outward World, *viz.*, its *Fire*, and *Light*, and *Air*, must have such a *State* and *Birth* within you, as they have without you, before you can be an Inhabitant or Partaker of the Life of this World; that is, Fire must be in you, must be the *same Fire*, have the same *Place* and *Nature* within you, have the same Relation to the *Light* and *Air* that is within you, as it has without you, or else the Fire of the *outward World*, cannot keep up, or have *any Communion* with your own Life.

The Light of this World can signify nothing to you, cannot reach or enrich you with its Powers and Virtues, if the same Light is not arisen in the *same Manner* in the kindling of your own Life, as it arises in the outward World.

The *Air* also of this World can do you no Good, can be no

Blower up and Preserver of your Life, but because it has the *same Birth* in you, that it has in outward Nature. And therefore it must be a Truth of the greatest Certainty, that so it must of all Necessity be with Respect to the *Kingdom of God*, or that *Life* which is to be had in the *Beatific Presence* of God; it must, by an absolute Necessity, have the *same Birth* within you, as it has without you, before you can enter into it, or become an Inhabitant of it: If you are to live, and be eternally blessed in the *triune Life*, or Beatific Presence of God, that Triune Life, must, of the utmost Necessity, first make itself *creaturely* in you; it must *be* and *arise* in you, as it does without you, before you can possibly enter into any Communion with it.

Now is there any Thing more plain and Scriptural, more easy to be conceived, more pious to be believed, and more impossible to be denied, than all this? And yet this is all that I have said, in two Propositions in the Treatise upon *Christian Regeneration*: It is there said, 'Man was created by God *after his own Image*, ' and *in his own Likeness*, a Living Mirror of the Divine Nature; 'where *Father, Son, and Holy Ghost* each brought forth their 'own Nature in a Creaturely Manner.' Now, what is this, but saying, That the Holy Trinity brought forth a Creature in its own Likeness, standing in a creaturely Birth of the Divine, triune Life? If it did not stand thus, how could it have a Likeness of the Holy Trinity? Or how could it have its *Form* or *Creation* from the Holy Trinity? Or how could it without this triune Life in itself, enter into, or be a Partaker of the triune Life or Presence of God? In the next Proposition it is said; 'In it, 'that is, in this created Image of the Holy Trinity, the Father's 'Nature generated the Divine *Word*, or *Son* of God, and the 'Holy Ghost proceeded from them both as an amiable, moving 'Life of both. This was the *Likeness* or *Image* of God, in which 'the first Man was created, a true Offspring of God, in whom 'the Divine Birth sprung up as in the Deity, where Father, Son, ' and Holy Ghost, saw themselves in a creaturely manner.'

Now, what is this, but saying in the plainest Manner, only thus much, that the triune, creaturely Life stood in the *same Birth* and Generation of its threefold Life, as the Deity doth, whose Image, Likeness, and Offspring it is? And can it possibly be otherwise; for if the Creature cometh from the Father, Son, and Holy Ghost, as their *created Image* and *Likeness*, must not That which it hath from the Father, be of the *Nature* of the Father, That which it hath from the Son, be of the *Nature* of the Son, and That which it hath from the Holy Ghost, be of the *Nature* of the Holy Ghost? And must they not therefore stand in the Creature in such Relation to one another, as they do in the Creator? If it is the Nature of the Father to *generate*, if it is the Nature of the Son to be *generated*, if it is the Nature of the Holy Ghost to *proceed* from both, must not That which you have from the Father generate in you, That which you have from the Son be *generated* in you, and that which you have from the Holy Ghost, *proceed* from both in you? All which is only saying this plain and obvious Truth, that That Being, or *created Life*, which you have from Father, Son, and Holy Ghost, must stand in such a *triune Relation* within you as it does without you; that having this threefold Likeness of God, you may be capable of entering into an Enjoyment of his *triune, beatific* Life or Presence.

For, consider again this Instance, with regard to the Life of this World. The *Fire*, and *Light*, and *Air*, of outward Nature, must become *creaturely* in you; that is, you must have a Fire that is your *own creaturely* Fire, you must have a Light that is generated by, or from your *own Fire*, a *Breath* that proceeds from your *own Fire* and *Light*, as the *Air* of outward Nature proceeds from its Fire and Light: You must have all this *Nature* and *Birth* of Fire, and Light, and Air in your own creaturely Being, or you cannot possibly *live in*, or have a Life from the Fire, and Light, and Air of *outward Nature*: No Omnipotence can make you a *Partaker* of the Life of this outward World, without having the Life of this outward World *born in* your own creaturely Being. And therefore, no Omnipotence can make you a *Partaker* of the Beatific Life or Presence of the Holy Trinity, unless that Life stands in the *same triune State* within you, as it does without you.

The Nature of this World must become *creatural* in you, before you can live, or have a Share in the Life of this World; the triune Nature of God must breathe forth itself to stand creaturely in you, before you can live, or have a Share in the Beatific Life or Presence of the triune God.

Now, is not all this strictly according to the very outward *Letter*, and inward *Truth* of the most important Articles of the Christian Religion? For what else can be meant by the Necessity of our being born again of the *Word*, or Son of God, being born of the *Spirit* of God, in order to our Entrance into the Kingdom of Heaven? Is not this saying, that the triune Life of God must first have *its Birth* in us, before we can enter into the triune, beatific Life, or Presence of God? What else is taught us by that *new Birth* sought for by a *Baptism*, in the Name of the Father, Son, and Holy Ghost? Does it not plainly tell us, that the triune Nature of the Deity is *That* which wants to be born in us, and that our Redemption consists in Nothing

the Truths of the Gospel. 81

else but in the *Bringing forth* this new Birth in us, and that, being thus born again in the *Likeness* of the Holy Trinity, we may be capable of its threefold Blessing and Happiness? The New Testament tells us of the Impossibility of our being *redeemed*, but by the Son of God, of the Impossibility of our being made *holy*, but by the Holy Spirit of God: Now, how could we want any distinct Thing *particularly* from the Son of God, any distinct Thing, *particularly* from the Holy Ghost, in order to raise and repair our fallen Nature, how could *this Particularity* be thus *absolutely necessary*, but because the holy *threefold Life* of the Deity must stand *within* us, in the Birth of our own Life, as it does without us, that so we may be capable of living in God, and God in us.

Search to Eternity, why no *Devil*, or *Beast* can possibly be a *Partaker* of the Kingdom of Heaven, and there can only this *one Reason* be assigned for it, because neither of them have the *triune, holy Life* of God in them: For every created Thing does, and must, and can only want, seek, unite with, and enjoy That *outwardly*, which is of the *same Nature* with itself. Remove a *Devil* where you will, he is still in Hell, and always at the *same Distance* from Heaven; he can touch, or taste, or reach Nothing but what is in Hell. Carry a *Beast* where you please, either to *Court*, or to *Church*, he is yet at the *same infinite Distance* from the Joys and Fears either of *Church*, or *Court*, as the Beasts that never saw any Thing else but their own Kind: And all this is grounded solely on this Eternal Truth; namely, That no Being can rise *higher* than its *own* Life reaches. The *Circle* of the *Birth* of Life in every Creature is its necessary *Circumference*, and it cannot possibly reach any further; and therefore it is a joyful Truth, that Beings created to *worship* and *adore* the Holy Trinity, and to enter into the beatific Life and Presence of the triune God, must, of all Necessity, have the *same triune Life* in their own Creaturely Being. And now, what can be so glorious, so edifying, so ravishing, as this Knowledge of God and ourselves? The very Thought of our standing in this *Likeness* and *Relation* to the Infinite Creator and *Being* of all Beings, is enough to kindle the Divine Life within us, and melt us into a continual Love and Adoration: For how can we enough love and adore that Holy Trinity which has created us in its own Likeness, that we might live in an Eternal Union and Communion with it? Will anyone call this an *irreverent* Familiarity, or *bold* Looking into the Holy Trinity, which is nothing else but a thankful Adoration of it, as our Glorious Father and Creator? It is our best and only Acknowledgment of the greatest Truths of the Holy Scriptures; it is the Scripture

Doctrine of the Trinity kept in its own Simplicity, separated from *Scholastic Speculations*, where the three in God, are only distinguished by that threefold Share that they have in the Creation and Redemption of Man. When we thus know the Trinity in ourselves, and adore its high Original in the Deity, we are possessed of a Truth of the greatest Moment, that enlightens the Mind with the most solid and edifying Knowledge, and opens to us the fullest Understanding of all that concerns the Creation, Fall, and Redemption of Man.

Without this Knowledge, all the Scripture will be used as a *dead Letter*, and formed only into a *figurative*, *historical* System of Things, that has no Ground in Nature ; and learned Divines can only be learned in the Explication of Phrases, and verbal Distinctions.

The first Chapters of *Genesis* will be a Knot that cannot be untied ; the Mysteries of the Gospel will only be called *fœderal Rites*, and their inward Ground reproached as enthusiastic Dreams ; but when it is known, that the *triune Nature* of God was brought forth in the *Creation* of Man, that it was lost in his *Fall*, that it is *restored* in his *Redemption*, a never-failing Light arises in all Scripture, from *Genesis* to the *Revelation*. Every Thing that is said of God, as Father, Regenerator, or Sanctifier of Man ; every Thing that is said of Jesus Christ, as Redeeming, forming, dwelling in, and quickening ; and of the Holy Spirit, as moving and sanctifying us : Every Thing that is said of the Holy Sacraments, or promised in and by them, has its deep and inward Ground *fully discovered;* and the whole Christian Religion is built upon a *Rock*, and that Rock is *Nature*, and God will appear to be doing every Good to us, that the God of all Nature can possibly do. The Doctrine of the Holy Trinity is wholly practical ; it is revealed to us, to discover our high Original, and the Greatness of our Fall, to show us the deep and profound Operation of the triune God in the Recovery of the Divine Life in our Souls ; that by the Means of this Mystery thus discovered, our Piety may be rightly directed, our *Faith* and *Prayer* have their proper Objects, that the Workings and Aspirings of our own Hearts may co-operate, and correspond with that triune Life in the Deity, which is always desiring to manifest itself in us ; for as every Thing that is in us, whether it be Heaven, or Hell, rises up in us by a *Birth*, and is generated in us by the Will-spirit of our Souls, which kindles itself either in Heaven, or Hell ; so this Mystery of a triune Deity manifesting itself, as a *Father* creating, as a *Son*, or *Word*, regenerating, as a *Holy Spirit* sanctifying us, is not to entertain our Speculation with dry, metaphysical Distinctions of the Deity, but to show us from what a Height and Depth we are fallen, and to excite such a Prayer and Faith, such a Hungering and Thirsting after this triune Fountain of all Good, as may help to generate and bring forth in us that first Image of the Holy Trinity in which we were created, and which must be born in us before we can enter into the State of the Blessed: Here we may see the Reason, why the Learned World has had so many fruitless Disputes about this Mystery, and why it has been so often a Stone of Stumbling to Philosophers and Critics; it is because they began to reason about that, which never was proposed to *their Reason*, and which no more belongs to human Learning and Philosophy, than *Light* belongs to our *Ears*, or Sounds to our *Eyes*. No Person has any *Fitness*, nor any *Pretence*, nor any *Ground* from Scripture, to think, or say any Thing of the Trinity, till such Time as he stands in the State of the Penitent Returning *Prodigal*, weary of his own sinful, shameful Nature; and desiring to renounce the World, the Flesh, and the Devil, and then is he *first* permitted to be baptized *into the Name of the Father, Son, and Holy Ghost*: This is the *first Time* the Gospel *teaches*, or calls anyone to the Acknowledgment of the Holy Trinity. Now, as this Knowledge is first given in Baptism, and there only as a Signification of a triune Life of the Deity, which must be regenerated in the Soul; so the Scriptures say Nothing afterwards to this Baptized Penitent concerning the Trinity, but only with Regard to *Regeneration*, everywhere only showing him how Father, Son, and Holy Ghost, all equally Divine, must draw, awaken, quicken, enlighten, move, guide, cleanse, and sanctify the new-born Christian: Is it not therefore undeniably plain, that all abstract Speculations of this Mystery, how it is in itself, how it is to be *ideally* conceived, or Scholastically expressed by us, are a Wandering from that true Light, in which the Trinity of God is set before us, which is only revealed as a Key, or Direction to the true Depths of that Regeneration, which is to be sought for from the triune Deity? But to go on in a further Account of the Creation.

23. Now, as all Creatures, whether intellectual, animate, or inanimate, are Products, or Emanations of the *Divine Desire*, created *out of* the Father, who from Eternity to Eternity generates the Son, whence the Holy Spirit eternally proceeds; so every intelligent, created Being, not fallen from its State, stands in the *same Birth*, or *generating Desire*, it generates in its Degree, as God the Father generates eternally the Son, and is blessed and perfected in the Divine Life, by having the Holy Spirit arise up in it.

Hence it is, that those Angels which stood, and continued in the *same Will* and *Desire* in which they came out from God, willing and desiring as God from all Eternity had *willed* and *desired*, were by the Rising up of the Holy Spirit in them, *confirmed* and *established* in the Divine Life, and so became eternally and inseparably united with the ever-blessed triune Deity.

On the other hand, those Angels which did not keep their *Will* and *Desire* in its first created *Tendency*, but raised up an *own Will* and *Desire*, which own Will and Desire was their direct, *full* choosing and desiring to *be*, and *do* something which they could not be, and do in God, and is therefore properly called their aspiring to be *above* God, or to be without any *Dependence* upon him; these Angels, by thus going *backwards* with their Will and Desire *out of*, or *from* God and the *Divine Truth*, could only find, or generate *That* which had the *utmost Contrariety* to God and the Divine Birth, and so became under a Necessity of finding themselves in an Eternal *State, Spirit* and *Life* that was *directly contrary* to all that is good, holy, amiable, blessed and Divine.

Now, the *Will* and *Desire* in every Creature is *generating*, and *efficacious*, strictly according to the State and Nature of that Creature;* therefore, Eternal Beings in an Eternal State, must have an Eternal Power and Efficacy in the Working of their Wills and Desires: When therefore those Angels, with all the Strength of their Eternal Desires, turned away from, and contrary to God and the Divine Birth, they could become Nothing else, but Beings eternally separated and broken off from all that was God and Goodness: For Eternal Beings that stood only in an eternal State, acting with all their Vigour, not doubting, but strongly willing, could not do anything that had only a *Temporal Nature* and *Effect*, because they stood not in such a Nature or such a World, and therefore what they willed and generated with all their Nature, (which was a Contrariety to God) that became the Eternal State of their Nature. And this is the Birth and Origin of Hellish Beings.

God had done all to them and for them, that he had done to and for the Angels that stood; he had given them the same holy *Beginning* of their Lives, had brought them forth out of himself in the *same Tendency*, that which was the Nature of other Angels, was theirs; he could not make any established, fixed, and unchangeable Angels, because the Life of every Thing must be a *Birth*, and *willing* Beings must have a *Birth* of their *Wills;* he could not make them *fixed*, because every

---

* See *Way to Divine Knowledge*, pages 139-160.

Thing that comes from God, must *so* come from him, *as* it was in him, a *self-existent* and *self-moving* Power, and therefore no Goodness of God could hinder their having a *Self-motion*, because they were, and could be Nothing else but Creatures brought forth *by*, and *out* of his own *self-existent* and *self-moving* Nature.

God is all Good, and every Thing that comes out from him, as his Creature, Product, or Offspring, must come forth in *that State* of Goodness, which it had in Him ; and every Creature, however high in its Birth from God, must in the Beginning of its Life, have a *Power* of joining with or departing from God, because the Beginning of its Life is nothing else but the Beginning of its *own Self-motion* as a Creature ; and therefore no Creature can have its State or Condition *fixed*, till it gives itself up either wholly unto God, or turns *wholly* from him ; for if it is an Intelligent Creature, it can only be so, by having the Intelligent Will of God derived into it, or made creaturely in it ; but the Intelligent Will brought into a creaturely Form, must be *That* which it was in the Creator, and therefore must be the same *self-existent* and *self-moving* Power that it was before it became creaturely in any Angel or Spirit. And thus the Cause and Origin of Evil, wherever it is, is absolutely and eternally separated from God.

24. Again : As all Intelligent Beings can no way attain their Happiness and Perfection, but by standing with their Will and Desire united to God, in the *same Tendency* in which the Father eternally generateth the Son, from whence the Holy Spirit proceedeth as the Finisher of the triune, beatific Life, so the same Thing is manifestly proved to us by the lowest kind of Beings that are in this visible World ; for all *Vegetables*, by their Attraction or Astringency, which is *their Desire*, and is an *Outbirth* of the Divine Desire, reach their utmost Perfection by the *same Progress*, that is, by getting a Birth of the *Light* and *Spirit* of this outward World into them, and so become infallible, though remote Proofs that no Life can be brought to its proper Perfection in the Creature, till the Image of the *triune Life* of God, is, according to the State and Capacity of the Creature, formed in it : Look where you will, every Thing proclaims and proves this great Truth. The Christian Doctrine of the Salvation of Mankind by a Birth of the Son, and Holy Spirit of God in them, is not only written in Scripture, but in the *whole State* and *Frame* of Nature, and of every Life in this World ; for every perfect Fruit openly declares, that it can have no Goodness in it, till the *Light* and *Spirit* of this World has done that to it and in it, which the Light and Spirit of

God must do to the Soul of Man, and therefore is a full Proof, that it is as absolutely necessary for every Human Creature to desire, believe, and receive the Birth of the Son and Holy Spirit of God to save it from its own Wrath and Darkness, as it is necessary for every Fruit of the Earth to be raised and regenerated from its own Bitterness and Sourness, by receiving the Light and Spirit of this World into it.

25. Some Learned Men, willing to discover the Image of the Holy Trinity in the Creation, have observed *three Properties* both in Body and Spirit, which they supposed to be a proper Likeness of the Trinity. But all this is Nothing to the Matter.

For as the Holy Trinity is a *threefold Life* in God, so the Image of the Trinity is only found in a *threefold Life* in the Creature; for it is the *whole Birth*, or Generation of the Thing itself, whether it be corporeal or spiritual, that stands in such a *threefold State* as the Holy Trinity doth, that is the *proper Likeness* or Image of the Trinity. As there is one infinitely perfect Deity, because this one Deity is Father, Son, and Holy Spirit, so every Creature that is an original Production of the Deity, or in its proper State of Perfection, stands in its whole Being, or generating as the Deity doth, and neither hath, nor ever can have any Perfection, but because the Triune Nature of God is manifested and brought forth in it; for Perfection of Life *in* God, and a Perfection of Life *derived* from God, must stand in the same threefold State, and that which is a Life from the Deity, must have a Life of the Trinity in it.

26. Take away *Attraction*, or *Desire* from the Creature of this World, and you annihilate the Creature; for where there is no Attraction or Desire, there can be no Nature or Being; and therefore Attraction or Desire shows the Work of the Creator in every Thing, or what is meant by the *Divine Fiat*, or Creating Power. Now, what is it which this *Attraction* or *Desire* wants, hungers, draws and reaches after? Nothing else but the *Light* and *Spirit* of this World. What is the *true, deep,* and *infallible* Ground of this? Why does this Desire *thus* work in every Life of this World? It is because the Eternal Will in the Deity, is a *Desiring* or *Generating* the Son, from whence the Holy Spirit of God proceeds: And therefore Attraction, which is an *Out-birth* of the Divine Desire, stands in a perpetual Desiring of the Light and Spirit of this World, because they are the two *Out-births* of the Light and Holy Spirit of God. What rational Mind can help being charmed with this wonderful Harmony and Relation betwixt God, Nature, and Creature?

27. And now, my dear Reader, if you are either *Arian*, or *Deist*, be so no longer: The Ground is dug up from under you,

and neither Opinion has any Thing left to stand upon; you may wrangle and wrest the Doctrine of Scripture, because it is only taught in Words; but the Veil is now taken off from Nature, and every *Plant* and *Fruit* will teach you with the Clearness of a Noon-day Sun, these two great Truths; *First*, That Father, Son, and Holy Spirit are one Being, one Life, one God: *Secondly*, That the Soul, which is dead to the Paradisaical Life, must be made alive again by the Birth of the Son and Holy Spirit of God in it, in the same Manner as a *dead Seed* is, and only can be brought to Life in this World, by the Light and Spirit of this World.

If you are an *Arian*, don't content yourself with the Numbers that are with you, or with a Learned Name or two that are on your Side: *Arianism* has never yet been recommended by the Genius and Learning of a *Baronious*, or *Bellarmin;* and nothing but a poor, groping, purblind Philosophy, that is not able to look either at God, Nature, or Creature, hath ever led any Man into it: For it is a Truth proclaimed by all Nature and Creature, that there is a *threefold Life* in God, and every Thing that is, whether it be *happy*, or *miserable*, perfect or imperfect, is only so, because it has, or has not the *triune Nature* of God in it.

A *beginning* Fruit is like a *Poison;* a *Seed*, for a while, is shut up in a *hard Death*. Why are they both at *first* in this State? It is because each of them stands *as yet* only in that *first Birth* of Nature, which is but a *Beginning Manifestation* of the Deity. Let the Light of the Sun, and the Spirit of this World be born in them, and then the sour, astringent Fruit, and the *dead Seed* becomes a perfect, vegetable Life, and is in its kind perfect, for this *one only* Reason, because the triune Life of the Deity is truly manifested in it.

28. If you are a *Deist*, made so, either by the disorderly State *of your own* Heart, or by Prejudices taken from the Corruptions and Divisions of Christians, or from a Dislike of the Language of Scripture, or from an Opinion of the Sufficiency of a Religion of Human Reason, or from whatever else it may be, look well to yourself, Christianity is no Fiction of Enthusiasm, or Invention of Priests.

If you can show, that the Gospel proposes to bring Men into the Kingdom of Heaven by any other Method, than that, which *Nature* requires to make any Creature a living Member of this World, then I will acknowledge the Gospel not to be founded in Nature.

But if what the Gospel saith of the absolute Necessity, that the fallen Soul be born again of the Son and Holy Spirit of God, is the very same which all temporal Nature saith of every Thing that is to enter into the Life of this World, *viz.*, that it cannot partake of the Life of this World, till the Light and Spirit of this World is born in it; then does not all Nature in this World, and every Life in it, declare, that the Christian Method of Salvation is as *necessary* to raise fallen Man, as the Sun and Spirit of this World is, to bring a Creature alive into it?

Now, as there is but one God, so there is but *one Nature*, as unalterable as that God from whom it arises, and whose Manifestation it is; so also there is but *one Religion* founded in Nature, and but one Salvation *possible* in Nature. Revealed Religion is nothing else but a Revelation of the *Mysteries* of Nature, for God cannot reveal, or require any Thing by a spoken or written Word, but that which he reveals and requires by *Nature*; for *Nature* is his great *Book* of Revelation, and he that can only read its Capital Letters, will have found so many Demonstrations of the Truth of the written Revelation of God.*

But to show, that there is but one Salvation *possible* in Nature, and that Possibility solely contained in the Christian Method: Look from the Top to the Bottom of all Creatures, from the highest to the lowest Beings, and you will find, that *Death* has but *one Nature* in all Worlds, and in all Creatures: Look at *Life* in an Angel, and Life in a *Vegetable*, and you will find, that *Life* has but *one* and the *same* Form, one and the same Ground in the whole Scale of Beings: No Omnipotence of God can make that to be Life, which is not Life, or that to be Death, which is not Death, according to Nature; and the Reason is, because Nature is nothing else but God's own outward Manifestation of what he inwardly is, and can do; and therefore no Revelation from God can teach, or require any Thing but that which is taught and required by God in, and through Nature. The Mysteries of Religion therefore, are no higher, nor deeper than the Mysteries of Nature, and all the *Rites, Laws, Ceremonies, Types, Institutions* and *Ordinances* given by God from *Adam* to the Apostles, are only typical of something that is to be done, or instrumental to the doing of that, which the *unchangeable Working* of Nature requires to be done. As sure therefore as there is but one and the same Thing that is *Death*, and one and the same Thing that is *Life* throughout all Nature, whether temporal or eternal, so sure is it, that there is but one Way to Life or Salvation for fallen Man. And this Way, let it be what it will, must and can be only that, which has its *Reason* and *Foundation* in *that* one Universal Nature, which is the one unchange-

---

* *Spirit of Love*, Part II., pages 134-149.

able Manifestation of the Deity. For if there is but *one Thing* that is Life, and one thing that is Death throughout all Nature, from the highest *Angel* to the hardest *Flint* upon Earth, then it must be plain, that the *Life* which is to be raised or restored by Religion, must, and can only be restored according to Nature: And therefore, true Religion can only be the Religion of Nature, and Divine Revelation can do nothing else, but reveal and manifest the Demands and Workings of Nature.

29. Now, the one great Doctrine of the Christian Religion, and which includes all the rest, is this, that *Adam*, by his Sin, *died* to the Kingdom of Heaven, or that the *Divine Life* extinguished in him; That he cannot be *redeemed*, or restored to this first *Divine Life*, but by having it kindled or regenerated in him by the Son and Holy Spirit of God: Now, that which is here called *Death*, his losing the Light and Spirit of the Kingdom of Heaven, and that which is here made necessary to make him *alive* again to the Kingdom of Heaven, is that *very same* which is called, and is *Death* and *Life* throughout all Nature, both temporal and eternal: And therefore, the Christian Religion requiring this Method of raising Man to a Divine Life, has its infallible Proof from all Nature.* Consider Death, or the Deadness that is in a *hard Flint*, and you will see what is the *Eternal Death* of a fallen *Angel*: The *Flint* is dead, or in a State of Death, because its *Fire* is bound, compacted, shut up, and imprisoned; this is its Chains and Bands of Death: A *Steel* struck against a *Flint* will show you, that every Particle of the Flint consists of this *compacted Fire*.

Now, a fallen Angel is in no other State of Death, knows no other Death than this: It is in its whole Spiritual, Intelligent Being, nothing else, but that *very same* which the Flint is, in its insensible Materiality, *viz.*, an imprisoned compacted, darkened Fire-spirit, shut up, and tied in its own Chains of Darkness, as the Fire of the Flint; and you shall see by and by, that the Flint is changed from its first State into its present Hardness of Death, in the same Manner, and by the same Means, as the Heavenly Angel is become a fiery Serpent in the State of Eternal Death.

Now, look at every Death that can be found betwixt that of a fallen Angel, and that of a hard Flint, and you will find that Death enters nowhere, into no kind of Vegetable, Plant, or Animal, but as it has entered into the *Angel*, and the *Flint*, and stands in the same manner in every Thing wherever it is.

Now, that a fallen Angel, is nothing else but a Fire-spirit

---

* *Spirit of Love*, Part II., page 117, &c.

imprisoned in the same manner as a Flint is an imprisoned Fire, is plain from the Scripture Account of them; not only because all the wrathful Properties of a Fire *without Light*, are ascribed to them as their essential Qualities, but because the *Place* of their Habitation, or the *State* of their Life, is a *Fire* of *Hell*. For how could it be possible, that a *hellish Fire* should be the Eternal *State* of their Life, unless their *Nature* was such a Fire? Must not their painful Condition arise from *their Nature*, and their Misery be only a Sensibility of themselves, of that which they have made themselves to be? Therefore, if Fire *shut up* in Darkness, is the Nature of Hell, it can only be so, because such a darkened Fire is the *very Nature* of a fallen Angel. Or how again could the Human Soul, which has withstood its Salvation in this Life, be said to fall into *Eternal Death*, or the Fire of Hell, if the Soul itself did not become *that Fire* of Hell? For when you say the Soul enters into Hell, you say neither more nor less, than if you had said, that Hell enters into the Soul; therefore, the State of Hell, and the State of the Soul in Hell, is one and the same Thing. If therefore Hell is a State of Fire shut up, and imprisoned from all Communion with Light, then the same dark, imprisoned Fire must be the Nature of the fallen Angel and lost Soul; and thus, what your Eyes see to be the *Death* or *Deadness* of a Flint, is that same Thing, or that *same State* of the Thing, which the Scripture assures you, to be the *Eternal Death* of a fallen Angel, and a lost Soul. Here also you may see a plain Proof of what I have elsewhere declared concerning the fallen Soul; that considered *without* its Redeemer in it, or the *in-spoken Word* of Life given to *Adam* at his Fall, it is in itself, as a fallen Soul, the *same dark, fiery* Spirit, as the Devils are; and that the Reason why Men wholly given up to Wickedness, and who have *suppressed* the Redeeming Power of God in their Souls, do not become *fully sensible* of this State of their Souls, is this, because the Soul, while it is in *this Flesh* and *Blood*, is capable of being *softened, assuaged,* and *comforted* in some Degree or other, by the Influences of the *Sun* and *Spirit* of this World, as all other Creatures and Beings are. And if it was not thus, how could it be a plain, constant Doctrine of Scripture, that when the *Unredeemed Soul* departs this Life, it is incapable of anything but Hell? Is not this directly saying, that Hell, or the Sensibility of Hell was only hid and suppressed in such a Soul, by the Life and Light of this World shining upon it.

Now what I have said of the sad Condition of the Soul at the *Fall*, that it lost the Divine Life, or the Birth of the Son and Holy Spirit of God in it, and so became of the *same dark, fiery*

Nature, as the Devils, is not possible to be denied, without denying the most universally received Doctrine of Scripture.

Is it not a fundamental Doctrine of Scripture, that *Adam* and all his Posterity had been *left* in a State of *Eternal Death*, or Damnation, unless Jesus Christ had become their Redeemer, and taken them out of their natural State? But how can you believe, or own they had been *left* in this State, without believing and owning that they were *in* it? Or, how can you with the Scripture believe, that by the Fall they became *Heirs* of Eternal Death and Damnation with the Devils, unless you believe and affirm, that by the Fall they became of a hellish, diabolical Nature? Or how can you hold, that by the Fall they *wanted* to be delivered from the State of the Devils, and yet not allow, that by the Fall, they got the Nature of the Devils? Can any Thing be more absurd and inconsistent? Is it not the same Thing as saying, that God made them Heirs of Eternal Death and Hell, before they were by Nature fit for it, or before they had extinguished in themselves the Divine Life which was at first brought forth in them.

Again: It is a Scripture Doctrine of the utmost Certainty and Importance, that those Souls which have *totally* resisted and withstood all that God has done in them and for them by his Son Jesus Christ, will, at their Departure from the Body, be incapable of any Thing but *Eternal Death*, or a hellish Condition. Now, how can you possibly hold this Doctrine of Scripture, without holding at the same Time, that the Soul was in that State by the Fall, before it had received its Redeemer, as it is then in, when it has *refused* to receive him; for all that you can say of a lost Soul is only this, that it has *lost* its Redeemer, and therefore is only in the Condition of that Soul which has *not received* him: And therefore, if a lost Soul is only an unredeemed Soul, it must be plain, that the Soul, *before* it had received its Redeemer, was in the miserable Condition, and had the miserable Nature of a Lost Soul; and therefore, the only Difference between the fallen Soul, and the lost Soul is this, they are both in the *same need* of a Saviour, both have the *same miserable* Nature, because they have him *not;* but the one has the Offer of him, and the other has refused to accept of Him: But his final Refusal of him, has only left him in Possession of that *fallen State* of a hellish Condition, which it had before a Saviour was given to it; and therefore, it is a Truth of the utmost Certainty, that *Adam*, by his Fall, died to the Divine Life, and that by this Death, his Soul became of the *same Nature* and *Condition* with the fallen Angels; and that therefore *that new Birth* or Regeneration, which he is to obtain by his Redeemer Jesus Christ, is nothing else but the bringing back his Soul into the Kingdom of Heaven, by a *Birth* of the Son and Holy Spirit of God brought forth in it, that so the Life of the triune God may be in him *again*, as it was at his *Creation*, when his Soul was first breathed forth from the triune God. Is there any Thing more great, more glorious, or more consistent than these Truths? Or is there any Possibility of denying any Part of them, without giving up the whole? Or is there any Reason, why a Christian should be loath to believe this, and this alone, to be the true State of that Regeneration which is so absolutely required by the Gospel? Is it an unreasonable or uncomfortable Thing to be told, that our Regeneration is a true and real Regaining that heavenly, Divine, immortal Life which at first came forth from God, and which alone can enter into the Kingdom of Heaven?

Say that *Adam* did not die a real Death at his Transgression, that he did not lose a Divine, immortal Life, Light and Spirit, that he did not then first become a mere earthly, mortal, Diabolical Animal in the true and proper Sense of the Words, but that these Things could only be affirmed of him in a figurative Form of Speech; say this, and then tell me what Reality you have left in any Article of our Salvation?

But if all these Things must be said of fallen Man according to the strictest Truth of the Expression, then the Gospel Regeneration, by a Birth of the Son and Holy Spirit of God, arising a *second Time*, in the Soul of Man, must mean such a real Birth of a new heavenly Life, as the proper Sense of the Words denote.

30. But to return now to my Argumentation with the Deist.

I have plainly shown you, that there is, and can be but one kind of Death through all Nature, whether temporal or eternal; and this I have done, by showing that *Eternal Death* in an *Angel*, is the same Thing, and has the same Nature, as the hard Death that is in a senseless Flint. But if it be a certain Truth, that Death has but *one Way* of entering into, or possessing any Being from the highest of spiritual to the lowest of material Creatures, then, though nothing else could be offered, it must be an infallible Consequence, that *Life* has but one Way of being *kindled* throughout all Nature, and that therefore there can be but *one true* Religion, and that only can be it, which hath the *one only way* of kindling the heavenly Life in the Soul.

Now, look where you will, the Birth or kindling of Life through all Nature shows you, that the Way of Gospel Regeneration, or Raising the Divine Life again in the fallen Soul, is that one and the same Way, by which every kind of Life is, and must be raised, wherever it is found. The Gospel saith, unless the fallen Soul be born again from above, be born again of the Word, or Son, and the Spirit of God, it cannot see, or enter into the Kingdom of Heaven: Now here it says a Truth, as much confirmed and ratified by all Nature, as when it is said, except a Creature hath the Light and Spirit of this World born in it, it cannot become a living Animal of this World: Or, except a *Seed* have the Light and Spirit of this World incorporated in it, it cannot become a *Vegetable* of this World, either as Plant, Fruit, or Flower. Ask now wherein lies the absolute Impossibility, that the fallen Soul should be raised to its Divine Life, without a *Birth* of the *Son* and Holy *Spirit* of God in it, and the true Ground of this Impossibility is only this, because a *Seed* shut up in its own cold hardness, cannot possibly be raised into its highest Vegetable Life, but by a *Birth* of the *Light* and *Spirit* of this World rising up in it.

On the other hand, ask why a *Seed* cannot possibly become a Vegetable Life, till the Light and Spirit of this World has been incorporated, or generated in it; and the only true Ground of it is, because a fallen Soul can only be raised to a Divine Life, or become a Plant of the Kingdom of Heaven, by receiving the Birth of the Light and Spirit of God into it. For the true Reason, why Life is in *such a Form*, and rises in *such* a Manner in the lowest Creature living, is because it does, and must arise in the *same manner*, and stand in the *same Form* in the highest of Living Creatures: For Nature does, and must always act and generate in *one* and the *same unchangeable* Manner, because it is nothing else but the *Manifestation* of one unchangeable God.

It is *one* and the *same* Operation of Light and Spirit, that turns Fire into every Degree and kind of Life that can be found either in temporal or eternal Nature: It is one and the same Operation of Light and Spirit, that upon one State of Fire, raises only a *vegetable* Life, upon another State of Fire, raises an *animal* Life, upon another State of Fire, raises an *intellectual* and *angelical* Life.

There is no State or Form of Death in any Creature, but where some kind of Fire is shut up from Light and Spirit, nor is there any kind of Life but what is kindled by the same Operation of Light and Spirit upon some sort of Fire.

A *Fruit* must first stand in a *poisonous, sour, astringent, bitter*, and *fiery* Agitation of all its Parts, before the Light and Spirit of this World can be generated in it. And thus Light and Spirit operate upon one sort of Fire in the Production of a vegetable Life.

94 *An Appeal to all who doubt*

An *Animal* must be conceived in the same manner, it must begin in the *same Poison,* and when Nature is in its *fiery Strife,* the Light and Spirit of this World kindles up the true animal Life.

Thus also there is but one kind, or State of Death that can fall upon any Creature, which is nothing else, but its *losing the Birth* of Light and Spirit in itself, by which it becomes an imprisoned, dark Fire. In an Animal, Vegetable, or mere Matter, it is a senseless State of imprisoned Fire; in an Angel, or intellectual Being, as the Soul of Man, it is a *self-tormenting, self-generating, fiery* Worm, that cannot lose its Sensibility, but is in a State of Eternal *Death,* because it is separated *eternally* from that Light and Spirit, which alone can raise a Divine Life in any intellectual Creature.

And thus it is plain, beyond all Possibility of Doubt, that there is neither *Life* nor *Death* to be found in any Part of the Creation but what sets its infallible Seal to this Gospel Truth, that fallen Man cannot enter into the Kingdom of Heaven any other Way, than by being born again of the Son and Holy Spirit of God.

31. And here, my Friend, you may with Certainty see what a poor, groundless *Fiction,* your Religion of *Human Reason* is; its Insignificancy and Emptiness is shown you by every Thing you can look upon.

Salvation is a *Birth of Life,* but Reason can no more bring forth *this Birth,* than it can kindle Life in a *Plant,* or *Animal:* You might as well write the Word *Flame,* upon the outside of a *Flint,* and then expect that its imprisoned Fire should be *kindled* by it, as to imagine, that any *Images,* or *Ideal Speculations* of Reason painted in your Brain, should raise your Soul out of its State of Death, and kindle the Divine Life in it. No: Would you have Fire from a *Flint;* its House of Death must be *shaken,* and its Chains of Darkness *broken off* by the Strokes of a *Steel* upon it. This must of all Necessity be done to your Soul, its *imprisoned Fire* must be awakened by the *sharp Strokes* of Steel, or no true Light of Life can arise in it: All Nature and Creature tells you, that the Heavenly Life must begin in you from the same Causes, and the same Operation as every earthly Life, whether vegetable, or animal, does in this World.*

Now, look where you will, all Life must be generated in this Manner: First, an *Attraction,* or an *astringing* Desire, must work itself into an *anguishing Agitation,* or *painful Strife;* this Attraction become restless, and highly agitated, is that *first Poison,* or

---

* *Way to Divine Knowledge,* page 162, &c.

Strife of the *Properties* of Nature, which is and must be the *Beginning* of every *Vegetable* or *Animal* Life; it is by this *Strife*, or inward *Agitation*, that it reaches and gets a *Birth* of the Light and Spirit of this World into it, and so becomes a Living Member, either of the animal or vegetable World.

Now, this must be your Process, a *Desire* brought into an *anguishing State;* or the *bitter Sorrows* and *fiery Agitations* of Repentance, must be the *Beginning* of a Divine Life in your Soul; 'tis by this awakened Fire, or inward Agitation, that it becomes capable of being regenerated, or turned into an heavenly Life, by the Light and Holy Spirit of God.

Nothing is, or can possibly be Salvation, but this regenerated Life of the Soul: How vain and absurd would it be, to talk of a Creature's being made a Member of a vegetable or animal Kingdom, through an *outward Grace* or *Favour?* or by any *outward Thing* of any kind? For does not Sense, Reason, and all Nature force you to confess, that it is absolutely impossible for *any Thing* to become a *Living Member* of the animal or vegetable Kingdom, but by having the animal or vegetable Life *raised* or brought forth in it? Therefore, does not Sense and Reason, and all Nature join with the Gospel in affirming, that no Man can enter into the Kingdom of Heaven, till the *Heavenly Life*, or that which is the Life in Heaven, *be born* in him?

The Gospel says to the fallen, earthly Man, that he must be *born again from above*, before he can see, enter into, or become a Living Member of the Kingdom that is above.

Now, he that understands this to be a *figurative Saying*, that requires no *real Birth* of a *real Life* that is only above, but that an earthly Man may enter into the Life of Heaven, by only carrying this figurative Saying along with him, is as absurd, as ignorant, and offends as much against Sense, Reason, and all Nature, as he who holds, that it is a *figurative Expression*, when we say that nothing can enter into the vegetable Kingdom, till it has the *vegetable Life* in it, or be a Member of the Animal Kingdom, till it hath the Animal Life born in it.*

And if some Learned Men will say, that it is *Religious Enthusiasm* to place our Salvation, or Capacity for the Kingdom of Heaven in the *inward Life* or *Birth* of *Heaven* derived into our Souls, they are only as learned as those who should call it *Philosophical Enthusiasm* to place the true Nature of a Vegetable, or Animal, in its getting the *inward, real Birth* of a Vegetable and Animal Life. But to return to the Deist.

You act as if God was a Being that had an *arbitrary, discre-*

---

* *Way to Divine Knowledge,* page 159.

tionary Will, or Wisdom, like that of a great Prince over his Subjects, who will reward Mankind according as their Services appeared to him. And so you fancy, that your Religion of Reason may appear as valuable as a Religion that consists of Forms, and Modes, Ordinances, and Doctrines of Revelation; but your Idea of the last Judgment is a Fiction of Reason that knows nothing rightly of God. God's last rewarding, is only his last separating every Thing into its own Eternal Place; it is only putting an end to all temporary Nature, to the Mixture of Good and Evil that is in Time, and leaving every Thing to be *That* in *Eternity*, which it has made itself to be in *Time*. Thus it is that our Works follow us, and thus God rewards every Man according to his Deeds.*

During the Time of this World, God may be considered as the good Husbandman; he sows the Seed, the End of the World is the Harvest, the Angels are the Reapers; if you are *Wheat*, you are to be gathered into the Barn, if you are *Tares*, it signifies nothing, *whence*, or *how*, or by what *Means* you are become so; Tares are to be rejected, because they are Tares, and Wheat to be gathered by the Angels, because it is Wheat: This is the Mercy, and Goodness, and Discretionary Justice of God that you are to expect at the last Day. If you are not Wheat, that is, if the heavenly Life, or the Kingdom of God, is not grown up in you, it signifies nothing what you have chosen in the stead of it, or why you have chosen it, you are not *That*, which alone can help you to a Place in the Divine Granary.

God wants no Services of Men to reward, he only wants to have *such a Life* quickened and raised up in you, as may make it *possible* for you to enter into, and live in Heaven.

He has created you out of his own *Eternal Nature*, and therefore you must have either an Eternal Life, or Eternal Death according to it. If eternal Nature standeth *in you*, as it doth *without* you, then you are born again to the Kingdom of Heaven; but if Nature works contrary in you to what it does in Heaven, then you are in Eternal Death: And here lies the Necessity of our being *born* again of the *Word* and *Spirit* of God, in order to the Kingdom of Heaven. It is because we are created out of that eternal Nature which is the *Kingdom of Heaven*; 'tis because we are *fallen out* of it into a Life of temporal Nature, and therefore must have the Life of eternal Nature *re-kindled* in us, before we can possibly enter into the Kingdom of Heaven: Therefore, look where you will, or at what you will, there is only one Thing to be done, we want

---

* *Way to Divine Knowledge*, pages 169-183.

Nothing else, but to have the *Light World*, or the life of Eternal Nature kindled again in our Souls, that *Life*, and *Light*, and *Spirit* may be *That* in our Souls, which they are in Eternal Nature, out of which our Souls were created; that so we may be heavenly Plants growing up to the Kingdom of Heaven.*

You deceive yourself with fancied Notions of the Goodness of God; you imagine, that so perfect a Being cannot damn you for so *small* a Matter, as *choosing* a Religion according to your *own Notions*, or for not joining yourself with this, or that Religious Society.

But all this is great Ignorance of *God*, and *Nature*, and *Religion*. God has appointed a Religion, by which Salvation is to be had according to the *Possibility* of Nature, where no Creature will be saved, or lost, but as it works with, or contrary to Nature. For as the God of Nature cannot himself act *contrary* to Nature, because Nature is the *Manifestation* of himself, so every Creature having its Life in, and from *Nature*, can have only *such* a Life, or *such* a Death as is according to the *Possibility* of Nature: And therefore, no Creature will be saved, by an *arbitrary* Goodness of God, but because of its *Conformity* to Nature, nor any Creature lost by a Want of Compassion in God, but because of its Salvation being *impossible*, according to the *whole State* of Nature.

It is not for Notional, or Speculative Mistakes, that Man will be rejected by God at the last Day, or for *any Crimes* that God could *over-look*, if he was so pleased; but because Man has continued in his *unregenerate State*, and has resisted and suppressed that *Birth of Life*, by which alone he could become a Member of the Kingdom of Heaven. The *Goodness* and *Love* of God have no *Limits* or *Bounds*, but such as his Omnipotence hath: And every Thing that hath a *Possibility* of partaking of the Kingdom of Heaven, will *infallibly* find a Place in it.

God comes not to Judgment to display any Wrath of his own, or to inflict any Punishment as from Himself upon Man: He only comes to declare, that all temporary Nature is at an End, and that therefore, all Things must be, and stand in their own Places in Eternal Nature: His Sentence of *Condemnation*, is only a leaving them that are lost, in such a Misery of their *own Nature*, as has finally rejected all that was possible to relieve it.

You fancy that God will not reject you at the last Day, for having not received this, or that *Mode*, or *Kind* of Religion: But here all is Mistake again. You might as well imagine, that no particular *kind* of Element was necessary to extinguish

---

* *Way to Divine Knowledge*, pages 186-195.

Fire, or that *Water* can supply the *Place* of Air in kindling it, as suppose that no *particular kind* of Religion is absolutely necessary to raise up such a Divine Life in the Soul as can only be its Salvation; for Nature is the *Ground* of all Creatures, it is God's Manifestation of himself, it is his Instrument in, and by which he acts in the Production and Government of every Life; and therefore a Life that is to belong to *this* World, must be raised according to *temporal* Nature, and a Life that is to live in the next World, must be raised according to *Eternal* Nature.

Therefore, all the particular *Doctrines, Institutions, Mysteries,* and *Ordinances* of a revealed Religion that comes from the God of Nature, must have their *Reason, Foundation,* and *Necessity* in Nature; and then your renouncing such a revealed Religion, is renouncing *all* that the God of Nature can do to save you.

When I speak of Nature as the true Ground and Foundation of Religion, I mean nothing like that which you call the Religion of *Human Reason,* or *Nature;* for I speak here of *Eternal Nature,* which is the Nature of the *Kingdom of Heaven,* or that Eternal State, where all redeemed Souls must have their Eternal Life, and live in Eternal Nature by a Life derived from it, as Men and Animals live in temporal Nature, by a Life derived from it; for, seeing Man stands with his Soul in Eternal Nature, as certainly as he lives outwardly in temporal Nature, and seeing Man can have nothing in this World, neither Happiness, nor Misery from it, but what is according to temporal Nature, so he can with his Soul, attain nothing, nor suffer nothing in the next World, but what is according to the Eternal Nature of that World; and therefore, it is an infallible Truth, that that *particular* Religion can *alone* do us any Good, or help us to the Happiness of the next World, which works *with,* and *according* to Eternal Nature, and is able to *generate* that Eternal Life in us. But your Notion of a Goodness of God that may be expected at the last Day, is as groundless, as if you imagined, that God would then stand over his Creatures in a compassionate kind of *weighing* or *considering* who should be saved, and who damned, because a good-natured Prince might do so towards Variety of Offenders.

But hear how the God of Nature himself speaks of this Matter: *Behold, I have set before thee, Life and Death, Fire and Water,—choose whither thou wilt.* Here lies the *Whole* of the Divine Mercy; 'tis all on *this side* the Day of Judgment: Till the End of Time, God is *compassionate* and *long-suffering,* and continues to every Creature a *Power* of choosing Life or Death, Water or Fire; but when the End of Time is come, there is an End of Choice, and the last Judgment is only a putting everyone into the full and sole Possession of *That* which he has chosen.

But your Notion of a Goodness of God at the last Day supposes, that if a Man has erroneously chosen *Death* instead of *Life*, *Fire* instead of *Water*, that God will not suffer such a Creature to be deprived of Salvation through a *mistaken Choice;* but that in such a Creature, he will make *Death* to be *Life*, and *Fire* to be *Water*. But you might as well expect, that God should make a Thing to be, and not to be at the same Time; for this is as possible as to make Hell to be Heaven, or Death to be Life: For Darkness can no more be Light, Death can no more be Life, Fire can no more be Water in any Being through a Compassion of God towards it, than a *Circle* could be a *Square*, a Falsehood a Truth, or *two* to be more than *three*, by God's looking upon them.

32. Our Salvation is an *Entrance* into the Kingdom of Heaven; now, the *Life*, *Light* and *Spirit* of Heaven must as necessarily be in a Creature before it can *live* in Heaven, as the Life, Light and Spirit of this World must be in a Creature before it can *live* in this World: Therefore the *one only* Religion that can save any one Son of fallen *Adam*, must be that which can *raise* or *generate* the Life, Light and Spirit of Heaven in his Soul, that when the Light and Spirit of this World leaves him, he may not find himself in eternal Death and Darkness.

Now if this Light and Spirit of Heaven is *generated* in your Soul as it is generated in Heaven, if it arises up in your Nature *within* you, as it does in eternal Nature *without* you, (which is the Christian new Birth, or Regeneration) then you are become capable of the Kingdom of Heaven, and nothing can keep you out of it; but if you die without this Birth of the Eternal Light and Spirit of God, then your Soul stands in the *same Distance* from, and *Contrariety* to the Kingdom of Heaven, as Hell does: If you die in this unregenerate State, it signifies nothing *how* you have lived, or *what* Religion you have owned, all is left undone that was to have saved you: It matters not what *Form* of Life you have appeared in, what a Number of decent, engaging or glorious Exploits you have done either as a *Scholar*, a *Statesman*, or a *Philosopher*; if they have proceeded only from the Light and Spirit of this World, they must die with it, and leave your Soul in that Eternal Darkness, which it must have, so long as the Light and Spirit of Eternity is not generated in it.

And this is the true Ground and Reason, why an outward *Morality*, a *Decency* and *Beauty* of Life and Conduct with respect to this World, arising only from a *Worldly Spirit*, has nothing of Salvation in it: He that has his Virtue only from this World, is only a *Trader* of this World, and can only have a Worldly Benefit from it. For it is an undoubted Truth, that every Thing is necessarily bounded by, or kept within the Sphere of its *own Activity;* and therefore, to expect Heavenly Effects from a Worldly Spirit, is Nonsense: As *Water* cannot rise higher in its Streams, than the Spring from whence it cometh, so no Actions can ascend further in their Efficacy, or rise higher in their Value, than the *Spirit* from whence they proceed. The Spirit that comes from Heaven is always in Heaven, and whatsoever it does, tends to, and reaches Heaven: The Spirit that arises from this World, is always in it; it is as worldly when it gives *Alms*, or prays in the *Church*, as when it makes *Bargains* in the *Market*. When therefore the Gospel saith, He that gives Alms to be seen of Men, hath his Reward; it is grounded on this general Truth, That every Thing, every Shape, or kind or degree of Virtue that *arises* from the *Spirit* of this World, has nothing to expect but *That* which it can receive from this World: For every Action must have its Nature, and Efficacy according to the Spirit from whence it proceeds. He that loves to see a *Crucifix*, a worthless Image, solely from this Principle, because from his Heart he embraces Christ as his suffering Lord and Pattern, does an Action poor, and needless in itself, which yet by the Spirit from whence it proceeds, *reaches* Heaven, and *helps* to kindle the heavenly Life in the Soul. On the other hand, he that from a *selfish Heart*, a *Worldly Spirit*, a Love of Esteem, distinguishes himself by the most rational Virtues of an exemplary Life, has only a Piety that may be reckoned amongst the *perishable* Things of this World.

33. You (the *Deist*) think it a *Partiality* unworthy of God, when you hear that the *Salvation* of Mankind is attributed and appropriated to *Faith* and *Prayer* in the Name of Jesus Christ. It must be answered, *First*, That there is *no Partiality* of any kind in God; every Thing is accepted by him according to its *own Nature*, and receives all the Good from him that it can possibly receive: *Secondly*, That a Morality of Life, not arising from the *Power* and *Spirit* of Jesus Christ, but brought forth by the Spirit of *this World*, is the same Thing, has the same Nature and Efficacy in a Heathen, as a Christian, does only the *same* worldly Good to the one, as it does to the other; therefore, there is not the least Partiality in God, with respect to the *Moral Works* of Mankind, considered as arising from, and directed by the Spirit of this World.

Now, were these the *only Works* that Man could do, could he only act from *the Spirit* of this World, no *Flesh* could be saved, that is, no earthly Creature, such as Man is, could possibly *begin* to be of a heavenly Nature, or have a heavenly Life *brought* forth in him; so it is only a Spirit from Heaven derived into the fallen Nature, that makes *any Beginning* of a heavenly Life in it, that can lay the *Possibility* of its having the least Ability, Tendency, and Disposition towards the Kingdom of Heaven. This Spirit derived from Heaven, is the *Birth* of the Son of God, given to the Soul as its *Saviour, Regenerator,* or *Beginner* of its Return to Heaven; it is that *Word* of Life, or *Bruiser* of the Serpent, that was *in-spoken* into the first fallen Father of Men; 'tis this *alone* that gives to all the Race of *Adam* their *Capacity* for Salvation, their *Power* of being again Sons of God; and therefore, Faith and Prayer in the *Name* of Jesus Christ, or Works done in the *Spirit* and *Power* of Jesus Christ can *alone* save the Soul, because the Soul can have *no Relation* to Heaven, *no Communion* with it, *no Beginning* or *Power* of Growth in the heavenly Life, but solely by the Nature and Name of Jesus Christ *derived* into it. God's Redemption of Mankind is as universal as the Fall: It was the one Father of all Men that fell, therefore, all his Children were born into his fallen State: It was the *one Father* of all Men that was redeemed by the *in-spoken Word* of Life into him; therefore, all his Children are born into his State of Redemption, and have as certainly the same Bruiser of the Serpent in the *Birth* of their Life from him, as they have from him a *Serpentine Nature* that is to be bruised.

Hence it was, that this *Bruiser* of the Serpent, when born of a Virgin, and come to die for the World, saith of himself, 'I am 'the Way, the Truth, and the Life; no Man cometh unto the 'Father but by me.' Hence also the Apostle saith, 'There is 'no other Name under Heaven given among Men, whereby we 'must be saved,'—because he is that *same* saving Name, or Power of Salvation which from the *Beginning* was given to *Adam*, as an in-spoken *Word* of Life, or Bruiser of the Serpent: And therefore, as sure as *Adam* had *any Power* of Salvation *derived* into him from Jesus Christ, so sure was it, that the Apostle *must tell* both Jews and Heathens, that there *was no Salvation in any other.*

Therefore, though Jesus Christ is the *one only* Saviour of all that can anywhere, or at any Time be saved, yet there is no *Partiality* in God, because, this same Jesus Christ, who came in Human Flesh to the Jews in a certain Age, was that *same Saviour* who was given to *Adam*, when all Mankind were in his Loins; and who, through all Ages, and in all Countries, from the first Patriarchs to the End of the World, is the common Saviour, as he is the common *Light that lighteth every Man* that cometh into the World, and that *Principle* of *Life* both in Jews and Heathens, by which they had any Relation to God, or any *Power*, or *Right*, or *Ability* to call him Father. When therefore you look upon the Gospel as *narrowing* the Way of Salvation, or limiting it to those, who only know and believe in Jesus Christ, since his Appearance in the Flesh, you mistake the *whole Nature* of the Christian Redemption.

And when you reject *this Saviour* that then appeared, and *died* as a Sacrifice upon the *Cross*, you don't renounce a *particular kind* of Religion, that was given *only* at a certain Time to one Part of the World, but you renounce the *one Source* and *Fountain* of all the Grace and Mercy that God *can* bestow upon Mankind, you renounce your Share of that first Covenant which God made with *all Men* in *Adam*, you go back into his *first fallen* State, and so put yourself into that Condition of Eternal Death, from which there is no Possibility of Deliverance, but by that one Saviour whom you have renounced.

And now, my dear Friend, beware of Prejudice, or Hardness of Heart: One careless, or one relenting Thought upon all that is here laid before you, may either quite shut out, or quite open an Entrance for true Conviction. I have shown you what is meant by Christian Redemption, and the absolute Necessity of a *new* and *heavenly Birth*, in order to obtain your Share of a heavenly Life in the next World: I have confirmed the Truths of the Gospel, by Proofs taken from what is undeniable in Nature: And I readily grant you that nothing can be true in revealed Religion, but what has its *Foundation* in Nature; because a Religion coming from the God of Nature, can have no other End but to reform, and set right the Failings, Transgressions, and Violations of Nature. When the Gospel saith that Man fallen from the State of his Creation, and become an earthly Animal of this temporal World, must be born again of the Son and Holy Spirit of God, in order to be a heavenly Creature; 'tis because all Nature saith, that an immortal, eternal Soul, must have an *immortal, eternal* Light and Spirit, to make it live in Eternal Nature, as every Animal must have a *temporal* Light and Spirit, in order to live in temporary Nature. Must you not therefore either deny the *Immortality* of the Soul, or acknowledge the Necessity of its having an *Eternal* Light and Spirit? When the Gospel saith, that nothing can *kindle* or *generate* the heavenly Life, but the Operation of the *Light* and *Spirit* of Heaven, it is because all Nature saith, that no temporal Life can be raised but in the *same manner* in temporary Nature. Must you not therefore be forced to confess, that Nature and the Gospel both preach the *same Truths.*

Light and Spirit must be wherever there are *living* Beings: And there must be the same Difference betwixt the Light and Spirit of different Worlds, as there is betwixt the Worlds themselves. *Hell* must have its Light, or it could have no *living* Inhabitants, but its Light is not so *refreshing*, not so *gentle*, not so *delightful*, not so *comfortable* as flashing Points of Fire in the thickest Darkness of Night; and therefore their Light is called an *Eternal Darkness*, because it can never *disperse*, but only horribly *discover* Darkness: Hell also must have its *Spirit;* but it is only an incessant Sensibility of *wrathful Agitations*, of which the Thunder and Rage of a Tempest is but a low, shadowy Resemblance, as being only a little outward Eruption of *That Wrath*, which is the inward, restless Essence of the Spirit of Hell; and therefore that Life, though it be a living Spirit, is justly called an *Eternal Death.*

The Light and Spirit of God admit of no Delineation or Comparison, they are only so far known to anyone, as they are brought into the Soul by a Birth of themselves in it.

Now consider, I pray you: The Light and Spirit of this World can no more be the Light and Spirit of *immortal Souls*, than *Grass* and *Hay* can be the Food of Angels; but is as different from the Light and Spirit of Heaven, as an Angel is different from a Beast of the Field. When therefore the Soul of a Man departs from his Body, and is *eternally* cut off from *all* temporal Light and Spirit, what is it that can keep such a Soul from falling into *Eternal Darkness*, unless it have in itself, that *Light* and *Spirit*, which is of the same Nature with the Light and Spirit of Eternity, so that it may be in the Light of Heaven or Eternal Nature, as it was in the Light of this World in temporary Nature.

Light and Spirit there must be in every Thing that lives, but the Death of the Body takes away the Light and Spirit of this World; if therefore the Light and Spirit of Heaven be *not born* in the Soul when it loses the Body, it can only have that Light and Spirit, which is the very *Death* and *Darkness* of Hell.

When Man lost the Light and Spirit of his Creation, he lost it by turning the *Will* and *Desire* of his Soul into an Earthly Life; this was his Desire of *knowing Good and Evil* in this World. His Fall therefore consisted in this, his Soul lost its first *innate, in-breathed* Light and Spirit of Heaven, and instead of it, had only the Light and Spirit of Temporary Nature, to keep up for a Time such a Life in him from this World, as the proper Creatures of this World have: And this is the Reason, why Man, the noblest Creature that is in this World, has yet various Circumstances of Necessity, Poverty, Distress and Shame, that are not common to other Animals of this World. 'Tis because the Creatures of this Life are here *at home*, are the proper Inhabitants of this World, and therefore that Womb out of which they are born, has provided them with all that they want; but Man being only *fallen* into it, and as a Transgressor, must in many Respects find himself in such Wants as other Creatures have not. *Transitory Time* has brought them forth, and therefore they can have no Pain, nor Concern, nor Danger in *passing away;* because it is the *very Form* of their Nature, to begin, and to have an End: And therefore the God of Nature has no outward Laws, or Directions for the Creatures of this World.

But the Soul of Man being *not born* of the Light and Spirit of this transitory World, but only standing a while as a *Stranger* upon Earth, and being under a *Necessity* of having either the Nature of an Angel, or a Devil, when it *leaves* this World, is met by the Mercy and Goodness of the God of Nature, is inwardly and outwardly called, warned, directed, and assisted *how* to regain that Light and Spirit of Heaven which it lost, when it fell under the temporary Light and Spirit of this World. And this is the whole Ground and End of revealed Religion, *viz.*, to kindle such a *Beginning* or *Birth* of the Divine Light and Spirit in the Soul, that when Man must take an Eternal Leave of the Light and Spirit of this World, he may not be in a State of Eternal Death and Darkness.

Now, seeing the Light and Spirit of Heaven or Eternal Nature, is as different from the Light and Spirit of this World, as an Angel is from an Animal of the Field, if you have lived here only to the Spirit and Temper of this World, governed by its Goods and Evils, and only wise according to its Wisdom, you must die as *destitute* of the Light and Spirit of Heaven, as the Beasts that perish. You have now an *Aversion* and *Dislike*, or at least, a *Disbelief* of the Doctrines of Christian Regeneration, you struggle against *this Kind* of Redemption, you would have no Salvation from the *Light* and *Spirit* of Eternity regenerated in your Soul; where then must you be, when the Light and Spirit of this World leaves you?

Do you think that the Light and Spirit of God will then *seize* upon you, *shine* up in you by an *outward Force*, though they never could *be born* in you? Or do you think, that the Light and Spirit of God can *now be generating* themselves in you, and ready to appear, as soon as you have ended a Life, that has continually *resisted* them, and would have no *new Birth* from them? Or that God, by a compassionate Goodness, will not suffer you to be in that Condition, into which your *own Will* has brought you? No, my Friend, the *Will* that is in you, must do *That* for you, which the Will that was in Angels did for those that *stood*, and for those that *fell*.

God's Goodness or Compassion is always in the *same* infinite State, always *flowing forth*, in and through all Nature in the same infinite Manner, and nothing wants it, but that which cannot receive it: Whilst the Angels stood, they stood encompassed with the infinite Source of all Goodness and Compassion, God was communicated to them in as high a Degree as their Nature could receive; and they fell, not because he ceased to be an infinite, open Fountain of all Good to them, but because they had a Will which must direct itself.

For the Will, at its first arising in the Creature, can be subject to no outward Power, because it has no outward Maker; as it stands in a creaturely Form, God is its true Creator; but as a *Will*, it has no *outward Maker*, but is a Ray, or Spark, derived from the *Unbeginning* Will of the Creator, and is of the same Nature in the Creature, as it was in the Creator, *self-existent, self-generating, self-moving*, and *uncontrollable* from without; and there could not possibly be a *free Will* in the Creature, but by its being *directly* derived, or propagated from the same Will in the Creator, for Nothing can be free *now*, but that which *always* was so.

But if the free Will of God, which is above and superior to Nature, be communicated to the Creature, then the Creature's free Will must have the same Power over its *one Nature*, that the Will of God has over that Eternal Nature, which is his own Manifestation: And therefore, every free Creature must have, and find its *own* Nature in *this*, or *that* State, as a *Birth* from the free Working of its own Will. And here appears the true Reason, why no Creatures of this World can commit Sin; 'tis because they have no Will that is *superior* to Nature: Their Will in every one of them, is only the Will of Nature; and therefore let them do what they will, they are always doing that which is *natural*, and consequently, not sinful. But the Will of Angels and Men being an *Offspring*, or *Ray*, derived from the Will of God, which is *superior* to Nature, stands chargeable with the State and Condition of their Nature; and therefore it is, that the Nature of the Devil, and the Nature of fallen Man is imputed to both of them, as their Sin, which could not be, but because their Will was uncontrollable, and gave Birth and Being to that State and Condition of Nature, which is called, and is their Sin.

Therefore, O Man! look well to thyself, and see what Birth thou art bringing forth, what Nature is growing up in Thee, and be assured, that stand thou must, in that State in Nature, which the Working of thy own Will has brought forth in Thee, whether it be happy or miserable. Expect no Arbitrary Goodness, of God towards Thee, when thou leavest this World; for that must grow for ever which hath grown here. God hath created thee in Nature, his Mercy hath shown Thee all the Laws and Necessities of Nature, and how Thou mayest rise from Thy Corruption, according to the Possibilities of Nature, and He can only save Thee by thy conforming to the Demands of Nature: The Greatness of the Divine Mercy and Favour towards all Men appears in this, that when all Nature had failed, and Mankind could from Nature have nothing but Eternal Death, that God brought such a Second *Adam* into the World, as being God and Man, could make Nature begin its Work again, where it failed in the first *Adam*.

The *free Grace* and Mercy by which we are said in the Scripture to be *saved*, is not an arbitrary Good Will in God, which saves whom he pleases; as a Prince may forgive some, and not forgive others, merely through his own Sovereign Grace and Favour: Nothing of this Kind hath any Place in God, or in the Mystery of our Redemption; but the Mercy and Grace, by which we are saved, is therefore free, because God hath freely, and from his own Goodness, put us into a *State* and Possibility of Salvation, by freely giving us Jesus Christ, (the Divine and Human Nature united in one Person) as the only Means of regenerating that first Divine and Human Life, which the whole Race of Mankind had lost. In this sense alone it is, that all our Salvation is wholly owing to the free Grace of God, that is, our *State*, and *Possibility*, and *Means* of attaining Salvation is wholly owing to his free Grace in giving us Jesus Christ; but our Salvation, considered as a *finished Thing*, is not, cannot be found by any Act of God's free Grace towards us, but because *all That* is done, altered, removed, suppressed, quickened, and recovered by us in the *State* of our Nature, which the free Grace of God had furnished us with the Possibility and Means of doing. If Nature and Creature had no Share in working out our Salvation; if it was all free Grace, effected against, and without the Powers of Nature, how comes it, that the fallen Angels are not to be redeemed as well as Man? Must we say that God is less good to them than he is to us? Or if they are not redeemed, can there be any other Reason for it, but because it is an Impossibility in Nature? Must not an infinite Good do all the Good that is wanted, and is possible to be done? If free Grace can do what it pleases, if it wants no Concurrence of Nature and Creature, how can any Being, whether Man or Angel, be eternally miserable, but through an Eternal Defect in the Goodness of God towards it? Shall we call that infinite Goodness, which sets Bounds and Limits to itself, and which could do more Good, but will not?

The Truth of the Matter is this, God is as infinite and boundless in Love and Goodness, as he is in *Power*, but his Omnipotence can only do that which is possible, and nothing is possible but that which hath its Possibility in Nature; because Nature is God's first Power, his great, universal Manifestation of his Deity, in and through, and by which all his infinite Attributes break forth, and display themselves: So that to expect, that God should do any Thing that is above, or contrary to this Nature, is as absurd as to expect that God should act above, or contrary to himself: As God can only make a Creature to be in, and through, and by Nature; so the Reason why he cannot make a Creature to be, and not to be at the same Time, is only this, because it is contrary to Nature. Let no Man therefore trust to be saved at the last Day, by any *arbitrary* Goodness, or *free Grace* of God; for Salvation is, and can be nothing else, but the having *put off* all that is damnable and hellish in our Nature, which Salvation can be found by no Creature but by its own full conforming to, and concurring with those Mysterious Means, which the free Grace of God hath afforded for the Recovery of our first, perfect, glorious State in Nature.

Chapter II.

Of Eternal and Temporal Nature. How Nature is from God, and the Scene of his Action. How the Creatures are out of it. Temporal Nature created out of that which is eternal. The fallen Angels brought the first Disorders into Nature. This World created to repair those Disorders. Whence Good and Evil is in every Thing of this

World. How Heaven and Hell make up the Whole of this World. How the Fire of this World differs from eternal Fire; and the Matter of this World from the Materiality of Heaven. Eternal Nature is the Kingdom of Heaven, the beatific Manifestation of the triune God. God is mere Love and Goodness. How Wrath and Anger come to be ascribed to him. Of Fire in general. Of the Unbeginning Fire. Of the Spirituality of Fire. How Fire comes to be in material Things. Whence the Possibility of kindling Fire in the Things of this World. Every Man is, and must be the Kindler of his own Eternal Fire, &c.

1. WAS there no *Nature*, there could be no Creature, because the Life of every Creature is, and can be nothing else, but the Life of *that Nature* out of which it was created, and in which it has its Being. Eternal Beings must have their Qualities, Nature, Form and Manner of Existence out of *Eternal Nature*, and temporal Beings out of temporary Nature: Was there no Eternity, there could be no Time, was there nothing infinite, there could be nothing finite; therefore we have here two great fundamental Truths that cannot be shaken; *First*, That there is, and must be, an *Eternal Nature;* because there is a Nature that is temporary, and that it must be that to Eternal Creatures, which temporal Nature is to temporal Creatures: *Secondly*, That everywhere, and in all Worlds, *Nature* must stand between God and the Creature, as the Foundation of all mutual Intercourse; God can transact nothing with the Creature, nor the Creature have any Communion with God, but in, and by *that Nature*, in which it stands.

I hope no one will here ask me for Scripture Proofs of this, or call these Truths *Nostrums*, because they are not to be found in the *same Form* of Expression in some particular Text of Scripture. Where do the Holy Writings tell us, that a Thing cannot be, and not be at the *same Time* ? Or that every *Consequence* must arise from *Premises* ? And yet the Scripture is continually supposing both these Truths, and there could be no Truth in the Scripture, or anywhere else, if these Things were not undeniable.

There is nothing said of Man throughout all Scripture, but what supposes him to stand *in Nature*, under a necessity of choosing something that is *natural,* either Life or Death, Fire or Water. There is nothing said of God with relation to Creatures, but what supposes him to be the God of *Nature*, manifesting himself in and through Nature, calling, assisting and directing every Thing to its highest *natural* State. Nature is the Scene of his Providence, and all the Variety of his governing Attributes display themselves by his various Operations in and through Nature : Therefore it is equally certain, that what God does to any Creature, must be done through the *Medium* of Nature, and also what the Creature does toward God, must be done in and through the Powers of *that Nature* in which it stands. No temporary Creature can turn to God, or reach after him, or have any Communion with him, but in, and according to that Relation which temporary Nature bears to God ; nor can any Eternal Beings draw near to, or unite with God in any *other manner*, than that in which Eternal Nature is united with him. Would you know, why no Omnipotence of God can create Temporal Animals but out of temporary Nature, nor eternal Animals but out of Eternal Nature ; it is because no Omnipotence of God can produce a visible *Triangle,* but out of, and by three visible *Lines;* for, as *Lines* must be before there can be any *lineal Figures,* so *Nature* must be before there can be *natural Creatures.*

2. Every Thing that is in Being, is either God, or Nature, or Creature ; and every Thing that is not God, is only a Manifestation of God ; for as there is nothing, neither Nature, nor Creature, but what must have its Being in, and from God, so every Thing is, and must be according to its Nature, more or less a *Manifestation* of God. Everything therefore, by its Form and Condition, speaks *so much* of God, and God in every Thing, speaks and manifests *so much* of himself. Temporary Nature is this beginning, created System of *Sun, Stars,* and *Elements ;* 'tis temporary Nature, because it begins and hath an End, and therefore is only a temporary Manifestation of God, or God manifested according to transitory Things.

3. Properly and strictly speaking, nothing *can begin* to be: The Beginning of every Thing is nothing more, than its beginning to be in a *new State*. Thus *Time* itself does not begin to be, but Duration, which always was, began to be measured by the Earth's turning round, or the rising and setting of the Sun, and that is called the Beginning of Time, which is, properly speaking, only the Beginning of the Measure of Duration: Thus it is with all temporal Nature, and all the Qualities and Powers of temporal Beings that live in it: No Quality or Power of Nature *then* began to be, but such Qualities and Powers as had been from all Eternity, began then to be in a *new State*. Ask what Time is, it is nothing else but something of Eternal Duration become *finite, measurable*, and *transitory?* Ask what *Fire, Light, Darkness, Air, Water*, and *Earth* are; they are, and can be nothing else, but some eternal Things become *gross, finite, measurable, divisible*, and *transitory?* For if there could be a temporal Fire that did not *spring* out of Eternal Fire, then there might be Time that did not come out of Eternity.

'Tis thus with every temporary Thing, and the Qualities of it; 'tis the Beginning of Nothing, but only of a *new State* of something that existed before: Therefore all temporary Nature is a Product, Offspring, or Out-birth of Eternal Nature, and is nothing else but so much of Eternal Nature changed from its eternal to a temporal Condition. *Fire* did not begin to be, Darkness did not begin to be, Light did not begin to be, Water and Earth did not begin to be, when this temporary World first appeared, but all these Things came out of their *Eternal State*, into a lower, divided, compacted, created and transitory State. Hearing, Seeing, Tasting, Smelling, Feeling, did not then begin to be, when God first created the Creatures of this World, they only came to be Qualities and Powers of a lower, and more imperfect Order of Beings than they had been before.

Figures, and their Relations, did not then begin to be, when Material *Circles* and *Squares*, *&c.*, were first made, but these Figures and Relations began then to appear in a lower State than they had done before: And so it must be said of all temporal Nature, and every Thing in it. It is only *something* of Eternal Nature separated, changed, or created into a new, temporary State and Condition.

4. Now it may be asked, why was Eternal Nature thus degraded, debased, and changed from its Eternal State of Perfection? Will anyone say, that God of his own Will changed Eternal Nature, which is the *Glorious Manifestation* of his Power and Godhead, the *Seat* of his holy Residence, his *Majestic Kingdom* of Heaven, into this poor, miserable Mixture of Good

and Evil, into this impure State of Division, Grossness, Death, and Darkness? No. It is the highest of all Absurdities, to say so. Now, we sufficiently know from Scripture, that a whole Hierarchy, or Host of Angels, renounced their Heavenly Life, and thereby raised up a *Kingdom* that was not Heavenly. Could they not have inflamed and disordered outward Nature in which they lived, they could not have destroyed the Heavenly Nature in themselves: For every Thing must be according to the State of that World in which it lives; and therefore, the State of outward Nature, and the State of inward Nature in the Angels must stand and fall together; and as sure as a whole Kingdom of Angels lost their heavenly Life, so sure it is, that their whole Kingdom lost its heavenly State and Condition: And therefore, it is an undeniable Truth, founded on Scripture Evidence, that *same Part* of Eternal Nature was changed from its *first State* of Glory and Perfection, *before* the Creation of Temporary Nature; therefore, in the Creation of this poor, gross, disordered, perishable, material World, one of these two Things was done, either God took the *spoiled Part* of Heaven or Eternal Nature, and created it into this *Temporary State* of Good and Evil; or he degraded, and brought down some Part of the Kingdom of Heaven from its Glory and Perfection, into *this Mixture* of Good and Evil, Order and Disorder in which the World stands. He could not do this *latter*, without bringing Evil into Nature, as the Devil had done, and therefore we may be sure he did not do it; but if he did the former, then the Creation of this lower World, was a glorious Act, and worthy of the infinite Goodness of God, it was putting an End to the Devil's working Evil in Nature, and it was putting the Evil that was brought into Nature, in a way of being finally overcome, and turned into Good again. Will anyone now call these Things *whimsical Speculations?* Can any Thing be thought of *more worthy* of God, more *conformable* to Nature, or more *consonant* to all revealed Religion? But perhaps you will say, how could the Angels spoil or destroy that glorious Kingdom of Eternal Nature in which they dwelt. It may be answered, how could it possibly be otherwise? How could they live in Eternal Nature, unless Nature without them, and Nature within them, mutually *mixed* and *qualified* with each other? Would you have such mighty Spirits, with their eternal Energies, have less Power in *that Nature*, or Kingdom in which they dwelt, than a kindled Piece of *Coal* hath in this World? For every Piece of *Coal* set on Fire, adds so much Heat to outward Nature, and so far alters and changes the State of it.

5. Now, let it be supposed, not only that a Piece of *Coal,* but

that the Whole of every Thing in this World, that could either give or receive Fire was made to burn, what Effect would it have upon the whole Frame of Nature? Would not the whole State of Things, the Regions, Places, and Divisions of the Elements, and all the Order of temporal Nature be quite destroyed?

When therefore *every Angelical Life* kindled itself in Wrath, and became thereby divided, darkened, and separated from God, the same Kindling, Darkening, Dividing and Confusion must be brought forth in their Natural Kingdom, because they lived in Nature, and could have neither Love, nor Wrath, but such as they could exert in and by the Powers of Nature.

Now, all Fire, wherever it is, is either a Fire of Wrath, or a Fire of Love: Fire not overcome or governed by *Light*, is the Fire of *Wrath*, which only tears in Pieces, consumes and devours all that it can lay hold of, and it *wills* nothing else: But *Light* is the Fire of *Love*, it is meek, amiable, full of kind Embraces, lovingly spreading itself, and giving itself with all its Riches into every Thing that can receive it. These are the *two Fire*s of Eternal Nature, which were but one in Heaven, and can be only one wherever Heaven is; and it was the *Separation* of these two Fires that changed the Angels into Devils, and made their Kingdom a Beginning of Hell.

Now, either of these two Fires, wherever it is kindled in animate or lifeless Things, communicates its own kind of Heat in some Degree to outward Nature, and so far alters and changes the State of it: The Wrath of a *Man*, and the Wrath of a *Tempest* do *one* and the *same Thing* to outward Nature, alter its State in the same Manner, and only differ in their Degree of doing it.

Fire kindled in a material Thing, can only communicate with the Materiality of Nature; but the Fire of a wrathfully-inflamed Man, being a Fire both of Body and Soul, communicates a *two*fold Heat, it stirs up the Fire of outward Nature, as Fire does in a *Coal*, and it stirs up the Wrath of Hell as the Devils do.

The Fire of Love kindled by the Light and Spirit of God in a truly regenerated Man, communicates a twofold Blessing, it outwardly joins with the meek Light of the Sun, and helps to overcome the Wrath of outward Nature; it inwardly co-operates with the Power of Good Angels, in resisting the Wrath and Darkness of Hell: And it would be no Folly to suppose, that if all human Breath was become a *mere, unmixed* Wrath, that all the Fire in outward Nature would immediately break forth, and bring that Dissolution upon outward Nature, which will arise from the last Fire. Therefore it is necessary, that a whole Kingdom of Angels should kindle the *same* Wrath and Disorder in outward Nature that was in themselves; for being in eternal Nature, and communicating with it, as temporal Beings do in temporal Nature, what they did in themselves, must be done in that Nature or Kingdom in which they lived, and moved, and had their Being.

What a powerful Fire there is in the Wrath of a Spirit, may be seen by the Effects of human Wrath; one sudden Thought shall in a Moment discolour, poison, inflame, swell, distort and agitate the *whole Body* of a Man. Whence also is it, that a diseased Body infects the Air, or that malignant Air infects a healthful Body? Is it not because there is, and must be an inseparable Qualifying, Mixing and Uniting betwixt Nature and those Creatures that live in it? Now, all Diseases and Malignities, whether in Nature or Creature, all proceed from the sinful Motions of the *Will* and *Desires* of the Creature. This is as certain, as that Death and all that leads to it, is the *sole Product* of Sin; therefore it is a certain Truth, that all the Disorder that ever was, or can be in Nature, arises from that Power which the Creature hath in and upon Nature; and therefore, as sure as a whole Host of Heavenly Beings raised up a fiery, wrathful, dark Nature in themselves, so sure is it, that the same wrathful, fiery, dark Disorder was raised up in that Kingdom, or Nature, in which they had their Being.

6. Now the Scriptures nowhere say in express Words, that the *Place* of this World was the Place of the Angels that fell, and that their fallen, spoiled and disordered Kingdom, was by the Power of God, *changed* or *created* into this temporary State of Things in which we live; this is not expressly said, because it is plainly implied and fully signified to us by the most general Doctrines of Scripture; for if we know, both from Nature and Scripture, that this World is a *Mixture* of Good and Evil, do not we enough know, that it could only be created out of *That* which was Good and Evil? And if we know that Evil cannot come from God, if we know that the Devil had actually brought it forth *before* the Creation of this World; are we not enough told, that the Evil which is in this World, is the Evil that was *brought forth* into Nature by the Devil? And that therefore the Matter of this World, is that *very Materiality* which was spoiled by the fallen Angels? How can we need a particular Text of Scripture to tell us, that the *Place* of this World was the Place of the *Angels* before their *Fall*, when the whole Tenor of Scripture tells us, that it is the Place of their Habitation *now*? For how could they have, or find Darkness, but in that *very Place*, where they had extinguished the Light? What could they have to do with us, or we with them, but that we are entered into *their Possessions*, and

have their Kingdom made over to us? How could they go about amongst us as roaring Lions, seeking whom they may devour, but that our Creation has brought us amongst them? They cannot *possibly* be anywhere, but where they fell, because they can live nowhere but in the *Evil* which they have brought forth; they can have no Wrath and Darkness but where they broke off from Light and Love; they can communicate with no outward Nature but that which fell with them, and underwent the same Change as they did: Therefore, though St. *Jude* saith with great Truth, that they *left their own Habitation*, yet, it is only as they left their own Angelical Nature, not departed from it into a distant Place, but deformed and changed it; so that the Heaven that was within them, and without them, is *equally left*, because both within them, and without them, they have no Habitation but a fiery Darkness broken off from the Light of God.

And therefore, as Man by his Creation is brought into a Power of Commerce with those fallen Angels, who must live, and could only act in that Part of Nature which they had deformed, it is plain, that this Creation placed him in *that System* of Things, which was formed and created out of their fallen Kingdom, because they can act, or be acted upon nowhere else.

7. And this is the one true, and only Reason, why there is Good and Evil throughout all temporal Nature and Creature; 'tis because all this temporary Nature is a Creation out of that Strife of Evil against Good which the fallen Angels had brought into their Kingdom. No subtle, *evil Serpent* could have been generated, no *Tree of Knowledge* of Good and Evil could have sprung out of the Earth, but because Nature in this World was *that Part* of Eternal Nature which the fallen Angels had *corrupted;* and therefore, a Life made up of Good and Evil could be brought forth by it. Evil and Good was in the Angelical Kingdom as soon as they set *their Wills* and *Desires* contrary to God, and the Divine Life. Had God permitted them to go on, their whole Kingdom had been like themselves, all over *one unmixed* Evil, and so had been incapable of being created into a redeemable State: But God put a Stop to the Progress of Evil in their Kingdom, he came upon it *whilst* it was in Strife, and *compacted* or *created* it all into a new, temporary, material State and Condition; whence these two Things followed: *First*, That the fallen Angels lost their Power over it, and could no further kindle their *own Fire* in it, but were as chained Prisoners, in an Extent of Darkness which they could neither get out of, nor extend any further: *Secondly*, This new Creation being created out of this *begun Strife*, stood as yet in

the *Birth* of Life, and so became capable of being assisted and blessed by God; and finally, at the End of Time, restored to its first heavenly State.

Now, the Good and Evil that is in this World is *that same* Good and Evil, and in the *same Strife* that it was in the Kingdom of the fallen Angels, only with this happy Difference, there it was under the Devil's Power, and in a Way to be wholly evil; here it is in a new compacted, or created State under the Providence and Blessing of God, appointed to bring forth a *new kind* of Life, and display the Wonders of Divine Love, till such Time as a new Race of Angelical Creatures born in this Mixture of Good and Evil, shall be fit to receive the Kingdom of *Lucifer*, restored to its first Glory?

Is there any Part of the Christian Religion that does not either *suppose* or *speak* this great Truth, any Part of outward Nature that does not *confirm* it? Is there any Part of the Christian Religion that is not made more intelligible, more beautiful and edifying by it? Is there any Difficulty of outward Nature that is not totally removed and satisfied by it?

How was the Philosophy of the Ancient Sages perplexed with the State of Nature? They knew God to be all Goodness, Love, and Perfection, and so knew not what to do with the Misery of Human Life, and the Disorders of outward Nature, because they knew not *how* this Nature came into its *present State*, or from whence it was descended. But had they known, that temporal Nature, all that we see in this whole Frame of Things, was only the *sickly, defiled* State of Eternal Things put into a temporary State of *Recovery*, that Time and all transitory Things were only in this War and Strife, to be finally delivered from all the Evil that was brought into Eternal Nature, their Hearts must have praised God for this Creation of Things as those *Morning Stars* did, that *shouted for Joy* when it was first brought forth.

8. From this true Knowledge of the *State*, and *Nature*, and *Place* of this Creation, what a Reasonableness, Wisdom, and Necessity does there appear in the hardest Sayings, Precepts and Doctrines of the Gospel? He that thus knows what this World is, has great Reason to be glad that he is born into it, and yet still greater Reason to rejoice, in being called out of it, preserved from it, and shown how to escape with the Preservation of his Soul. The Evils that are in this World, are the Evils of *Hell*, that are tending to be nothing else but Hell; they are the *Remains* of the Sin and Poison of the fallen Angels: The Good that is in this World are the Sparks of *Life* that are to generate *Heaven*, and gain the Restoration of the first Kingdom of

Lucifer. Who therefore would think of any Thing, desire any Thing, endeavour any Thing, but to resist Evil in every Kind, under every Shape and Colour ? Who would have any Views, Desires and Prayers after any Thing, but that the *Life* and *Light* of Heaven may rise up in Himself, and that God's Kingdom may come, and his Will be done in all Nature and Creature?

Darkness, Light, Fire and Air, Water and Earth, stand in their temporary, created Distinction and Strife, for no other End, with no other View, but that they may obtain the *one Thing needful,* their first Condition in Heaven : And shall Man that is born into Time for no other End, on no other Errand, but that he may be an Angel in Eternity, think it hard to live as if there were but one Thing needful for him ? What was the poor *Politics,* the earthly *Wisdom,* the *Ease, Sensuality,* and *Advancements* of this World for us, but such Fruits as must be eaten in Hell ? To be swelled with Pride, to be fattened with Sensuality, to grow great through Craft, and load ourselves with earthly Goods, is only living the Life of Beasts, that we may die the Death of Devils. On the other hand, to go starved out of this World, rich in nothing but heavenly Tempers and Desires, is taking from *Time* all that we came for, and all that can go with us into Eternity.

9. But to return to the further Consideration of Nature. As all temporary Nature is nothing else but eternal Nature brought out of its kindled, disordered Strife, into a created or compacted Distinction of its *several Parts,* so it is plain, that the Whole of this World, in all its *working Powers,* is nothing else but a Mixture of Heaven and Hell. There cannot be the smallest Thing, or the smallest Quality of any Thing in this World, but what is a Quality of *Heaven* or *Hell,* discovered under a temporal Form : Every Thing that is disagreeable to the *Taste,* to the *Sight,* to our *Hearing, Smelling* or *Feeling,* has its Root and Ground, and Cause, *in* and from *Hell,* and is as surely in its Degree the *Working* or *Manifestation* of Hell in this World, as the most diabolical Malice and Wickedness is: The *Stink* of Weeds, of Mire, of all *poisonous,* corrupted Things, *Shrieks,* horrible *Sounds, wrathful Fire, Rage of Tempests,* and *thick Darkness,* are all of them Things that had *no Possibility* of Existence, till the fallen Angels disordered the *State* of their Kingdom ; therefore, every Thing that is disagreeable and horrible in this Life, every Thing that can afflict and terrify our Senses, all the Kinds of natural and moral Evil, are only *so much* of the Nature, Effects, and Manifestation of Hell : For Hell and Evil are only two Words for *one* and the *same* Thing : The Extent of one is the Extent of the other, and all that can be

ascribed to the one, must be ascribed to the other. On the other hand, all that is sweet, delightful and amiable in this World, in the *Serenity* of the Air, the *Fineness* of Seasons, the *Joy* of Light, the *Melody* of Sounds, the *Beauty* of Colours, the *Fragrancy* of Smells, the *Splendour* of precious Stones, is nothing else but Heaven *breaking through* the Veil of this World, *manifesting* itself in such a Degree, and darting forth in such Variety *so much* of its own Nature. So that Heaven and Hell are not only as near you, as constantly showing and proving themselves to all your Senses, as *Day* and *Night*, but Night itself is nothing else but Hell breaking forth in *such a Degree*, and the Day is nothing else but a certain *Opening* of Heaven, to save us from the Darkness that arises from Hell.

O Man! consider thyself, here thou standest in the earnest, perpetual Strife of Good and Evil, all Nature is continually at work to *bring about* the great Redemption; the whole Creation is travailing in Pain, and laborious Working, to be delivered from the *Vanity* of Time, and will thou be asleep? Everything thou hearest, or seest, says nothing, shows nothing to Thee, but what either eternal Light, or eternal Darkness hath *brought forth;* for as Day and Night divide the whole of our Time, so Heaven and Hell divide the whole of our Thoughts, Words and Actions. Stir which way thou wilt, do, or design what thou wilt, thou must be an *Agent* with the *one* or with the *other*. Thou canst not stand still, because thou livest in the *perpetual Workings* of temporal and eternal Nature; if thou workest not with the Good, the Evil that is in Nature carries thee along with it: Thou hast the Height and Depth of Eternity in Thee, and therefore be doing what thou wilt, either in the *Closet*, the *Field*, the *Shop*, or the *Church*, thou art sowing *That* which grows and must be reaped in Eternity. Nothing of thine can vanish away, but every Thought, Motion, and Desire of thy Heart has its *Effect* either in the Height of Heaven, or the Depth of Hell: And as Time is upon the Wing, to put an End to the *Strife* of Good and Evil, and bring about the last great *Separation* of all Things into their Eternal State, with such Speed art Thou making Haste either to be wholly an Angel, or wholly a Devil: O! therefore awake, watch and pray, and join with all thy Force with that Goodness of God, which has created Time and all Things in it, to have a happy End in Eternity.

10. Temporal Nature opened to us by the Spirit of God, becomes a *Volume* of holy Instruction to us, and leads us into all the Mysteries and Secrets of Eternity: For as every Thing in temporal Nature is *descended* out of that which is eternal, and stands as a *palpable, visible Out-birth* of it; so when we know

how to separate the *Grossness, Death,* and *Darkness* of Time from it, we find what it is in its eternal State. Fire, and Light, and Air in this World are not only a true Resemblance of the Holy Trinity in Unity, but are the Trinity itself in its most *outward, lowest* kind of Existence or Manifestation; for there could be no Fire, Fire could not *generate* Light, Air could not *proceed* from both, these three could not be thus united, and thus divided, but because they have their *Root* and *Original* in the Triunity of the Deity. Fire *compacted, created, separated* from Light and Air, is the *Elemental Fire* of this World: Fire uncreated, uncompacted, unseparated from Light and Air, is the *heavenly Fire* of Eternity: Fire kindled in any material Thing is only Fire *breaking out* of its *created, compacted* State; it is nothing else but the awakening the *Spiritual Properties* of that Thing, which being thus stirred up, strive to get rid of that material *Creation* under which they are imprisoned: Thus every kindled Fire, with all its Rage and Fierceness, tears and divides, scatters and consumes that *Materiality* under which it is imprisoned; and were not these *Spiritual Properties* imprisoned in Matter, no material Thing could be made to burn. And this is another Proof, that the Materiality of this World is come out of a higher, and spiritual State, because every Matter upon Earth can be made to *discover* Spiritual Properties concealed in it, and is indeed a Compaction of nothing else. Fire is not, cannot be a *material* Thing, it only makes itself visible and sensible by the Destruction of Matter: Matter is its *Death* and *Imprisonment,* and it comes to Life but by being able to agitate, divide, shake off, and consume that Matter which held it in Death and Bondage; so that every Time you see a Fire kindled, you see Nature striving in a *low degree* to get rid of the Grossness of this material Creation, and to do that which can alone be done by the *last Fire,* when all the inward, spiritual Properties hid in every Thing, in *Rocks,* and *Stones,* and *Earth,* in *Sun,* and *Stars,* and *Elements,* shall by the last Trumpet be awakened and called forth: And this is a certain Truth, that Fire could *nowhere* now be kindled in any material Thing, but for *this Reason,* because all material Nature was created to be restored, and stands by Divine Appointment in a *Fitness* and *Tendency* to have its Deliverance from this created State, by *Fire;* so that every Time you see a Piece of Matter *dissolved* by Fire, you have a *full Proof,* that all the Materiality of this World is appointed to a Dissolution by Fire; and that then, (O glorious Day!) Sun and Stars, and all the Elements will be delivered from Vanity, will be again that *one eternal, harmonious, glorious* Thing which they were, before they were compacted into *material* Distinctions and Separations.

11. The Elements of this World stand in great *Strife* and *Contrariety*, and yet in great Desire of *mixing* and *uniting* with each other; and hence arises both the *Life* and *Death* of all Temporal Things: And hereby we plainly know that the Elements of this World were once *one undivided* Thing; for Union can *nowhere* be desired, but where there has first been a *Separation;* as sure therefore as the Elements desire each other, so sure is it, that they have been *parted* from each other, and are only Parts of some *one Thing* that has been divided. When the Elements come to *such* a Degree of Union, a Life is produced; but because they have still a *Contrariety* to each other, they soon destroy again that same Life which they had built, and therefore every four-elementary Life is short and transitory.

Now, from this undeniable State of Nature, we are told these following great Truths: 1. That the *four* Elements are only *four Parts* of That, which before the Creation of this World, was only a *one Element,* or one *undivided Power* of Life. 2. That the Mortality of this Life is wholly and solely owing to the *divided State* of the Elements. 3. That the true, immortal Life of Nature, is only *there* to be found, where the four Elements are only *one Thing*, mere *Unity* and *Harmony;* where Fire and Air, Water and Earth, have a much more *glorious* Union than they have in *Diamonds* and precious *Stones:* For in the brightest Diamonds the four Elements still partake of their divided State, though to our Eye they appear as only *one glorious* Thing; but the Beauty of the *Diamond* is but a *Shadow*, a low Specimen of *that Glory* which will shine through all Nature, when Fire and Air, Water and Earth shall be again that *one Thing* which they were, before the Fall of Angels and the Creation of this World. 4. That the Body of *Adam* (being formed for Immortality) could not possibly have the *Nature,* or be made out of the *divided State* of the Elements. The Letter of Scripture absolutely demonstrates this; for if Sickness, Sorrow, Pain, the Trouble of Heat and Cold, all so many Forerunners of Death, can *only be* where the Elements are in *Division* and *Contrariety;* and if, according to Scripture, these Calamities did not, could not *possibly* touch *Adam* till he fell, then it is plain from Scripture, that before his Fall, the Division and Contrariety of the Elements was not in him: And that was his Paradisaical Nature, in and by which he stood in a State of Superiority over all the Elements of this World. 5. That the Body of *Adam* lost its one Elementary Glory and Immortality, and then first became *gross, dark, heavy Flesh* and *Blood*, under the Power of the four Elements, when he *lusted* to eat, and *actually* did eat of that Tree, which had its Good and Evil from the *divided State* of the Elements. 6.

Hence we also know, with the greatest Certainty, the Mystery of the Resurrection of the Body, that it consists *wholly* and *solely* in the reducing the four-Elementary Body of this World, to its *first, one Elementary* State, and then everyone has that *same Body* raised again that died, and *all* that *Adam* lost is *restored*. For if the Body is mortal, and dies because it is become a Body of the *four Elements*, it can only be raised *immortal*, by having its four Elements reduced again into *one:* And here lies the *true Sameness* of the Body that died, and that which rises again. But to proceed :

12. As all the four Elements, by their *Desiring*, and wanting to be *united* together, prove that they are only four grossly divided *Out-births* of That which before was *only one* heavenly, harmonious Element, so every single Element fully demonstrates the same Thing ; for every single Element, though standing in its *created Contrariety* to every other, has yet in its *own* divided State, all the four Elements *in itself:* Thus the *Air* has every Thing in it that is in the Earth, and the Earth has in itself every Thing that is in Fire, Water and Air, only in a different Mixture and Compaction ; were it not so, had not every Element in some Degree the *whole Nature* of them all, they could not possibly mix, and qualify with one another ; and this may well pass for a Demonstration, that *That* out of which the four Elements are descended, was *one harmonius* Union of them all, because every one of the four, has *now*, and must have in its divided State, all the four in itself, though not in Equality ; for if the four must be together, though unequally lodged in every single Element, it is plain, the four must have been *one harmonious* Thing, before they were brought into four *unequal Separations:* And therefore, as sure as there are four warring, disagreeing Elements in *Time*, so sure is it, that *That* which is now in this fourfold Division, was and is in Eternity, *one*, in an heavenly, harmonious Union, keeping up an Eternal, joyful, glorious Life in *Eternal Nature*, as its four broken Parts bring forth a poor, miserable, transitory Life in temporal Nature.

13. All *Matter* in this World is only the Materiality of Heaven *thus* altered. The Difference between *Matter* in this World and *Matter* in the other World, lies wholly and solely in this ; in the one it is *dead*, in the other it is *living* Materiality. It is dead Materiality in this World, because it is *gross, dark, hard, heavy, divisible, &c.* It is in this State of Death, because it is *separated*, or *broken* off from the Eternal *Light*, which is the true Life, or the Power of Life in every Thing.

In eternal Nature or the Kingdom of Heaven, Materiality stands in Life and Light ; it is the Light's *glorious Body*, or that

Garment wherewith Light is *clothed*, and therefore has all the Properties of Light in it, and only differs from Light, as it is its *Brightness* and *Beauty*, as the *Holder* and *Displayer* of all its Colours, Powers and Virtues. But the same Materiality in this World, being created or compacted into a Separation from Fire united with Light, is become the Body of *Death* and *Darkness*, and is therefore *gross, thick, dark, heavy, divisible, &c.*, for Death is nothing else but the shutting up, or shutting out the *united Power* of Fire and Light: This is the *only Death* that ever did, or can happen to any Thing, whether earthly or heavenly. Therefore, *every Degree* of Hardness, Darkness, Stiffness, *&c.*, is a Degree of Death; and herein consists the Deadness of the Materiality of this World. When it shall be raised to Life, that is, when the *United Power* of Fire and Light shall *kindle* itself through all temporal Nature, then *Hardness, Darkness, Divisibility, &c.*, will be all extinguished together.

That the *Deadness* of the Earth may, and certainly will be brought to Life by the *united Power* of Fire and Light, is sufficiently shown us by the Nature and Office of the *Sun*. The *Sun* is the *united Power* of Fire and Light, and therefore the Sun is the Raiser of Life out of the *Deadness* of the Earth; but because Fire and Light as united in the Sun, is only the Virtue of temporary Fire and Light, so it can only raise a short and fading, transitory Life. But as sure as you see, that Fire and Light united in the Sun, can change the *Deadness* of the Earth, into such a beautiful Variety of a Vegetable Life, so sure are you, that this dark, gross Earth, is in its State of Death and Darkness, only for this Reason, because it is *broken off* from the united Power of Fire and Light: For as sure as the outward Operation of the Fire and Light of the Sun can change the Deadness of the Earth into a *Degree* of Life, so sure is it, that the Earth lies in its present Deadness, because it is separated from its *own Eternal* Fire and Light: And as sure as you see, that the Fire and Light of the Sun can raise a *temporal Life* out of the Earth, so sure is it, that the united Power of *Eternal* Fire and Light can, and will turn all that is earthly, into its *first State* of Life and Beauty. For the Sun of this World, as it is the Union of temporal Fire and Light, has no Power, but as it is the *outward Agent*, or Temporary *Representative* of Eternal Fire and Light, and therefore it can only do that in part, and imperfectly in Time, which by the Eternal Fire and Light will be *wholly* and *perfectly* done in Eternity. And therefore every Vegetable Life, every Beauty, Power, and Virtue which the Sun calls forth out of the Earth, tells us, with a *Divine Certainty*, that there will come a Time, when all that is hid in the Deadness, Grossness, and Darkness of the Earth, will be again called up to a Perfection of *Life* and *Glory of Beauty.*

14. How has the Philosophy of the *Schools* been puzzled with the *Divisibility* of Matter! It is because human Reason, the Mistress of the Schools, partakes of the *Deadness* of the Earth; and the Soul of Man must first have the Light of *Eternal Life* rise up in him, before he can *see* or *find* out the Truths of Nature. Human Reason knew nothing of the Death of the Matter, or the Nature and Reason of its temporary Creation, and so thought Death and Divisibility to be *essential* to Matter; but the Light of God tells every Man this infallible Truth, that *God made not Death* in any Thing, that he is a God of Life, and therefore, every Thing that comes from him, comes into a *State* of Life. Matter is thick, hard, heavy, divisible, and the like, only for a *Time*, because it is *compacted* or *created* into Thickness, Hardness, and Divisibility only for a Time: These are only the Properties of its *temporal*, created State, and therefore are no more *essential* to it than the Hardness of *Ice* is essential to Water. Now, that the Creation of the Matter of this World is nothing else but a *Compaction*, that all the Elements are *separated Compactions* of That which before was free from such a Compaction, is plain from Scripture. For we are told, that all the Material Things and Elements of this World, are to have their created State and Nature taken from them, by being *dissolved* or *melted:* But if this be a Scripture Truth, then it is equally true from Scripture, that their Creation was only a Compaction; and a Compaction of *something* that stood before according to its own Nature, absolutely free from it. *Mortality, Corruptibility*, and *Divisibility*, are not essential Properties, but temporary Accidents, they are in Things, as *Diseases* and *Sickness* are, and are as separable from them; and that is the true Reason, why this *Mortal can put on Immortality, this Corruptible can put on Incorruptibility*, and this Divisible put on Indivisibility: For when the four Elements shall be dissolved and loosed from their *separate Compaction* from one another, when Fire and Air, Water and Earth, shall be *a one* much more glorious and harmonious Thing than they are now in the brightest Diamond, then the *Divisibility* of this redeemed Materiality will be more impossible to be *conceived*, than the *Distance* between Fire and Water in a *Diamond.*

15. The Reason why all inanimate Things of this World tend towards their utmost Perfection in their Kind, lieth wholly and solely in this Ground; it is because the four Elements of this World were once the one Element of the *Kingdom* of the fallen Angels; and therefore, Nature in this World is *always*

labouring after its *first* Perfection of Life, or as the Scripture speaks, the ' whole Creation travaileth in Pain, and groaneth to 'be delivered from its present Vanity :' And therefore it is, that all Vegetables and Fruits naturally grasp after every Kind and Degree of Perfection they can take in; endeavouring with all their Power, after that *first Perfection* of Life which was before the Fall of the Angels. Every *Taste* and *Colour*, and *Power* and *Virtue*, would be what it was before *Lucifer* kindled his dark, fiery, wrathful Kingdom ; but as this cannot be, so when every Fruit and Flower has worked itself *as far* towards a heavenly Perfection as it can, it is forced to wither and rot, and become a *Witness* to this Truth, that neither Flesh nor Blood, nor Fruit, nor Flower, can reach the Kingdom of God.

16. All the Misery and Imperfection that is in Temporary Nature, arises from the divided State of the Elements: Their Division is that which brings all Kinds and Degrees of Death and Hell into this World, and yet their being in a certain Degree in one another, and always endeavouring after their *first Union*, is so much of the Nature and Perfection of Heaven still in them. The Death that is in this World, consists in the Grossness, Hardness and Darkness of its Materiality. The Wrath that is in this World consists in the kindled Division of its Qualities, whence there arises a contrary Motion and Fermentation in all its Parts, in which consists both the Life and Death of all its Creatures. This Death and this Wrath is the Nature of Hell in this World, and is the Manifestation of the *Disorders* which the fallen Angels have occasioned in Nature. The Heaven in this World began when God said, *Let there be Light*, for so far as Light is in any Thing, *so much* it has of Heaven in it, and of the *Beginning* of a heavenly Life : This shows itself in all Things of this World, chiefly in the Life-giving Power of the *Sun*, in the *Sweetness* and *Meekness* of Qualities and Tempers, in the *Softness* of Sounds, the *Beauty* of Colours, the *Fragrancy* of Smells, and *Richness* of Tastes and the like ; thus far as any Thing is tinctured with *Light*, so far it shows its *Descent* from Heaven, and its partaking of something heavenly and paradisaical. Again, *Love* or Desire of Union, is the other Part of Heaven that is visible in this World. In Things without Life, it is a *senseless Desire*, a friendly *mixing* and *uniting* of their Qualities, whereby they strive to be again in that first State of Unity and Harmony in which they existed, before they were kindled into Division by *Lucifer*. In rational Creatures, it is *Meekness, Benevolence, Kindness* and *Friendship* amongst one another : And thus far they have Heaven and the Spirit of God in them, each in their Sphere, being and doing

that to one another, which the Divine Love is and does to all.

Again, the Reason why Man is naturally taken with beautiful Objects, why he admires and rejoices at the Sight of *lucid* and *transparent* Bodies, and the *Splendour* of precious Stones, why he is delighted with the *Beauty* of his own Person, and is fond of his Features when adorned with *fine Colours*, has this only true Ground, 'tis because he was created in the *greatest Perfection* of Beauty, to live amongst all the Beauties of a *glorious Paradise:* And therefore Man, though fallen, has this strong *Sensibility* and reaching Desire after all the *Beauties*, that can be picked up in fallen Nature. Had not this been his Case, had not *Beauty*, and *Light*, and the *Glory* of Brightness been his *first State* by Creation, he would now no more want the Beauty of Objects, than the *Ox* wants to have his Pasture enclosed with beautiful Walls, and painted Gates. Every Vanity of fallen Man shows our first Dignity, and the Vanity of our Desires are so many Proofs of the *Reality* of that which we are fallen from. Man wants to see himself in Riches, Greatness and Power, because Human Nature came first into the World in that State; and therefore, what he had in *Reality* in Paradise, that is he vainly seeking for, where he is only a poor Prisoner in the Valley and Shadow of Death.

17. All Beings that are purely of this World, have their Existence in and Dependence upon temporal Nature. God is no Maker, Creator or Governor of any Being or Creature of this World, *immediately*, or by himself, but he creates, upholds and governs all Things of this World, by, and through, and with temporal Nature: As temporary Nature is nothing else but Eternal Nature *separated, divided, compacted,* made *visible* and *changeable* for a Time, so Heaven is nothing else but the *beatific Visibility*, the *Majestic Preference* of the abyssal, unsearchable, triune God: 'Tis that Light with which the Scripture saith, God is *decked as with a Garment*, and by which he is manifested and made visible to *heavenly Eyes* and *Beings;* for Father, Son, and Holy Ghost, as they are the triune God, *deeper* than the Kingdom of Heaven or Eternal Nature, are invisible to all created Eyes; but that *beatific Visibility* and *outward Glory* which is called the Kingdom of Heaven, is the *Manifestation* of the Father, Son, and Holy Ghost, in, and by, and through the glorious Union of *Eternal Fire*, and *Light*, and *Spirit*. In the Kingdom of Heaven, these are three and one, because their Original, the Holy Trinity, is so, and we must call them by the Names of Fire, and Light, and Spirit; because all that we have of Fire, and Light, and Spirit in this World, has

its *whole Nature* directly from them, and is indeed nothing else but the Fire, and Light, and Spirit of Eternity, brought into a *separated, compacted,* temporal State. So that to speak of a heavenly Fire, has no more *Grossness* and *Offence* in it, than when we speak of a heavenly *Life*, a heavenly *Light*, or heavenly *Spirit;* for if there is a heavenly Light and Spirit, there must of all necessity be a heavenly Fire; and if these Things were not in Heaven in a *glorious State* of Union, they never could have been here in this *gross State* of a temporal Compaction and Division: So that as sure as there are Fire, and Light, and Air in this World, in a *divided, compacted,* imperfect State, in which consists the Life of temporary Nature and Creatures, so sure is it, that Fire, and Light, and Spirit are in the Kingdom of Heaven, united in *one Perfection* of Glory, in which consists the beatific Visibility of God, the Divine Nature, as communicable to heavenly Beings.

18. The Kingdom of Heaven stands in this *threefold Life*, where three are one, because it is a Manifestation of the Deity, which is three and one; the Father has his *distinct* Manifestation in the Fire, which is always *generating* the Light; the Son has his *distinct* Manifestation of the *Light*, which is always *generated* from the Fire; the Holy Ghost has his *Manifestation* in the Spirit, that always *proceeds* from both, and is always *united* with them.

It is this Eternal Unbeginning Trinity in Unity of Fire, Light, and Spirit, that constitutes *Eternal Nature*, the *Kingdom of Heaven*, the *heavenly Jerusalem*, the *Divine Life*, the *beatific Visibility*, the *Majestic Glory* and *Presence* of God. Through this Kingdom of Heaven, or Eternal Nature, is the invisible God, the incomprehensible Trinity *eternally breaking* forth, and manifesting itself in a boundless Height and Depth of blissful Wonders, opening and displaying itself to all its Creatures as in an infinite Variation and endless Multiplicity of its Powers, Beauties, Joys and Glories. So that all the Inhabitants of Heaven are for ever Knowing, Seeing, Hearing, Feeling, and variously enjoying all that is great, amiable, infinite and glorious in the Divine Nature.

Nothing ascends, or comes into this Kingdom of Heaven, but that which descended, or came out of it, all its Inhabitants must be innate Guests, and born out of it.

19. God considered in himself, as distinct from this Eternal Nature, or Kingdom of Heaven, is not the *immediate* Creator of any Angels, Spirits, or Divine Beings; but as he creates and governs all temporal Beings *in*, and *by*, and *out* of temporal Nature, so he creates and governs all Spiritual and Heavenly

Beings *in*, and *by*, and *out* of Eternal Nature: This is as absolutely true, as that no Being can be *temporal*, but by partaking of temporal Nature, nor any Being eternal, but by partaking of the eternal, Divine Nature; and therefore, whatever God creates is not created *immediately* by *himself*, but in and by, and out of *that Nature*, in which it is to live, and move, and have its Being, temporal Beings out of temporal Nature, and eternal Beings out of the heavenly Kingdom of Eternal Nature: And hence it is, that all Angels, and the Souls of Men are said to be born of God, Sons of God, and Partakers of the *Divine Nature*, because they are formed out of *that* Eternal Nature, which is the *unbeginning Majesty* of God, the *Kingdom* of *Heaven*, or *Visible Glory* of the Deity. In this Eternal Nature, which is the Majestic Clothing, or Glory of the triune God, manifested in the glorious Unity of Divine Fire, Light, and Spirit, have all the created Images of God, whether they be Angels or Men, their Existence, Union and Communion with God; because Fire, and Light, and Spirit have the *same Union* and *Birth* in the Creature, as in the Creator: And hence it is, that they are so many various Mirrors of the Deity, penetrated with the Majesty of God, receiving and returning back Communications of the Life of God. Now, in this Ground, that is, in this Consideration of God, as manifesting his Holy Trinity through *Nature* and *Creature*, lieth the solid and true Understanding of all that is so variously said of God, both in the Old and New Testament with Relation to Mankind, both as to their Creation, Fall, and Redemption. God is to be considered throughout, as the God of Nature, only manifesting himself to all his Creatures in a Variety of Attributes in and by Nature; creating, governing, blessing, punishing, and redeeming them according to the *Powers, Workings*, and *Possibilities* of Nature. Fire, Light, and Spirit in *harmonious Union*, is the substantial Glory, the beatific Manifestation of the triune God, visible and communicable to Creatures formed out of it. All intelligent, holy Beings were by God formed and created out of, and for the Enjoyment of this Kingdom of Glory, and had Fire, and Light, and Spirit, as the triune Glory of their created Being: And herein consisted the infinite Love, Goodness and Bounty of God to all his Creatures: It was their being made Creatures of this Fire, Light, and Spirit, Partakers of that *same Nature* in which the Holy Trinity had stood from all Eternity *gloriously manifested*. And thus they were Creatures, Subjects, and Objects of the Divine Love; they came into the nearest, highest Relation to God; they stood in, and partook of his own *manifested Nature*, so that the outward Glory and Majesty of the triune God, was the very *Form*, and *Beauty*, and *Brightness* of their own created Nature. Every Creature which thankfully, joyfully, and absolutely gave itself up to this blessed Union with God, became absolutely fixed in its first created Glory, and incapable of knowing anything but Love, and Joy, and Happiness in God to all Eternity: Thus in this State, all Angels and Men came first out of the Hands of God. But seeing *Light* proceeds from Fire by a *Birth*, and the Spirit from both, and seeing the *Will* must be the *Leader* of the Birth, *Lucifer* and *Adam* could both do as they did, *Lucifer* could *will* strong *Might* and *Power*, to be greater than the Light of God made him, and so he brought forth a Birth of *Might* and *Power*, that was only mighty *Wrath* and *Darkness*, a Fire of Nature *broken off* from its Light. *Adam* could will the *Knowledge* of *temporal Nature*, and so he lost the Light and Spirit of Heaven for the Light and Spirit of this World: And had Man been left in this State of temporary Nature, without a Redeemer, he must, when the Light of this World had left him, have found himself in the same absolute Wrath and Darkness of Nature, which the fallen Angels are in.

20. Now, after these two Falls of two Orders of Creatures, the Deity itself came to have *new* and *strange* Names, new and unheard of Tempers and Inclinations of *Wrath, Fury*, and *Vengeance* ascribed to it. I call them *new*, because they began at the *Fall;* I call them *strange*, because they were *foreign* to the Deity, and could not *belong* to God in himself: Thus God is in the Scriptures said to be *a Consuming Fire*. But to whom? To the fallen Angels, and lost Souls. But *why*, and *how* is he so to them? It is because those Creatures have lost *all* that they had from God, but *Fire;* and therefore God can only be *found* and *manifested* in them, as a *Consuming Fire*. Now, is it not justly said, that God, who is nothing but infinite Love, is yet in *such Creatures* only a Consuming Fire, and that though God be nothing but Love, yet they are under the *Wrath* and *Vengeance* of God, because they have only *that Fire* in them, which is broken off from the Light and Love of God, and so can know, or feel nothing of God, but *his Fire* in them? As Creatures they can have no Life, but what they have *in* and *from* God; and therefore, that wrathful Life which they have, is truly said to be a *Wrath of God* upon them. And yet it is as strictly true, that there is no Wrath in God himself, that he is not changed in *his Temper* towards the Creatures, that he does not cease to be one and the same *infinite Fountain* of Goodness, *infinitely flowing forth* in the Riches of his Love upon all and every Life; but the Creatures have changed *their State* in *Nature*, and so the God of Nature can only be *manifested* in and to them, according

to their *own State* in Nature : And this is the true Ground of rightly understanding all that is said of the *Wrath* and *Vengeance* of God in and upon the Creatures. It is only in *such* a Sense as the *Curse* or *Unhappiness* of God may be said to be upon them, not because any Thing cursed, or unhappy can be *in*, or come *from* God, but because they have made *that Life* which they must have in God, to be mere *Curse* and *Unhappiness* to them : For every Creature that lives, must have its Life in and from God, and therefore God must be in every Creature; this is as true of Devils, as of Holy Angels: But how is God in them ? Why only as he is manifested in *Nature*. Holy Angels have the *triune* Life of God in them, therefore God is in them all *Love, Goodness, Majesty* and *Glory*, and theirs is the Kingdom of Heaven. Devils have *nothing* of this triune Life left in them, but the *Fire* of Eternal Nature *broken off* from all Light and Joy ; and therefore the Life that they can have in and from God, is only a Life of *Wrath* and *Darkness*, and theirs is the Kingdom of Hell: And because this Life is a Strength of Life which they must have *in* and *from* God, and which they cannot *take out* of his Hands; therefore, is their cursed, miserable, wrathful Life truly and justly said to be the *Curse*, and *Wrath*, and *Vengeance* of God in and upon them, though God himself can no more have Wrath and Vengeance, than he can have *Mischief* and *Malice* in him : For this is a glorious, twofold Truth, that from God considered as in himself, nothing can come from Eternity to Eternity, but infinite Love, Goodness, Happiness, and Glory ; and also that infinite Love, Goodness, Happiness and Glory are, and will be for ever and ever flowing forth from him in the *same boundless, universal, infinite* manner ; he is the same infinitely overflowing Fountain of Love, Goodness and Glory after, as before the *Fall* of any Creatures ; his Love, and the infinite Workings of it can no more be *lessened,* than his Power can be increased by any outward Thing; no Creature, or Number of Creatures can raise any Anger in him, 'tis as impossible as to cast *Terror*, or *Darkness*, and *Pain* into him, for nothing can come into God from the Creature, nothing can be in him, but that which the Holy Trinity in Unity is in itself. All Creatures are Products of the infinite, triune Love of God ; nothing *willed,* and *desired,* and *formed* them, but *infinite Love,* and they have all of them all the Happiness, Beauty and Excellency that an infinitely powerful Love can reach out to them : The same infinite Love *continues still* in its *first creating* Goodness, willing, desiring, working, and doing nothing with regard to all Creatures, but what it willed, did, and desired in the *Creation* of them : This God over Nature and Creature, darts *no more* Anger at Angels when fallen, than he did in the Creation of them: They are not in *Hell*, because Father, Son, and Holy Ghost are *angry* at them, and so cast them into a Punishment, which their Wrath had *contrived* for them; but they are in Wrath and Darkness, because they have done to the Light which *infinitely* flows forth from God, as that Man does to the Light of the Sun, who puts out his own Eyes: He is in Darkness, not because the Sun is *darkened* towards him, has *less Light* for him, or has lost all *Inclination* to enlighten him, but because he has put out that *Birth* of *Light* in himself, which alone made him capable of seeing in the Light of the Sun. It is thus with fallen Angels, they have extinguished in themselves that *Birth* of *Light* and *Love*, which was their *only Capacity* for that Happiness, which infinitely, and everywhere flows forth from God; and they no more have their Punishment from God himself than the Man who puts out his Eyes, has his Darkness from the Sun itself.

21. God, considered in himself, as the holy, triune God, is not the immediate Fountain and Original of Creatures; but God considered as *manifesting* himself in and through Nature, is the Creator, Father and Producer of all Things. The hidden Deity of Father, Son, and Holy Ghost, is from Eternity to Eternity, *manifested*, made *visible*, *perceivable*, *sensible* in the united Glory of Fire, Light and Spirit; this is the *beatific Presence*, the *glorious Out-birth* of the Holy Trinity; this is that eternal, universal Nature, which *brings* God into all Creatures, and all Creatures into God, according to that Degree and Manner of Life which they have in Nature: For the Life of Creatures must stand in Nature, and Nature is nothing else but God made *manifest*, *visible*, and *perceptible;* and therefore the Life of every Creature, be it what it will, a Life of Joy or Wrath, is only *so much* of God made *manifest* in it, and *perceptible* by it, and thus is God in some Creatures only a God of Wrath, and in others, only a God of Glory and Goodness.

No Creature can have Life, or live, and move, and have its Being in God, but by being formed out of, and living in this Manifestation of Nature. Thus far Hell and Heaven, Angels and Devils are *equally* in God, that is, they equally live, move, and have their Being in that *Eternal Nature*, which is the Eternal Manifestation of God: The one have a Life of Glory, Majesty, and Love, and Bliss, the other a Life of Horror, Fire, Wrath, Misery, and Darkness. Now, all this could not possibly be, there could be no Room for *this Distinction* between Creatures standing in Nature, the one could not possibly have a Life of *Majestic Bliss* and *Glory*, the other of *fiery Horror* and *Darkness*, but because the Holy, triune God is *manifested* in the *united* Glory and Bliss of Fire, Light, and Spirit. For the Creatures could only divide *That*, which there was in Nature to be divided, they could only divide *That*, which was *united*, and divisible; and therefore, as sure as Heaven is a splendrous Light of blissful Majesty, as sure as Hell is a Place of *fiery Wrath* and *Darkness*, so sure is it from the Scriptures, that Eternal Nature, which is from God, or a Manifestation of God, is a Nature of *united* Fire, Light, and Spirit, otherwise, some Creatures could not have the *blissful Glory* of Light, and others, a horrible, fiery Darkness for their *separate Portions*.

All therefore that has been said of an Eternal Nature, or Kingdom of Heaven, consisting of *united* Fire, Light, and Spirit, is not only to be looked upon as an Opinion well grounded, and sufficiently discovered by the Light of Nature, but as a *fundamental* Truth of revealed Religion, fully established by *all* that is said in the Scriptures both of Heaven and Hell. For if God was not *manifested, visible, perceptible* and *communicable*, in and by this *united* Fire, and Light, and Spirit, how could there be a Heaven of *glorious Majesty?* If this Fire of Heaven could not be *separated*, or *broken off* from its heavenly Light, how could there be a Hell in Nature? Or, how could those Angels which lost the Light of Heaven, have *thereby* fallen into a State of hellish Darkness, or Fire? Is not all this the greatest of Demonstrations, that the holy Triunity of God is, and must be manifested in Nature, by the Union of Fire, Light, and Spirit? And is not this Demonstration wholly taken from the very Letter of the most plain Doctrines of Scripture?

Hell and Wrath could have no *Possibility* of Existence, but because the Light, and Majesty, and Glory of Heaven, must of all necessity have its Birth *in* and *from* the Fire of Nature. An Angel could not have *become* a Devil, but because the Angelic *Light* and *Glory* had, and must have *its Birth* in and from the *Fire* of Life. And thus as a Devil was *found*, where angelic Light and Glory had its Existence, so a Hell was found, where heavenly Glory was *before;* and as the Devil is nothing but a Fire-spirit *broken off* from its Angelical Light and Glory, so Hell is nothing but the Fire of Heaven *separated* from its first Light and Majesty.

And here we have plainly found two Worlds in Eternity; not *possible* to be two, nor ever *known* to be two, but by such Creatures, as have in their own Natures, by their own Self-motion, separated the Fire of Eternal Nature from its Eternal Light, Spirit and Majesty. And this is also the Beginning, or first Opening of the *Wrath* of God in the Creature; which is, in other Words, only the Beginning, or first Opening of Pain

the Truths of the Gospel.

and Misery in the Creature, or the Origin of a hellish, tormenting State of Life.

22. And here, in this *dark wrathful* Fire of the fallen Creature, do we truly find that *Wrath* and *Anger* and *Vengeance* of God, that cleaves to Sin, that must be *quenched, atoned*, and *satisfied* before the Sinner can be reconciled to God; that is, before it can have again that *triune* Life of God in it, which is its Union with the holy Trinity of God, or its regaining the Kingdom of Heaven in itself.

Some have objected, that by thus considering the *fallen* Soul, as a *dark, wrathful* Fire-Spirit, for this Reason, because it has lost the *Birth* of the Son and holy Spirit of God in it, that this casts Reproach upon God the Father, as having *the Nature* of such a Soul in Him. But this is a groundless Objection, for this State of the Soul casts no more Reproach upon the *first*, than upon the second and third Persons of the holy Trinity. The fallen Soul, that has lost the Birth of the Son and holy Spirit of God in it, cannot be said to have *the Nature* of the Father left in it. This would be blasphemous Nonsense, and is no way founded on this Doctrine. But such a Soul must be said to have *a Nature* from the Father left in it, though a *spoiled* one, and this because the Father is the *Origin, Fountain* and *Creator* of all kind of Existence: Hell, and the Devils have their Nature from Him, because every Kind of Creature must have what it has of Life and Being from its Creator; but Hell and the Devils have not therefore *the Nature* of the Father in them. If it be asked what the Father is, as he is the first Person in the sacred Trinity, the Answer must be, that as such, He is the *Generator* of the Son and holy Spirit: This is *the Nature* of the Father; where *this generating* is not, there is not *the Nature* of the Father. Is it not therefore highly absurd to charge this Doctrine with ascribing *the Nature* of the Father to the *fallen* Soul, which asserts the Soul to be fallen, for *this Reason*, because it has quite *lost* and *extinguished* all Power and Ability for the *Birth* of the Son and holy Spirit in it? How could it be more roundly affirmed, or more fully proved, that the fallen Soul *hath not* the Nature of the Father left in it. But to proceed:

The Reader ought not to wonder, or be offended at the frequent mention of the Word *Fire*, which is here used to denote the true Nature, and State of the Soul. For both Nature and Scripture speak continually the same Language. For wherever there is mention of Life, Light, or Love in the Scriptures, there Fire is *necessarily* supposed, as being that in which all Life, and Light, and Love must necessarily arise; and therefore the Scriptures speak as often of Fire, as they do of Life, and

Light, and Love, because the one necessarily includes the other: For all Life, whether it be *vegetable, sensitive, animal,* or *intellectual,* is only a kindled Fire of Life in such a Variety of States; and every dead, insensitive Thing is only so, because its Fire is quenched, or shut up in a hard Compaction. If therefore we will speak of the *true Ground* of the fallen State of Men and Angels, we are not at Liberty to think of it under any *other Idea,* or speak of it in any *other manner,* than as the *darkened Fire* of their Life, or the Fire of their Life unable to kindle itself into Light and Love. Do not the Scriptures strictly confine us to this Idea of Hell? So that it is not any particular Philosophy, or affected Singularity of Expression, that makes me speak in this manner of the Soul, but because all Nature and Scripture forces us to confess, that the Root of all and every Life stands, and must necessarily stand in the *Properties* of Fire.

The holy Scriptures also speak much of Fire, in the Ideas which they give us, both of the Divine Nature, and of created Spirits, whether they be saved, or lost; the former as becoming Flames of heavenly Light and Love, the latter as dark Firebrands of Hell.*

No Description is, or can be given us either of Heaven or Hell, but where Fire is necessarily signified to be the *Ground* and *Foundation* both of the one and of the other. Why do all Languages, however distant, and different from one another, all speak of the Coldness of *Death,* the Coldness of *Insensibility*?

---

* Theologia fere supra omnes Sacrosanctam Ignis Figuram probasse reperitur. Eam enim invenies non solum *Retas igneas* fingere, sed etiam ignea animalia — quinetiam *Thronos igneos* esse dicit, ipsosq; summos Seraphim *incensos* esse ex ipso nomine declarat, eisq; Ignis & *Proprietatem* & *Actionem* tribuit: semperatq; ubiq; igneam figuram probat. Ac igneam quidem Formam significare arbitror cœlestium Naturarum *maximam* in Deo imitando *similitudinem*. Theologi summam, & formâ carentem essentiam *ignis Specie* multis locis describunt, quòd Ignis multas Divinæ, si dictu fas est, Proprietatis, *Imagines* ac *Species* præ se ferat. Ignis enim, qui sensu percipitur, in omnibus & per omnia sine admixtione funditur, secerniturq; a rebus omnibus, lucetq; totus simul, & abstrusus est, incognitusq; manet ipse per se—Cohiberi, vinciq; non potest—quicquid ipsi proprius quoquo modo adhibeatur, sui particeps facit. Renovat omnia vitali calore, illustrat aperto lumine; teneri non potest, nec misceri. Dissipandi vim habet, commutari non potest, sursum fertur, celeritate magna præditus est, sublimis est, nec humilitatem ullam ferre potest. Immobilis est, per se movetur, aliis motum affert; comprehendendi vim habet, ipse comprehendi non potest. Non eget altero: clam se amplificat: in materiis quæ ipsius capaces sunt, magnitudinem suam declarat. Vim efficiendi habet, potens est: omnibus præsto est; nec videtur: *Attritu* autem quasi *Inquisitione* quadam connaturaliter repente apparet, rursusq; ita avolat ut comprehendi, & detineri nequeat: in omnibus sui communionibus minui non potest—Multas etiam alias Ignis Proprietates invenire possumus, quæ propria sunt divinæ actionis. *S. Dionis. Arcop. de cœlesti Hierarci,* 56.

Why do they all agree in speaking of the *Warmth* of Life, the *Heat* of Passions, the *Burnings* of Wrath, the *Flames* of Love? It is because it is the Voice or Dictate of universal Nature, that Fire is the *Root* or *Seat* of Life, and that every Variety of human Tempers is only the various *Workings* of the Fire of Life.—It ought to be no Reason why we should think *grossly* of Fire, because it is seen in so many *gross Things* of this World? For how is it seen in them? Why only as a *Destroyer*, a *Consumer*, and *Refiner* of *all Grossness;* as a *Kindler* of Life, and Light out of Death and Darkness. So that in all the Appearances of Fire, even in earthly Things, we have Reason to look upon it as something of a heavenly, exalting, and glorious Nature; as that which disperses Death, Darkness, and Grossness, and raises up the Power and Glory of every Life.

If you ask what Fire is in its first, true, and unbeginning State, not yet entered into any Creature, It is the Power and Strength, the Glory and Majesty of eternal Nature; it is that which *generates, enriches, brightens, strengthens* and *displays* the Light of Heaven. It is that which makes the eternal Light to be majestic, the eternal Love to be flaming: For the *Strength* and *Vivacity* of Fire, must be both the Majesty of Light, and the Ardour of Love. It is the glorious *Out-birth*, the true *Representative* of God the Father *eternally generating* his only Son, Light and Word.

If you ask what Fire is in its own spiritual Nature, it is merely a *Desire*, and has no other Nature than that of a *working Desire*, which is continually its *own Kindler*. For *every Desire* is nothing else, but its *own striking* up, or its *own kindling* itself into some Kind and Degree of Fire. And hence it is that Nature (though reduced to great Ignorance of itself) has yet forced all Nations and Languages to speak of *its Desires*, as *cool, warm*, or *burning, &c.*, because every Desire is, so far as it goes, a *kindled Fire*. And it is to be observed, that Fire could have no Existence or Operation in material Things, but because all the Matter of this World has in it more or less of spiritual and heavenly Properties compacted in it, which *continually desire* to be delivered from their material Imprisonment. And the stirring up *the Desire* of these spiritual Properties, is the *kindling* of that *Heat*, and *Glance*, and *Light*, in material Things, which we call Fire, and is nothing else but their gloriously breaking, and triumphantly dispersing that hard Compaction in which they were imprisoned. And thus does every kindled Fire, as a *Flash* or *transitory opening* of heavenly Glory, show us in little and daily, but *true* Instances, the *Triumph* of the last Fire, when all that is spiritual and heavenly in this

World, shall kindle and separate itself from that, which must be the Death and Darkness of Hell.

Now the Reason, why there are spiritual Properties in all the material Things of this World, is only this, it is because the Matter of this World is the *Materiality* of the Kingdom of Heaven, brought down into a *created State* of Grossness, Death, and Imprisonment, by occasion of the Sin of those Angels, who first inhabited the Place, or Extent of this material World.

Now these heavenly Properties, which were brought into this *created* Compaction, lie in a *continual Desire* to return to their first State of Glory; and this is the *groaning of the whole Creation to be delivered from Vanity*, which the Apostle speaks of. And in this *continual Desire* lieth the kindling, and *all the Possibility* of kindling any Fire in the Things of this World. Quench *this Desire*, and suppose there is nothing in the *Matter* of this World that desires to be restored to its first Glory, and then all the breaking forth of Fire, Light, Brightness, and Glance in the Things of this World, is utterly quenched with it, and it would be the same Impossibility to strike Fire, as to strike Sense and Reason out of a Flint.

24. But you will perhaps say, though this be a Truth, yet it is more *speculative* than *edifying*, more fitted to entertain the Curiosity, than to assist the Devotion of Christians. But stay awhile, and you shall see it is a Truth full of the most edifying Instruction, and directly speaking to the Heart.

For if *every Desire* is in itself, in its own Essence, the *kindling* of Fire, then we are taught this great practical Lesson, that our *own Desire* is the Kindler of our own Fire, the Former and Raiser of *that Life* which leads us. What our Desire kindles, that becomes the Fire of our Life, and fits us either for the majestic Glories of the Kingdom of God, or the dark Horrors of Hell: So that our *Desire* is all, it does all, and governs all, and all that we have and are, must arise from it, and therefore it is, that the Scripture saith, 'Keep thy Heart with all Diligence, for 'out of it are the Issues of Life.'

We are apt to think that our *Imaginations* and *Desires* may be played with, that they rise and fall away as nothing, because they do not always bring forth outward and visible Effects. But indeed they are the greatest Reality we have, and are the true *Formers* and *Raisers* of all that is real and solid in us. All outward Power that we exercise in the Things about us, is but as a *Shadow* in Comparison of that *inward Power*, that resides in our *Will, Imagination,* and *Desires;* these communicate with Eternity, and kindle a Life which always reaches either Heaven or Hell. This Strength of the inward Man makes all that is the

Angel, and all that is the Devil in us, and we are neither good nor bad, but according to the Working of that which is spiritual and invisible in us. Now our Desire is not only thus powerful and productive of real Effects, but it is always alive, always working and *creating* in us, I say creating, for it has no less Power, it perpetually generates either Life or Death in us : And here lies the Ground of the great Efficacy of *Prayer*, which when it is the Prayer of the Heart, the Prayer of Faith, has a kindling and creating Power, and forms and transforms the Soul into every Thing that its Desires reach after : It has the Key to the Kingdom of Heaven, and unlocks all its Treasures, it opens, extends, and moves that in us, which has its Being and Motion in and with the Divine Nature, and so brings us into a real Union and Communion with God.

Long *Offices* of Prayer sounded only from the Mouth, or impure Hearts, may Year after Year be repeated to no Advantage, they leave us to grow old in our own poor, weak State: These are only the poor Prayers of Heathens, who, as our Lord said, 'think to be heard by their much speaking.' But when the Eternal Springs of the purified Heart are stirred, when they stretch after that God from whence they came ; then it is, that what we ask, we receive, and what we seek, we find. Hence it is, that all those great Things are by the Scriptures attributed to Faith, that to it all Things are possible ; that it heals the Sick, saves the Sinner, can remove Mountains, and that all Things are possible to him that believeth ; 'tis because the Working of *Will* and *Desire* is the first Eternal Source of all Power, *that* from which every Thing is kindled into that Degree of Life in which it standeth ; 'tis because *Will* and *Desire* in us are *Creaturely Offsprings* of that first Will and Desire which formed and governed all Things ; and therefore, when the Creaturely Power of our Will, Imagination and Desire leaves off its Working in Vanity, and gives itself wholly unto God in a *naked* and *implicit* Faith in the Divine Operation upon it, then it is, that it does nothing in vain, it rises out of Time into Eternity, is in Union and Communion with God, and so all Things are possible to it. Thus is this Doctrine so far from being vainly speculative, that it opens to us the Ground, and shows us the Necessity and Excellency of the greatest Duties of the Gospel.

25. Now, as *all Desire* throughout Nature and Creature is but *one* and the *same* Thing, branching itself out into various Kinds and Degrees of Existence and Operation, so there is but *one Fire* throughout all Nature and Creature, standing only in different States and Conditions. The Fire that is in the *Light* of the Sun, is the same Fire that is in the *Darkness* of the Flint : That

Fire which is the Life of our Bodies, is the Life of our Souls; that which *tears* Wood in Pieces, is the same which upholds the beauteous Forms of Angels: It is the same Fire that burns *Straw*, that will at last melt the *Sun*, the same Fire that brightens a *Diamond*, is darkened in a *Flint:* It is the same Fire that kindles Life in an Animal, that kindled it in Angels: In an Angel it is an Eternal Fire of an Eternal Life, in an Animal it is the same Fire brought into a temporary Condition, and therefore can only kindle a Life that is temporary: The same Fire that is mere Wrath in a Devil, is the Sweetness of flaming Love in an Angel; and the same Fire which is the Majestic Glory of Heaven, makes the Horror of Hell.

Chapter III.

The true Ground of all the Doctrines of the Gospel discovered. Why Adam could make no Atonement for his Sins. Why, and how Jesus Christ alone could make this Atonement. Whence the Shedding of Blood for the Remission of Sins. What Wrath and Anger it is, that is quenched and atoned by the Blood of Christ. Of the last Sufferings of Christ. Why, and how we must eat the Flesh and drink the Blood of Jesus Christ.

WE have now, Worthy Reader, so far cleared the Way, that we have nothing to do, but to rejoice in the most open Illustration, and full Proof of all the great Doctrines of the Gospel, and to see all the Objections, which *Deists, Arians,* and *Socinians* have brought against the first Articles of our Faith, dashed to Pieces: For as soon as we but begin to know, that the holy, triune Deity from Eternity to Eternity *manifests* itself in *Nature,* by the *triune Birth* of Fire, Light and Spirit, and that all Angels and Men must have been created out of *this Nature;*

there is not a Doctrine in Scripture concerning the Creation, Fall, and Redemption of Man, but becomes the most plainly intelligible, and all the Mysteries of our Redemption are proved and confirmed to us, by all that is visible and perceptible in all Nature and Creature.

Here we have the plain Foundation of the whole Economy of all Religion from the Beginning to the End of Time, why the *Incarnation* of the Son of God, who is the Light of the World, must have before it the *fiery Dispensation* of the Father delivered from *Mount Sinai;* and after it, the *pouring* out, or *proceeding* forth of the Holy Spirit upon all Flesh; it is because the *triune Life* of the fallen race must be restored according to the *triune Manifestation* of the Holy Deity in Nature.

Here we know what the *Love,* and what the *Anger* of God is, what *Heaven* and *Hell,* an *Angel* and a *Devil,* a lost and a redeemed Soul are. The *Love,* and Goodness, and Blessing of God known, found, and enjoyed by any Creature, is nothing else but the Holy Trinity of God known, found, and enjoyed in the blissful, glorious, *triune Life* of Fire, Light and Spirit, *where* Father, Son, and Holy Ghost *perpetually* communicate their own nameless, numberless, boundless Powers, Riches and Glories to the created Image of their own Nature. The *Hell* in Nature, and the hellish Life in the Creature, the *Wrath* of God in Nature and Creature, is nothing else but the triune, holy Life broken and destroyed in *some Order* of Creatures, it is only the Fire of Heaven *separated* from its heavenly Light and Spirit. This is that Eternal *Anger,* and *Wrath,* and *Vengeance,* that must be *atoned, satisfied,* and *removed,* that eternal Fire that must be quenched, that eternal *Darkness* that must be changed into Light, or there is no *Possibility* in Nature, that the Soul of fallen Man should ever see the Kingdom of God: And here all the Doctrines of the *Socinians* are quite torn up by the Roots. For in this Ground appeareth the *absolute Necessity* of the Incarnation, Life, Sufferings, Death, Resurrection and Ascension of the Son of God. Here lieth the *full Proof,* that through *all Nature* there could no Redeemer of Man be found, but only in the Second Person of the adorable Trinity become Man. For as the Light and Spirit of Eternal Life, is the Light and Spirit of the Son and Holy Ghost manifested in Heaven, so the Light of Eternal Life could never come again into the *fallen Soul,* but from him *alone,* who is the *Light* of Heaven. He must be again in the Soul, as he was in it, when it was first breathed forth from the Holy Trinity, he must be manifested in the Soul, as he is in Heaven, or it can never have the Life of Heaven in it.

The *Socinians* therefore, or others, who think they pay a just

Deference to the Wisdom and Omnipotence of God, when they suppose there was no *absolute Necessity* for the Incarnation of the Son of God; but that God, if he had so pleased, could as well have saved Man some *other Way*, show as great Ignorance both of God and Nature, as if they should have said, that when God makes a *blind* Man to see by *opening* or *giving* him Eyes, there was no Necessity in the *Thing* itself, that *Sight* should be given in *that particular Way*, but that God, if he had so pleased, could have made him become a *seeing* Man in this World without *Eyes*, or *Light* of this World.

For if the *Son* of God is the *Light* of Heaven, and Man only wants to be redeemed, because he has *lost* the Light of Heaven; is it not absolutely impossible for Him to be redeemed any *other Way*, or by any other Thing, than by a *Birth* of this Son of God in him. Is not this Particularity the *one only* Thing that can raise fallen Man, as *seeing Eyes* are the one only Thing that can take away Blindness from the Man?

If *Adam* had been able to *undo* in himself all that he had *done*, if he could have *gone back* into that State from whence he was fallen, if he could have *raised up* again in himself that Birth of the Holy Trinity, in which he was created, *no Saviour* had been wanted for him; but because he could not do any Thing of this, but must be *That* which he had made himself to be, therefore the *Wrath* of Nature, or the Wrath of God *manifested* in Nature, abode upon him, and *this Wrath* must of all necessity be *appeased*, *atoned*, and *satisfied*, that is, it must be *kindled* into Light and Love, before he could again find, and enjoy the *God of Nature*, as a God of Light and Love.

Could *Adam* himself have done all that which I have just now mentioned, then his own Actions had *atoned* and *satisfied* the Divine Wrath, and had *reconciled* him to God: For nothing lost him the Love of God, but *That* which separated him from God; and nothing did, or ever can separate him from God, but the Loss of that *triune Life*, in which alone the Holy Trinity of Divine Love can dwell. If therefore *Adam* could have raised again in himself that *triune Life*, then his Sin, and the Wrath of God upon him, had been *only transitory;* but because he did That, which according to all the *Possibilities of Nature*, was unalterable; therefore he became a *Prisoner* of an eternal *Wrath*, an Heir of an *everlasting, painful* Life, till the Love of God, who is greater than Nature, should *do That* for him and in him, which he could by no Powers of Nature do for himself, nor the highest of Creatures do for him.

3. And here we see in the plainest Light, that there was *no Anger* in God *himself* towards the fallen Creature, because it was

purely and *solely* the infinite Love of God towards him, that did, and alone could raise him out of his fallen State: All Scripture, as well as Nature, obliges us to think thus of God. Thus it is the whole Tenor of Scripture, that 'God so loved the World, 'that he sent his only-begotten Son into it, that the World, 'through him, might be saved:' Is not this saying *more* than if it had been said, that there was *no Anger* in God himself towards fallen Man? Is he not expressly declared to be *infinitely* flowing forth in Love towards him? Could God be more infinite in Love, or more infinitely distant from all *Possibility* of Anger towards Man, when he first created him, than when he *thus* redeemed him? God out of pure and free Love gave his Son to be the Life of the World, *first*, as an *inspoken* and *ingrafted Word* of Life, as the *Bruiser* of the Serpent given to *all Mankind* in their Father *Adam*. This *Word* of Life, and *Bruiser* of the Serpent, was the *Extinguisher* of that Wrath of God that lay upon fallen Man. Now, will the Scriptures, which tell us that the Love of God sent his Son into the World, to redeem Man from that *hellish Wrath* that had seized him, allow us to say, that it was to extinguish a Wrath that was got into *God himself*, or that the Bruiser of the Serpent was to *bruise, suppress*, or *remove* something that Sin had *raised* in the Holy Deity *itself?* No surely, but to bruise, alter, and overcome an *Evil* in Nature and the Creature, that was become Man's *Separation* from the Enjoyment of the God of Love, whose Love still existed in its own State, and still followed him, and gave his only Son to make him capable of it. Do not the Holy Scriptures continually teach us, that the Holy Jesus became incarnate *to destroy the Works of the Devil*, to overcome Death and Hell that had taken Man captive? And is not this sufficiently telling us, *what* that Wrath was, and *where* it existed, which must be *atoned, satisfied*, and *extinguished*, before Man could again be alive unto God, or reconciled unto him, so as to have the triune Life of Light and Love in him? It was a Wrath of *Death*, a Wrath of *Hell*, a Wrath of *Sin*, and which only the precious, powerful Blood of Christ could change into a Life of Joy and Love: And when this Wrath of Death and Hell are *removed* from Human Nature, there neither is, nor can be any *other Wrath* of God abiding on it. Are not the Devils and all lost Souls justly said to be under the *eternal Wrath* of God, and yet in *no Wrath* but that which exists in Hell, and in their own Hellish Nature.

4. They therefore, who suppose the Wrath and Anger of God upon fallen Man, to be a *State* of Mind in God himself, to be a political kind of *just Indignation*, a Point of *Honourable Resentment*, which the Sovereign Deity, as Governor of the World,

ought not to recede from, but must have a *sufficient* Satisfaction done to his offended Authority, before he can, consistently with his Sovereign Honour, receive the Sinner into his Favour, hold the Doctrine of the *Necessity* of Christ's atoning Life and Death in a mistaken Sense. That many good Souls may hold this Doctrine in this Simplicity of Belief, without any more Hurt to themselves, than others have held the *Reality* of Christ's Flesh and Blood in the Sacrament under the Notion of the *Transubstantiation* of the Bread and Wine, I make no Manner of Doubt: But when Books are written to impose and require this Belief of others, as the only saving Faith in the Life and Death of Christ, it is then an Error that ceases to be innocent: For neither Reason nor Scripture will allow us to bring Wrath into God himself, as a Temper of his Mind, who is only infinite, unalterable, overflowing Love, as unchangeable in Love, as he is in Power and Goodness. The Wrath that was awakened at the Fall of Man, that then seized upon him, as its Captive, was only a *Plague*, or *Evil*, or *Curse* that Sin had brought forth in Nature and Creature: it was only the beginning of Hell: It was *such* a Wrath as God himself pitied Man's lying under it; it was *such* a Wrath as God himself furnished Man with a Power of overcoming and extinguishing, and therefore it was not a Wrath that was according to the *Mind, Will*, and *Liking*, or Wisdom of God; and therefore it was not a Wrath that was in God himself, or which was exercised by his Sovereign Wisdom over his disobedient Creatures: It was not *such* a Wrath, as when Sovereign Princes are angry at Offenders, and will not cease from their Resentment, until some political Satisfaction, or valuable Amends be made to their slighted Authority. No, no; it was such a Wrath as God himself hated, as he hates Sin and Hell, a Wrath that the God of all Nature and Creature so *willed* to be *removed* and *extinguished*, that seeing nothing less could do it, he sent his only begotten Son into the World, that all Mankind might be *saved* and *delivered* from it. For seeing the Wrath that was awakened and brought forth by the Fall, and which wanted to be appeased, atoned, and quenched, was the Wrath of *eternal Death*, and *eternal Hell*, that had taken Man captive; therefore God spared not the precious, powerful, efficacious Blood of the Holy Jesus, because that alone could extinguish this eternal Wrath of Death and Hell, and re-kindle Heaven and Eternal Life again in the Soul. And thus all that the Scriptures speak of the *Necessity* and *powerful* Atonement of the Life and Death of Christ, all that they say of the *infinite Love* of God towards fallen Man, and all that they say of the *Eternal Wrath* and *Vengeance* to which Man was become a Prey, have the most solid Foundation, and are all of them proved to be consistent, harmonious Truths of the greatest Certainty, according to the plain Letter of Scripture.

5. It is the Foundation of the Law and the Gospel, that *without shedding of Blood, there is no Remission of Sins;* and that the precious Blood of Christ could alone do this, could alone reconcile us to God, and deliver us from the Wrath to come. How, and why Blood, and only the Blood of Jesus Christ could do this, will appear as follows: *Adam* was created with a two-fold Respect, to be himself a glorious, living, eternal Image of the Holy, triune God, and to be a *Father* of a new World of like Beings, all descended from himself: When *Adam* fell, he lost both these Conditions of his created State; the Holy Image of God was extinguished, his Soul lost the Light and Spirit of Heaven, and his Body became earthly, bestial, corruptible Flesh and Blood, and he could only be a *Father* of a Posterity partly *diabolical*, and partly *bestial*.

Now, if the first Purpose of God was to stand, and to take Effect; if *Adam* was still to be the Father of a Race that were to become Sons of God, then there was an absolute Necessity that all that *Adam* had *done* in and to himself, and his Posterity, by the Fall, should be *undone* again; the *Serpent* and the *Beast,* that is, the Serpentine Life, and the bestial Life in Human Nature, must both of them be *overcome*, and *driven* out of it. This was the *one only*, possible Salvation for *Adam*, and every Individual of his Posterity.

Adam had killed that which was to have been immortal in him, he had raised that into a Life which never should have been alive in him, and therefore that which was to be *undone* and *altered* both in himself and his Posterity, was this, it was to part with a *Life* that he had raised up into Being, and to get *another Life*, which he had quite extinguished.

And here appears the true, infallible Ground of *all the Sacrifice,* and all the *Blood-shedding* that is necessary to redeem and reconcile Man to God. 'Tis because the earthly, fleshly, bestial, corruptible Life under the Elements of this World, is a Life *raised* and *brought* into Man by the Fall, is not that Life which God created, but is an Impurity in the Sight of God, and therefore cannot enter into the Kingdom of Heaven; 'tis a Life, or Body of Sin, brought forth by Sin, and the Habitation of Sin, and therefore it is a Life that must be *given up*, its Blood must be *poured out*, before Man can be released from his Sins: This is the *one only* Ground of all the *Shedding of Blood* in Religion. Had not a Life *foreign* to the Kingdom of God, and utterly *incapable* of it, been *introduced* by the Fall, there had been no possible Room for the *Death* of any Creature, or the *pouring out* any Blood, as serviceable and instrumental to the raising fallen Man.

6. But now, this bestial, animal Life which is thus to be given up, and its Blood poured out, is but the half, and lesser half of that which is required to deliver Man from all that the Fall has brought upon him. For the heavenly Life, the Birth of the Light and Holy Spirit of God which *Adam* had quite extinguished, was to be *kindled* or *regenerated* again ; also his *first, glorious, immortal* Body was to be regained, before he could become an Inhabitant of the Kingdom of Heaven : But for all this *Adam* had no Power. See here again the true and dreadful State of the *Fall*, it was the Fall into *such* a Life, as must be *slain* and *sacrificed* before the fallen Soul could come to God ; and yet this Death and Sacrifice of the Body, which was thus absolutely necessary, was the most dreadful Thing that could happen to Man, because *his own* Death, come when it would, would only remove him from the *Light* of this World into the Eternal Darkness, and hellish State of fallen Angels : And here we find the true Reason, why Man's own Death, though a Sacrifice *necessary* to be made, had yet nothing of *Atonement* or *Satisfaction* in it ; it was because it left the eternal Wrath of Nature, and the Hell that was therein, unquenched and unextinguished in the Soul, and therefore made no *Reconcilement* to God, no *Restoration* to the Creature of its *first State* and *Life* in God, but left the Soul in its dark, wrathful Separation from the Kingdom of Light and Love.

But here the amazing Infinity of Divine Love appeared, such a Mystery of Love as will be the universal Song of Praise to all Eternity. Here God, the second Person in the holy Trinity, took human Nature upon him, became a suffering, dying Man, that there might be found a Man, whose Sufferings, Blood and Death had Power to *extinguish* the Wrath and Hell that Sin had brought forth, and to be a *Fountain* of the first heavenly Life to the whole Race of Mankind.

It was *human Nature* that was fallen, that had lost its first heavenly Life, and got a bestial, diabolical Life in the stead of it. Now if *this* human Nature was to be restored, there was but *one possible* Way, it must go back to the State from whence it came, it must put off all that it had put on, it must regain all that it had lost : But the human Nature that fell, could do nothing of this, and yet all this must be done in and by *that* human Nature which is fallen, or it could never, to all Eternity, come out of the State of its Fall ; for it could not possibly come out of the State of its Fall, but by *putting off* all that, which the Fall had brought upon it. And thus stood Man, as to all the

Powers of Nature and Creature, in an *utter Impossibility* of Salvation, and had only a short Life of this World betwixt him and Hell.

7. But let us now change the Scene, and behold the Wonders of a *new Creation*, where all Things are called out of the *Curse* and *Death* of Sin, and created again to Life in Christ Jesus; where all Mankind are chosen and appointed to the *Recovery* of their first glorious Life, by a *new Birth* from a second *Adam*, who, as an *universal* Redeemer, takes the *Place* of the first fallen Father of Mankind, and so gives Life and Immortality, and Heaven to all that lost them in *Adam*.

God, according to the Riches of his Love, raised a Man out of the Loins of *Adam*, in whose mysterious Person, the *whole* Humanity, and the *Word* of God was personally united; that same *Word* which had been *inspoken* into *Adam* at his Fall, as a secret *Bruiser of the* Serpent, and *real Beginning* of his Salvation; so that in this second *Adam*, God and Man was one Person. And in this Union of the Divine and human Nature lies the *Foundation* and *Possibility* of our Recovery. For thus the holy Jesus became qualified to be the *second Adam*, or universal Regenerator of all that are born of *Adam* the first. For being himself *that Deity*, which as a *Spark* or *Seed* of Life was given to *Adam*, thus all that were born of *Adam* had also a *Birth* from him, and so stood under him, as their common Father and Regenerator of a heavenly Life in them. And it was this first inspoken *Word* of Life which was given to *Adam*, that makes all Mankind to be the *spiritual* Children of the *second Adam*, though he was not born into the World till so many Years after the Fall. For seeing the *same Word* that became their perfect Redeemer in the Fulness of Time, was in them from the Beginning, as a Beginning of their Redemption, therefore he stood related to all Mankind as a *Fountain* and *Deriver* of an heavenly Life into them, in the same *universal manner* as *Adam* was the Fountain and Deriver of a miserable Mortality into them.

And seeing also this great and glorious Redeemer had in himself the *whole Humanity*, both as it was *before* and after the *Fall, viz.*, in his inward Man the *Perfection* of the first *Adam*, and in his outward the *Weakness* and *Mortality* of the fallen Nature; and seeing he had all this, as the *Undoer* of all that *Adam* had done, as the *Overcomer* of Death, as the *Former* and *Raiser* of our heavenly Life, therefore it was, that all his Conquests over this World, Sin, Death, and Hell, were not the Conquests of a *single Person* that terminated in himself, but had their real *Effect* and efficacious *Merit* through *all* human

Nature, because he was the *appointed Father* and *Regenerator* of the whole human Nature, and as such, had that *same Relation* to it all as *Adam* had: And therefore as *Adam's* Fall, Sin and Death, did not, could not terminate in himself, because he was our *appointed Father*, from whom we must have such a State and Condition of Life as he had; so the Righteousness, Death, Resurrection and Ascension of Christ into the Kingdom of Heaven did not terminate in himself, but became ours, because he is our appointed *second Adam*, from whom we are to derive *such* a State and Condition of Life as he had; and therefore all that are *born again* of him, are certainly born into *his State* of Victory and Triumph over the World, Sin, Death and Hell.

8. Now here is opened to us the true Reason of the *whole Process* of our Saviour's Incarnation, Passion, Death, Resurrection and Ascension into Heaven: It was because fallen Man was to go through *all these Stages* as necessary Parts of his Return to God; and therefore, if Man was to go out of his *fallen State*, there must be a Son of *this fallen* Man, who, as a *Head* and *Fountain* of the whole Race, could do all this, could go back through all these Gates, and so make it *possible* for all the Individuals of human Nature, as being *born* of him, to inherit his *conquering Nature*, and follow him through all these Passages to eternal Life. And thus we see, in the strongest and clearest Light, both *why* and *how* the holy Jesus is become our great Redeemer.

Had he failed in any of these Things, had he not *been* all that he was, and *did* all that he did, he could not have made one full, perfect, sufficient Atonement and Satisfaction for the Sins of the whole World, that is, he could not have *been* and *done* that, which in the *Nature* of the Thing was *absolutely* necessary, and *fully* sufficient to take the whole human Race *out of* the Bondage and Captivity of their fallen State. Thus, had he not really had the Divine Nature in his Person, he could not have *begun* to be our *second Adam* from the Time of the Fall, nor could we have stood *related* to him as Children, that had received a *new Birth* from him. Neither could he have made a *Beginning* of a Divine Life in our fallen Nature, but that he was that God who could make Nature *begin again* where it had failed in our first Father. Without this Divinity in his Person, the Perfection of his Humanity would have been as helpless to us as the Perfection of an Angel. Again, had he not been *Man*, and in human Nature *overcome* Sin and Temptation, he could have been *no Saviour* of fallen Man, because nothing that he had done had been done *in* and *to* the fallen Nature. *Adam* might as well have derived Sin into the Angels by his Fall, as Christ had derived Righteousness into us by his Life, if he had not *stood* both in our Nature, and as the *common Father* and *Regenerator* of it; therefore his Incarnation was necessary to deliver us from our Sins, and accordingly the Scripture saith, 'he was manifest 'in the Flesh to destroy the Works of the Devil.' Again, if Christ had not *renounced* this Life, as heartily and thoroughly as *Adam* chose it, and declared absolutely for another Kingdom in another World; if he had not *sacrificed* the Life he took up in and from this World, he could not have been our Redeemer, and therefore the Scripture continually ascribes Atonement, Satisfaction, Redemption, and Remission of Sins to his *Sufferings* and *Death*. Again, had not our Lord entered into that State of *eternal Death* which fallen Man was eternally to inherit; had he not broken *from it* as its Conqueror, and rose again from the Dead, he could not have delivered us from the Effects of our Sins, and therefore the Apostle saith, 'If Christ be not risen, ye 'are yet in your Sins.' But I must enlarge a little upon the Nature and Merits of our Saviour's *last Sufferings*. It is plain from Scripture that *that Death,* which our blessed Lord died on the Cross, was *absolutely* necessary for our Salvation; that he, as our Saviour, *was to taste Death for every Man*—that as the *Captain of our Salvation, he was to be made perfect through Sufferings*—that there was no Entrance for fallen Man into Paradise till Christ had overcome that Death and Hell, or that first and second Death which stood between us and it.

Now the absolute Necessity of our Saviour's doing and suffering all this, plainly appears, as soon as we consider him as the *second Adam*, who, as such, is to *undo* all the Evil that the first *Adam* had done in human Nature; and therefore must enter into *every State* that belonged to this fallen Nature, *restoring* in every State that which was lost, *quickening* that which was extinguished, and *overcoming* in every State that by which Man was overcome. And therefore as *eternal Death* was as certainly brought forth in our Souls, as temporal Death in our Bodies, as this Death was a State that *belonged* to fallen Man, therefore our Lord was obliged to taste *this dreadful Death,* to enter into the *Realities* of it, that he might carry our Nature *victoriously* through it. And as fallen Man was to have entered into this eternal Death at his giving up the Ghost in this World, so the second *Adam*, as *reversing* all that the first had done, was to stand in this *second Death* upon the Cross, and die from it into that Paradise out of which *Adam* the first died into this World.

Now when the Time drew near that our blessed Lord was to enter upon his last great Sufferings, *viz.,* the *Realities* of that second Death through which he was to pass, then it was that all the *anguishing Terrors* of a lost Soul began to open themselves in him ; then all that eternal Death which *Adam* had brought into his Soul, when it lost the Light and Spirit of Heaven, began to be *awakened,* and *stirring* in the second *Adam,* who was come to stand in the *last State* of the fallen Soul, to be encompassed with that eternal Death and *Sensibility* of Hell, which must have been the everlasting State of fallen Man.

The *Beginning* of our Lord's Entrance into the terrible Jaws of this second *Death,* may be justly dated from those affecting Words, ' My Soul is exceeding sorrowful, even unto Death, tarry ' ye here with me and watch.' See here the Lord of Life reduced to such Distress as to beg the Prayers, Watching, and Assistance of his poor Disciples! A plain Proof that it was not the Sufferings of this World, but a State of *dreadful Dereliction* that was coming upon him. O holy Redeemer, that I knew how to describe the anguishing Terrors of thy Soul, when thou wast entering into eternal Death, that no other Son of Man might fall into it.

The Progress of these Terrors are plainly shown us in our Lord's *Agony* in the Garden, when the *Reality* of this eternal Death so broke in upon him, so awakened and stirred itself in him, as to force great Drops of Blood to sweat from his Body. This was that *bitter Cup* which made him withdraw himself, prostrate himself, and thrice repeat an earnest Prayer, that if it were possible, it might pass from him, but at the same Time heartily prayed to drink it according to the Divine Will.

This was that Cup he was drinking from the sixth to the ninth Hour on the Cross, nailed to the Terrors of a *two-fold Death,* when he cried out ' My God, my God, why hast thou for-'saken me ?'

We are not to suppose that our Lord's Agony was the Terrors of a Person that was going to be murdered, or the Fears of that Death which Men could inflict upon him ; for he had told his Disciples, not to fear them that could only kill the Body, and therefore we may be sure he had no such Fears himself. No, his Agony was his Entrance into the *last, eternal Terrors* of the lost Soul, into the real Horrors of that dreadful, eternal Death, which Man unredeemed must have died into when he left this World. We are therefore not to consider our Lord's Death upon the Cross, as only the Death of that mortal Body which was nailed to it, but we are to look upon him with wounded Hearts, as fixed and fastened in the State of that *two-fold Death,* which was due to the fallen Nature, out of which he could not come till he could say, ' It is finished ; Father, into thy Hands I ' commend my Spirit.'

In that Instant he gave up the Ghost of this earthly Life; and as a Proof of his having overcome all the Bars and Chains of Death and Hell, he rent the *Rocks*, opened the *Graves*, and brought the *Dead* to Life, and triumphantly entered into that long shut up Paradise, out of which *Adam* died, and in which he promised the Thief, he should that Day be with him.

When therefore thou beholdest the *Crucifix*, which finely represents to thy Senses the Saviour of the World hanging on the Cross, let not thy Thoughts stay on any Sufferings, or Death, that the Malice of Men can cause; for he hung there in greater Distress than any human Power can inflict, *forsaken* of God, *feeling, bearing*, and *overcoming* the Pains and Darkness of that eternal Death which the fallen Soul of *Adam* had brought into it. For as *Adam* by his Fall, or Death in Paradise, had nothing left in his Soul, but the *Nature, Properties* and *Life* of Hell, all which must have *awakened* in him in their full Strength, as soon as he had lost the Flesh, and Blood, and Light of this World, as this eternal Death was a *State* that belonged to Man by the Fall, so there was an *absolute* Necessity that the Saviour of Man should enter into all these awakened Realities of the last eternal Death, and come victoriously out of them, or Man had never been redeemed from them. For the fallen Nature could no way possibly be saved, but by its *own coming* victoriously out of every Part of its fallen State; and therefore all this was to be done by that Son of Man, from whom we had a Power of deriving into us his victorious Nature.

Lastly, if our blessed Lord was not ascended into Heaven, and set on the Right Hand of God, he could not deliver us from our Sins; and therefore the Scripture ascribes to him, as ascended, a perpetual Priesthood in Heaven: 'If any Man Sin,' saith St. *John*, 'we have an Advocate with the Father, Jesus 'Christ the Righteous, and he is the Propitiation for our Sins.'

All these Things therefore are so many equally essential Parts of our Saviour's Character, and he is the *one Atonement*, the *full Satisfaction* for Sin, the *Saviour* and *Deliverer* from the Bondage, Power, and Effects of Sin. And to ascribe our Deliverance from Sin, or the Remission of our Sins more to the *Life* and *Actions*, than to the *Death* of Christ, or to his Death more than to his *Resurrection* and *Ascension*, is directly contrary to the plain Letter and Tenor of the Scripture, which speaks of *all these* Things as *jointly* qualifying our Lord to be the *all-sufficient* Redeemer of Mankind; and when speaking separately of any of them, ascribes the *same* Power, Efficacy, and redeeming Virtue to one as to the other.

And all this is very plain from the Nature of the Thing; for since all these Things are necessary Parts or Stages of our Return to God, every one of them must have the same necessary Share in delivering us from our sinful State ; and therefore what our Saviour did, as living, dying, rising from the Dead, and ascending into Heaven, are Things that he did as equally necessary, and equally efficacious to our full Deliverance from all the Power, Effects, and Consequences of our Sins.

And here we may see, in the plainest Light, how Christ is said to bear *our Iniquities*, to be made *Sin for us*, and how his Sufferings have delivered us from the Guilt and Sufferings due to our Sins, and how we are *saved* by him. It is not by an *arbitrary, discretionary* Pleasure of God, accepting the Sufferings of an *innocent* Person, as a sufficient *Amends* or *Satisfaction* for the Sins of Criminals. This is by no means the true Ground of this Matter. In this View we neither think rightly of our Saviour, nor rightly of God's receiving us to Salvation through him. God is reconciled to us through Jesus Christ in *no other Sense* than as we are *new born, new created* in Christ Jesus. This is the only Merit we have from him. Jesus Christ was made Sin for us, he bore our Iniquities, he saved us, not by giving the *Merit* of his innocent unjust Sufferings as a *full Payment* for our *Demerits*, but he saved us because he made himself *one* of *us*, became a Member of *our Nature*, and *such a Member* of our Nature, as had *Power* to heal, remove, and overcome all the Evils that were brought into our Nature by the Fall. He bore our Iniquities and saved us, because he stood in our Nature as our *common Father*, as one that had the same Relation to all Mankind as *Adam* had, and from whom we can derive all the conquering Power of *his Nature*, and so are enabled to come out of our Guilt and Iniquities by having his Nature *derived* into us. This is the whole of what is meant by having our *guilty Condition transferred* upon him, and his *Merit* transferred upon us : Our Guilt is transferred upon him in *no other* Sense than as he took upon him the State and Condition of our fallen Nature, to bear all its Troubles, undergo all its Sufferings, till he had *healed* and *overcome* all the Effects of Sin. His *Merit* or *Righteousness* is imputed or derived into us in no other Sense, than as we receive from him a *Birth*, a *Nature*, a *Power* to become the Sons of God. Hence it appears, what vain Disputes the World has had upon this Subject, and how this edifying, glorious Part of Religion has been perplexed and lost in the Fictions and Difficulties of scholastic Learning. Some People have much puzzled themselves and others with this *Question*, How it is consistent with the Goodness and Equity of God to *permit*, or *accept* the Sufferings of an innocent Person as a

Satisfaction for the Guilt and Punishment of criminal Offenders? But this Question can only be put by those, who have not yet known the most fundamental Doctrine of the Gospel Salvation; for according to the Gospel, the *Question* should *proceed* thus, How it is consistent with the Goodness and Equity of God, to raise *such an innocent, mysterious Person* out of the Loins of fallen Man, as was able to *remove* all the Evil and Disorder that was brought into the fallen Nature? This is the only Question that is according to the true Ground of our Redemption, and at once disperses all those Difficulties which are the mere Products of Human Invention. The Short of the Matter is this:

Man considered as created, or fallen, or redeemed, is *That* which he is, because of his State in Nature; he can have no Goodness in him when created, but because he is brought into such a Participation of a *Goodness* that there is *in Nature;* he can have no Evil in him when *fallen*, but because he is fallen from his good State *in Nature;* he can no way be redeemed, but by being brought into his first State of Perfection *in Nature;* and therefore, this is an eternal, immutable Truth, that he can be redeemed by the God *of Nature*, only according to the *Possibilities* of Nature: And here lies the *true Ground*, the whole Reason of all that our Saviour *was*, and *did*, and *suffered* on our Account: It was because in and through *all Nature* there could be no other Relief found for us: It was because nothing less than *such a Process* of such a *Mysterious Person* could have Power to undo all the Evils that were done in and to the Human Nature; and therefore it is not only consistent with the Goodness and Equity of God to bring such a Mysterious Person into the World, but is the most infinite Instance of his most Infinite Love to all Mankind, that can possibly be conceived and adored by us. To proceed:

9. By the Fall of our first Father we have lost *our first, glorious* Bodies, that *eternal, celestial* Flesh and Blood which had as truly the Nature of Paradise and Heaven in it, as our present Bodies have the Nature, Mortality and Corruption of this World in them: If therefore we are to be redeemed, there is an *absolute Necessity* that our Souls be *clothed* again with this first paradisaical, or heavenly Flesh and Blood, or we can never enter into the Kingdom of God. Now, this is the Reason, why the Scriptures speak so particularly, so frequently, and so emphatically of the powerful Blood of Christ, of the great Benefit it is to us, of its *Redeeming, Quickening, Life-giving* Virtue; it is because our first Life, or heavenly Flesh and Blood is *born again* in us, or *derived* again into us from this Blood of Christ.

Our Blessed Lord, who died for us, had not only that outward

Flesh and Blood, which he received from the Virgin *Mary*, and which died upon the Cross, but he had also an holy Humanity of heavenly Flesh and Blood veiled under it, which was appointed by God to *quicken*, *generate*, and *bring forth* from itself, such an holy Offspring of immortal Flesh and Blood, as *Adam* the first should have brought forth before his Fall.

If our Lord Christ had not had a *heavenly Humanity*, consisting of such Flesh and Blood as is not of this World, he had not been so perfect as *Adam* was, nor could our Birth from him, raise us to *that Perfection*, which we had lost, nor could his Blood be said to *purchase*, *ransom*, *redeem*, and *restore* us; because, as it is heavenly Flesh and Blood that we have lost, so we can only have it *ransomed* and *restored* to us, by that Blood which is of the *same* heavenly and immortal Nature with that which we have quite lost. Our common Faith, therefore, obliges us to hold, that our Lord had the *Perfection* of the first *Adam's* Flesh and Blood united with, and veiled under that fallen Nature, which he took upon him from the Blessed Virgin *Mary*. Had he not taken our *fallen* Nature upon him, nothing that he had done, could have been of any Advantage to us, or brought any Ransom or Redemption to our fallen Nature; and had he not taken *our Nature* as it was *before* the Fall, he could not have been our *second* Adam, or a *Restorer* to us of *that Nature*, which we should have had from *Adam* if he had not fallen.

Now, what our Common Faith thus fully teaches, concerning a heavenly, as well as earthly Humanity, which our Lord had, is also plainly signified to us by several clear Texts of Scripture; as where he saith of himself, 'I am from above, ye are from 'beneath;' again, 'I am not of this World;' and further, 'No 'one ascends into Heaven, but he that came down from 'Heaven, even the Son of Man, who is in Heaven:' These and other Texts of the like Nature, which plainly speak of *something* in our Blessed Lord, which can neither be understood of his Divinity, nor of *that* Flesh and Blood which he received from the Virgin *Mary*, has forced some *Scholastic Divines* to hold the *Pre-existence* of our Saviour's Soul, which is an Opinion utterly inconsistent with our Redemption; for it is as necessary that our Lord should have a Soul as well as a Body derived from *Adam*, in order to be the Redeemer of *Adam's* Offspring: But all these Texts, which a Learning, merely *literal*, has thus mistaken, do only prove this great, necessary, and edifying Truth, that our Blessed Lord had a heavenly Humanity, which clothed itself with the Flesh and Blood of this World in the Womb of the Virgin; and from that heavenly Humanity, or Life-giving Blood it is, that our first heavenly, immortal Flesh and Blood is

the Truths of the Gospel. 151

generated and *formed* in us again; and therefore his Blood is truly the *Atonement*, the *Ransom*, the *Redemption*, the *Life* of the World; because it brings forth, and generates from itself the paradisaical, immortal Flesh and Blood, as *certainly*, as *really*, as the Blood of fallen *Adam* brings forth and generates from itself the sinful, vile, corruptible Flesh and Blood of this Life.

Would you further know, what Blood this is, that has this atoning, Life-giving Quality in it? It is that Blood which is to be received in the Holy Sacrament. Would you know, why it quickens, raises and restores the inward Man that died in Paradise? The Answer is from Christ himself, ' He that eateth ' my Flesh and drinketh my Blood, dwelleth in me, and I in ' him, that is, he is born of my Flesh and Blood.' Would you know, why the Apostle saith, ' That he hath purchased us by ' his Blood,' Acts xx. 28. 'That we have Redemption through ' his Blood,' Ephes. i. 7. Why he prays 'the God of Peace— ' through the Blood of the Everlasting Covenant, to make us ' perfect in every good Work to do his Will;' 'tis because the Holy Jesus saith, ' except we drink his Blood, we have no Life ' in us,' and therefore the drinking his Blood, is the same Thing as receiving *a Life* of heavenly Flesh and Blood from him: And all this is only saying, that our Saviour, the second *Adam*, must do *that* for us and in us, which the first *Adam* should have done; his Blood must be that to us by way of *Descent*, or *Birth* from him, which the Blood of our first Father, if he had not fallen, would have been to us; and as this Blood of an immortal Life is lost by the Fall, so he from whom we receive it again by a *secondary Way*, is justly and truly said, to *purchase*, to *redeem*, and *ransom* us by his Blood.

Now, there is but *one redeeming, sanctifying, Life-giving* Blood of Christ, and it is that which gave and shed itself under the Veil of that outward Flesh and Blood that was sacrificed upon the Cross; it is that Holy and Heavenly Flesh and Blood which is to be received in the Holy Sacrament; it is that holy, immortal Flesh and Blood which *Adam* had before the Fall, of which Blood, if we had *drank*, that is, if we had been *born* of it, we had not wanted a Saviour, but had had such Flesh and Blood as could have entered into the Kingdom of Heaven; had we received this holy, immortal Flesh and Blood from *Adam* before his Fall, it had been called our being *born* of his Flesh and Blood; but because we receive that same Flesh and Blood from Jesus Christ, our second *Adam*, by our *Faith*, our *Hunger* and *Desire* of it; therefore it is justly called our eating and drinking his Flesh and Blood.

And here we have another strong Scripture Proof, that our Saviour had heavenly Flesh and Blood veiled under that which he received from the Virgin *Mary*. For does not the Holy Sacrament undeniably prove to us, that he had a heavenly Flesh entirely different from that which was seen nailed to the Cross, and which was to be a heavenly, substantial Food to us; that he had a Blood entirely different from that which was seen to run out of his mortal Body, which Blood we are to drink of, and live for ever?

Now, that Flesh and Blood cannot enter into the Kingdom of God, is a Scripture Truth; and yet it must be affirmed to be a Truth according to the same Scriptures, that Flesh and Blood can, and must enter into the Kingdom of God, or else, neither *Adam*, nor any of his Posterity could enter in thither; therefore, it is a Scripture Truth, that there is a *Flesh* and *Blood* that has the Nature, the Likeness, and Qualities of Heaven in it, that is as wholly different from the Flesh and Blood of this World, as Heaven is different from the Earth. For if the Flesh and Blood that we now have, cannot possibly enter into the Kingdom of Heaven, and yet we must be Flesh and Blood, and Christ our Lord must be Flesh and Blood, for ever in Heaven; then it follows, that there is a real Flesh and Blood that has nothing of this World in it, that neither arises from it, nor is nourished by it, but will subsist eternally, when this World is dissolved and gone. Now, if this Flesh and Blood is lost by the Fall of our first Father, and if the Blood which we derive from him is the *Cause*, the *Seat*, and *Principle* of our mortal, corruptible, impure Life; if from the Blood of this first Father, all our Unholiness, Impurity and Misery is derived into us, then we may clearly understand what is meant by our being redeemed by the Blood of Christ, and why the Scriptures speak so much of his *atoning, quickening, Life-giving, cleansing, sanctifying* Blood; it is because it is to us the Reverse of the Blood of *Adam*, it is the *Cause*, the *Seat*, the *Principle* of our Holiness and Purity of Life; it is that from which we derive an immortal, holy Flesh and Blood in the same Reality from this second *Adam*, as we inherit a corrupt, impure, and earthly Flesh and Blood from our first *Adam*: And therefore that which would have been done to us by our *Birth*, if we had been born of the holy Blood of *Adam* unfallen, that we are to understand to be done to us, in and by the Holy Blood of Christ. For the Blood of Christ is that to us in the Way of Redemption, which the Blood of our first Father should have been to us in the Order of the Creation; for the Redemption has no other End, but to raise us from our Fall, to do that for us, which we should have had by the Condition of our Creation, if our Father had kept his State of Glory and Immortality ; and this is a certain Truth, that there would have been no eating the Flesh, and drinking the Blood of Christ in the Christian Scheme of Redemption, but that the Flesh and Blood which we should have had from *Adam*, must of all necessity be had, before we can enter into the Kingdom of Heaven.

10. Here therefore is plainly discovered to us, the true Nature, Necessity and Benefit of the Holy Sacrament of the Lord's Supper ; both why, and how, and for what End, we must of all necessity, eat the Flesh, and drink the Blood of Christ. No *figurative Meaning* of the Words is here to be sought for, we must eat Christ's Flesh, and drink his Blood in the *same Reality*, as he took upon him the *real Flesh* and *Blood* of the Blessed Virgin : We can have no real Relation to Christ, can be no true Members of his mystical Body, but by being real Partakers of that same kind of Flesh and Blood, which was truly his, and was his, for this *very End*, that through him, the same might be brought forth in us : All this is strictly true of the Holy Sacrament, according to the plain Letter of the Expression ; which Sacrament was thus instituted, that the *great Service* of the Church might continually show us, that the whole of our Redemption consisted in the receiving the *Birth, Spirit, Life* and *Nature* of Jesus Christ into us, in being born of him, and *clothed* with a heavenly Flesh and Blood from him, just as the whole of our Fall consists in our being born of *Adam's* sinful Nature and Spirit, and in having a vile, corrupt and impure Flesh and Blood from him.

But what Flesh and Blood are we to eat and drink ? Not such as we have already, not such as any Offspring of *Adam* hath, not such as can have its Life and Death by, and from the Elements of this World ; and therefore, not that outward, visible, mortal Flesh and Blood of Christ, which he took from the Virgin *Mary*, and was seen on the Cross, but a *heavenly, immortal* Flesh and Blood, which came down from Heaven, which hath the *Nature, Qualities,* and *Life* of Heaven in it, according to which our Lord said of himself, that he was a ' Son of Man come down from Heaven,' that ' he ' was not of this World,' that ' he was from Above,' *&c.*, that *very* Flesh and Blood which we should have received from *Adam*, if we had kept his first glorious and immortal Nature. For as the Flesh and Blood which we lost by his Fall, was the Flesh and Blood of *Eternal Life*, so it is the same Flesh and Blood of Eternal Life which is offered to us in the Holy Sacrament, that we may eat, and live for ever : This is the adorable Height and Depth of this Divine Mystery, which brings Heaven and Immortality again into us, and gives us *Power to become Sons of God.* Woe be to those who come to it with the Mouths of *Beasts*, and the Minds of *Serpents!* who, with impenitent Hearts, devoted to the Lusts of the Flesh, the Lusts of the Eyes, and the Pride of Life, for worldly Ends, outward Appearances, and secular Conformity, boldly meddle with those Mysteries that are only to be approached by those that are of a *pure Heart*, and who worship God in *Spirit and in Truth*. Justly may it be said of such, that they *eat and drink Damnation to themselves, not discerning*, that is, not regarding, not reverencing, not humbly adoring the Mysteries of the *Lord's* Body.

If you ask how the eating and drinking the Body and Blood of Christ, is the receiving that Flesh and Blood of Eternal Life, which we should have had from *Adam* himself, it is for this plain Reason, because the *same kind* of Flesh and Blood is in Christ, that was in *Adam*, and is in Christ as it was in *Adam*, for this *very End*, that it might *be derived* into all his Offspring : So that we come to the Sacrament of the Blessed Body and Blood of Christ, because he is *our Second Adam*, from whom we must now receive that eternal, celestial Flesh and Blood which we should have had from our first Father ; and therefore it is, that the Apostle saith, the ' first Adam was made a living Soul,' that is, had a *Life in himself*, which could have brought forth an eternal, ever-living Offspring ; but having brought forth a dead Race, *the last Adam*, as the Restorer of the Life that was lost, *was made a quickening Spirit*, because quickening again *that Life* which *Adam* as a *living Soul*, should have brought forth.

And thus we have the *plain* and *full Truth* of the most mysterious Part of this Holy Sacrament, delivered from the tedious Strife of Words, and that Thickness of Darkness which learned Contenders on all Sides have brought into it. The Letter and Spirit of Scripture are here both preserved, and the Mystery appears so amiable, so intelligible, and so beneficial, as must needs raise a true and earnest Devotion in everyone that is capable of hungering and thirsting after Eternal Life. And this true and sound Knowledge of the Holy Sacrament could never have been lost, if this Scripture Truth had not been overlooked ; namely, that Christ is *our second Adam*, that he is to do *that* for us, which *Adam* should have done ; that we are to have *that Life* from him, as a *Quickening Spirit*, which we should have had from *Adam* as a *living Soul;* and that our Redemption is only doing a *second Time*, or in a second *Way*, that which should have been done by the first Order of our Creation : This plain Doctrine attended to, would sufficiently show us, that the Flesh and Blood of *Eternal Life*, which we are to receive from

Christ, must be *that Flesh and Blood* of Eternal Life which we lost in *Adam*. Now, if we had received this immortal Flesh and Blood by our *Descent* from *Adam*, we must in the Strictness of the Expression have been said to partake of the Flesh and Blood of *Adam ;* so seeing we *now* receive it from Christ, we must in the same Strictness of the Expression, be said to be *real Partakers* of the Flesh and Blood of Christ, because he hath the same heavenly Flesh and Blood which *Adam* had, and for the *same End* that *Adam* had it ; namely, that it may come *by* and *through* him into us. And thus is this great Sacrament, which is a continual Part of our Christian Worship, a continual Communication to us of all the Benefits of our Second *Adam ;* for in and by the Body and Blood of Christ, to which the Divine Nature is united, we receive all that Life, Immortality, and Redemption, which Christ, as living, suffering, dying, rising from the Dead, and ascending into Heaven, brought to Human Nature ; so that this great Mystery is that, in which all the Blessings of our Redemption and new Life in Christ are centred. And they that hold a Sacrament short of *this Reality* of the true Body and Blood of Jesus Christ, cannot be said to hold that Sacrament of *Eternal Life*, which was instituted by our Blessed Lord and Saviour.

FINIS.

SOME ANIMADVERSIONS UPON Dr. *Trapp's* late REPLY.

HAD I the Spirit of an *Adversary*, or were inclined to find Entertainment for the *Satirical Reader*, it would not be easy for me to overlook the Opportunity which Dr. *Trapp's* Reply has put into my Hands; but as I don't want to lessen any Appearance of Ability which the Doctor has shown on this Occasion, or have any Wish that his *Pen* had not all its Advantages; so whatever *personally* concerns him, either as a *Writer*, a *Scholar*, a *Disputant*, a *Divine*, or a *Christian*, shall have no Reflection from me; and though by this means, some sort of Readers may be less pleased, yet, the more Christian Reader will be glad to find, that thus I must leave *two Thirds* of his Reply untouched; and as I neither have, nor (by the Grace of God) ever will have any *personal Contention* with any Man whatever, so all the *Triumph* which the Doctor has gained over me by that Flow of Wrath and Contempt which he has let loose upon me, I shall leave him quietly to enjoy.

It would be no Pleasure to me, nor Benefit to the World, to discover that *Malignity* of Spirit, that *undistinguishing Head*, that *diabolical Calumny*, that *shameful Ignorance*, that *unthinking* Temper, that *blundering* Mind, that *perverse Disposition*, that *indecent Sufficiency*, that *unbecoming Presumption*, that *nauseous* Dulness, that *Ignorance* of *Logic*, that *Insensibility* of Argument, that Want of *Grammar*, which he has so heartily laid to my Charge; and if he has any Readers that thank him for this, I shall make no Attempt to lessen their Number.

As I desire nothing for myself, or the Reader, but good *Eyes*, and a good *Heart*, seriously attentive to Things useful and edifying, and always open to the Light and Influence of the Holy Spirit of God, so I shall endeavour to say nothing but what is *suitable* to such a State of Mind, both in myself and the Reader.

The Doctor, by way of Plea for a certain Freedom in Drinking, had appealed to our Saviour's Miracle at the Marriage Feast, where he turned Water into Wine, *at a Time* when the Guests had already drank enough, and *had indulged something to Pleasure and Cheerfulness.* Therefore more Wine, or a Continuance of Drinking, when Man have *already indulged something to Pleasure and Cheerfulness*, has Authority from our Saviour's Conduct at the Feast.

One would imagine no one need be helped to look with a just Indignation at this Abuse and Profanation of our Lord's Miracle. Did the Saviour of the World *mean*, or *intend* to teach any Thing like this in what he did? Was this the *Spirit* of his Mind when he *thus timed* this Miracle, did he intend to convey *this Instruction* to them? Now, if our Lord had not this Spirit, did not mean *thus* to instruct the Feasters by thus *timing* his Miracle, Is it not a great Profanation of it to appeal to it for that Instruction, which was not meant or intended by it? Had any one of those *Guests* then present, come up to our Lord and said, Sir, we have heard indeed a Report that you require a Man to deny himself, to hate even his own Life in this World, and to forsake all that he hath in order to be your Disciple, but now we perceive, not by Words, but by your *miraculous Actions*, that you are *no Enemy* to these kind of Pleasures and Indulgences, since you have worked a Miracle to help us to *more Wine*, when we had already drank enough, and had *indulged something* to *Pleasure and Cheerfulness.* What would our Lord have said to so sagacious an Observer? Would he have told him, that *Flesh and Blood had not revealed* so great a Truth unto him? Would he have acquiesced in the *Propriety* and *Justness* of his Observation, and pronounced him rightly *disposed* to by one of his Disciples? But if such an Observation could not have been approved by our Lord as a *Sign* of a good Mind, how is the Doctor to be excused, who not only looks *thus* at it himself, but proposes it to the World to be considered in *that View?* In order to vindicate our Saviour's Conduct in this Matter, I ventured, without any Help from *Commentators* or *Schoolmen*, to tell the Doctor, ' That the Wine here spoken 'of, was not *common Wine*, and therefore had no Relation to 'our common Drinking—that it was not Wine from the Juice of 'the Grape—that it had nothing in it but what came from a 'heavenly Hand—that it must have in it the *Purity* and *Virtue* 'of him that made it—that it had as good Qualities in it, and 'was fitted to have the same Effect upon some that drank it as 'the Clay which he moistened with his Spittle had upon the 'Eyes of the Blind—that it was Water only *so altered*, and 'endued with such Qualities, as he pleased to put into it; and 'therefore we may be sure it was Water as *highly blessed* for their Use as they were capable of; we may be sure it was fitter to allay the Heat and Disorder of their Drinking, than if it had been Water *unaltered* by our Saviour. How suitable was this Miracle to a Feast? How worthy of so Divine a Person! to make them cooler by giving them Water made fitter for that Purpose, and to raise their Faith by its miraculously seeming to be the best of Wine.'*

Now how can it be proved that this Interpretation is not a true one, not a safe one, not a good one? That our Saviour could do all this which is here mentioned, that he could convert Water into a Wine of this Nature, is undeniable; therefore if it had not this Nature and Qualities in it, it could only be because he chose to make it as bad as that Wine, which has the *Curse* of the Earth in it. But who will undertake to prove that Wine thus brought forth by a Divine Power, must have the *Nature* of Wine that is squeezed from the Grape under the *Curse* of Sin?

The Doctor confutes my Interpretation, by calling it a *senseless, impious, profane, ridiculous Nostrum, a Whimsy of my own Brain, diluting the glorious Miracle into nothing*. He has also accepted the Help of a learned *Assistant*, one *Philoclericus*, who backs this Confutation by saying, that *it has evaporated the Miracle into nothing*. They both agree that I have brought it to nothing, and only differ in my manner of doing it. The one holds it to be by *Dilution*, and the other by *Evaporation*.

To set this Matter therefore in a *clear Light*, let it be supposed, that the *Ruler of the Feast* should have come to our Saviour, and said, Sir, having been surprised at the extraordinary Difference between the last Cup of Wine that was brought to me, and that which had been used in the Feast before, I called the *Bridegroom* to tell him my Wonder at that extraordinary Wine which he had kept to the last; but being since informed by them that drew it, that this Wine was by thy *Word of Power* drawn from Vessels brim full of Water, I now come to fall down before thee, and confess that thou art come from God, and hast given me a Wine that has *not the Nature* of the earthly Grape in it: But as God gave our Fathers *Manna* to eat, which was justly called *Angels' Food*, and *Bread from Heaven*, so this Wine, which thou by a *Divine Power* has given us, must be looked upon, not as the *poor Juice* of the Grape, but as Wine given us *from Heaven*.

Now had the Doctor and his *learned Assistant* been there, and

---

* *Serious Answer*, etc., page 48.

had been such Christians as they are now, they must both have fallen upon the Ruler of the Feast, as a *senseless, impious, profane, ridiculous* Wretch, that had *diluted* and *evaporated* our Lord's glorious Miracle into nothing : Though it was impossible in the Nature of the Thing, for all the Disciples of our Lord, though ever so full of Faith in him, to make higher Profession of the *Reality* of this glorious Miracle than the Ruler here has done ; and yet he has said nothing but what is said in the Account which I have given of the Wine. And indeed it must be strangely absurd for any one to suggest, that the *Reality* of the Miracle is hurt by this Account of the Wine. For is not as great a Divine Power required to change Water into a Wine, that has a *better Nature* and Qualities than common Wine, as to make it have no more Goodness and Virtue in it than is in the *ordinary Juice* from the Grape? Or is it not rightly called Wine by those that drew it, or by him that drank it, because it was Wine in Perfection, in such Perfection, as the Grape could never give since *Adam* brought the Curse into the World.

The Doctor says, he *believes* it was just the same sort of Wine as if it had been from the Juice of the Grape, and his Reason is, ' because it is a Part of his Faith that our Saviour had the Power ' of creating,' p. 56. Now this is the very worst Reason the Doctor could possibly have thought of. For the Doctor, I will venture to say, is so orthodox a Schoolman as to hold the common Notion of Creating, *viz.*, that it is a *Power of making something to be out of nothing.* But Wine thus created is the last Thing the Doctor should have had Recourse to ; *first*, because it is directly contrary to the Letter of the Text, which expressly saith, the Water was made Wine, therefore not a *created Wine.* Secondly, because Wine so created, could not possibly be *just the same Sort of Wine, as if it had been from the Juice of the Grape,* because as the Grape and every earthly Thing stands in a State of Evil, Corruption, and Curse through the Sin of the fallen Creatures, it is absolutely impossible that any Thing *immediately* created by God *out of Nothing,* should have any Thing of that Evil, Corruption, or Curse in it which Sin alone has brought into the Creatures.

The Truth of the Matter is, here was no more a *Creation* of Wine in this Miracle, than Wine is created *every Time* the Vine has ripe Grapes upon it. Water, together with Earth, is every Year turned into the Juice of the Grape by the Power of the Sun, from God's *eternal Word,* first saying, ' Let the Earth bring forth, ' the Fruit-tree yielding Fruit,' &c.

This same *eternal,* ever *speaking,* ever *operating Word* of God, being become Man, could as well turn Water into Wine in a quicker Way by his own Power, as by the Help of the Vine once in a Year. Seeing therefore this Wine was not raised from Water and Earth, according to the common Course of Vegetation in fallen Nature, but by the immediate Agency of the God of Nature upon Water alone, it is reasonable and absolutely necessary to suppose, that it was Wine very much freed from all that Evil, Wrath, and Curse, which is inseparable from the *ordinary Workings* of the present State of Nature. Hence it appears, that the Interpretation here given, is so far from being a profane, impious, senseless *Nostrum*, is so far from having any Thing of Force, or Fiction in it, that it is the *first*, most *easy*, *natural*, and *direct* Sense, in which the Miracle can be justly understood. And therefore every sober Christian ought to reject the Doctor's Use of this Miracle as inconsistent with Piety. Great Intemperance, we all know, is carried on by such as pretend not to exceed the lawful Bounds of Pleasure and Indulgence. And is it consistent with Christian Piety, or Prudence, to furnish such People with a Pretext for what they do, from our Saviour's Example and Conduct? Or is he to be blamed, who by a just, innocent, and safe Interpretation of the Miracle, leaves such People no Claim to its Authority? Surely it is a sad Mistake to draw Arguments for sensual Indulgence from him, who came to teach and save the World by every Kind and Degree of possible Self-denial.

But I shall add but one Argument more, which is sufficient of itself to show how unjustly the Doctor draws an Argument from our Saviour's turning Water into Wine, when more than was necessary had been already drank, and *something*, as he says, *had been indulged to Pleasure and Cheerfulness;* and my Argument is this: It is undeniably plain from the whole Story of this Matter, that there was no more Water turned into Wine than that *one Cup*, which was carried to the Ruler of the Feast, and therefore neither Foundation nor Excuse for the Doctor's Argument from it.

When the Vessels were empty, our Lord ordered them to be filled, and to be filled up to the Brim *with Water*. Such an Order as this must, at least in the Execution of it, draw the Eyes and Attention of many that were present. Not a Syllable is ever mentioned of any Wine in the Vessels; they are only represented to us as standing brimful of Water. Our Lord only bids a Servant to draw from these Pots thus full of Water, and what he drew and carried to the Ruler from Vessels full of Water, was such Wine as strangely surprised him with its peculiar Excellency. The Wine was only found in that Cup into which our Saviour ordered the Servant to draw, and bear to the Ruler, and as he gave this Command but once, so it is certain there was but this one Cup of miraculous Wine. A hasty Reader, that has his Eye upon the Increase of the Liquor, and wants to have an Argument for his Purpose from it, may hurry himself into a Fancy, that our Saviour made all the Water Pots stand brimful of Wine. But the Story itself plainly represents quite another Matter, and is only a Relation of *one Cup* of miraculous Wine. The Care that our Lord took, that all the Vessels should be filled with Water up to the Top, was not, that the Guests might have all the Wine these Vessels could hold, but that all the Vessels being filled up to the Top, and made visible to all Beholders, might be so many plain Proofs that the Wine which he ordered to be drawn, could only be drawn from one of those Vessels which so many Beholders saw to be brimful of Water, both before and after the Drawing of the Cup of Wine. And herein lay the Strength, and Certainty, and Glory of the Miracle; that so many Witnesses were forced to see and own, that by the Word of our Lord, Wine was drawn from Pots just filled, and still remaining full to the Top with Water. And when this Miracle had thus incontestably manifested itself, the whole Affair was over, and the Guests were left, not to rejoice over full Pots of Water turned into Wine, but to make sober Reflections upon the Divinity of that Person, who had put such an astonishing End to their Drinking. Great and holy Jesus! How like thyself, the Saviour of the World, hast thou acted at this Feast! How couldst thou more sink the Value, extinguish the Desire, suppress all Thoughts of Pleasure and Indulgence in earthly Wine, than by showing the Feasters, that from the poorest of the Elements thou couldst call forth such Wine as no Grape could give? How couldst thou more effectually take from them their sensual Joy, or more powerfully call them to deny themselves and come after thee, than by thus miraculously showing them, that the richest Delights of sensual Gratifications were far short of what thou couldst give to those, that would leave all earthly Delights for thee.

The next Thing of Importance which I shall speak to, shall be with Regard to what I have said to the Clergy. The miserable State of Religion, and the great Corruption of Manners, so incontestably apparent in this Island, gave me a just Occasion to desire all the Clergy, from the highest to the lowest in the Order, to consider their Conduct, and see how free they were from the common Corruption, and how justly every one could clear himself from having any Share in this general Depravity of Manners. I was not insensible that this was a dangerous Attempt, that would expose me to the Resentment of not a few of my Brethren: But as I wrote for no other End but to do as much Good as I could to those who were capable of it, so I had no Care but how to speak disagreeable Truths, in as Christian and inoffensive a manner as I could; how I have succeeded in this, is left to the World to judge. And as it is but too apparent, that the *Root* of all the Evil, which but too much spreads itself through the whole Body of the Clergy, is owing to a *worldly, trading* Spirit, too visible from the Top to the Bottom of the Order, so I pointed at it in the softest and most affecting manner that I could, in the following Words, grounded on a plain Apostolical Doctrine and Practice.

St. *Paul*, I had observed, had said, it was lawful for those that preach the Gospel to live by the Gospel, and yet makes it Matter of the greatest Joy and Comfort to himself that he had wholly abstained from this *lawful Thing*; and declares, it were better for him to die than that *this* Rejoicing should be taken from him. He appeals to his daily and nightly working with his own Hands, that so he might preach the Gospel *freely*, and not be chargeable to those that heard him. And this he said he did, not for want of Authority to do otherwise, but that he might make himself an Example unto them to follow him. Here, I say, 'What fine and awakening Instructions are here
'given to us of the *Clergy*, in a practical Matter of the greatest
'Moment? How ought every one to be frighted at the Thoughts
'of desiring or seeking a *second Living*, or of rejoicing at *great*
'*Pay* where there is but *little Duty*, when the Apostle's *rejoicing*
'consisted in *this*, that he had passed through all the Fatigues
'and Perils of preaching the Gospel without any Pay at all?
'How cautious, nay, how fearful ought we to be, of going so far
'as the secular Laws permit us, when the Apostle thought it
'more desirable to lose his Life, than to go so far as the very
'Law of the Gospel would have suffered him?

'It is looked upon as lawful to get several Preferments, and
'to make a Gain of the Gospel, by hiring others to do Duty for
'us at a lower Rate.—It is looked upon as lawful to quit a *Cure*
'of Souls of a small Income, for *no other* Reason, but because we
'can get another of a greater.—It is looked upon as lawful for a
'Clergyman to take the Revenues of the Church, which he
'serves, to his *own Use*, though he has more than a sufficient
'Competency of his own, and much more than the Apostle could
'get by his Labour.—It is looked upon as lawful for the Clergy
'to live in State and Equipage, to buy Purple and fine Linen
'out of the Revenues of the Church.—It is looked upon as
'lawful for Clergymen to enrich their Families, to bring up their
'Children in the fashionable Vanities, and corrupting Methods

'of a worldly and expensive Life, by Money got by preaching 'the Gospel of Jesus Christ. But now, supposing all this to be '*lawful*, what Comfort and Joy might we treasure up to our-'selves, what Glory and Honour might we bring to Religion, 'what Force and Power might we give to the Gospel, what 'Benefit and Edification should we do to our Neighbour, if we '*wholly* abstained from all these lawful Things? Not by work-'ing Day and Night with our own Hands, as the great Apostle 'did, but by limiting our Wants and Desires according to the 'plain Demands of Nature, and a religious Self-Denial.'

Now, there are but two possible ways of justly replying to this; *first*, either by showing that these Observations are falsely drawn from the Apostle's Doctrine and Practice, that I have mistaken the Spirit of St. *Paul*, and the Genius of the Gospel, that I am here doing what the Apostle would not do, was he here in Person, and representing such Things as Corruptions, which the Apostle would be glad to see flourishing in the Church of Christ: Or, *secondly*, that though these Things are plainly condemnable from the Apostle's Doctrine and Practice, yet they are not chargeable upon the Spirit, Temper and Practice of the Clergy of this Land. Now, though not a Word to the Purpose could possibly be said, but by one of these two Ways, yet the Doctor shuts his Eyes to both of them, and then pronounced the following Sentence upon Me, *That a Quaker, or Infidel, could not well have reflected with more Virulency upon the Clergy of our Church, than I have done in these Expressions.*

Must I then suppose, that the Doctor in his *Sermons*, never mentions any Failings that concerns his Auditors, or lays before them any of their unchristian Ways of Life? If he does, I desire to know how he clears himself from *virulently* reflect-ing upon them and their Christianity? The *Quakers*, and *Infidels*, are ready enough, and able enough to show, that most Congregations of Christians are sadly fallen away from the Religion of the Gospel; and does the Doctor forbear this Charge, is he ashamed to call his Flock to a more Christian Life, or afraid to remind them of their Departure from the Gospel, lest he should seem to join with Quakers and Infidels, who make great Complaints of the Corruptions of Christians? Or, how can the Doctor desire to be thought to have any *true Love* or *just Esteem* for those Christians, whom he is so often reminding of the Corruption and Depravity of their Manners, so contrary to the Religion of Jesus Christ? Now, if the Doctor knows how to untie this *Knot*, and to extricate himself from the Charge of *virulent reflecting* upon his Parishioners, as *Quakers* and *Infidels* do, then he has dissolved his Charge against me into a mere nothing.

If it was a Thing required of me I know no more how to raise in myself the least Spark of Rancour, or Ill-will towards the Clergy, as such, than I know how to work myself up into a Hatred of the Light of the Sun. It is as natural to me, to wish them all their Perfection, as to wish Peace and Happiness to myself both here and hereafter; and when I point at any Failings in their Conduct, it is only with such a Spirit as I would pluck a Brother out of the Fire.

In that Part of my *Answer*, which is addressed to the younger Clergy, I said, 'Lay this down for an infallible Principle; that 'an entire, absolute Renunciation of all worldly *interest*, is the 'only possible Foundation of that exalted Virtue, which your 'Station requires; without this, all Attempts after an exemplary 'Piety are in vain : (*and then, by way of Limitation and Explication* '*of this, it thus immediately follows :*) If you want any Thing from 'the World by way of *Figure* and *Exaltation*, you shut the 'Power of your Redeemer out of your own Souls, and instead 'of converting, you corrupt the Hearts of those that are about 'you. Detest therefore, with the *utmost Abhorrence*, all Desires 'of making your fortunes, either by *Perferments*, or *rich* '*Marriages*, and let it be your only Ambition, to stand at 'the *Top* of every Virtue, as visible Guides and Patterns to all 'that aspire after the Perfection of Holiness,' p. 61.

Now, one would imagine there was no Part of the Christian World, however corrupted by Division, where this Doctrine would not be admitted at least in Theory; or, that the Gospel of Christ should be thought to be reproached, where such Advice as this was given to young Divines: And yet it is of this very Advice, that Dr. *Trapp* says, 'he hopes they will have more Grace 'and Sense than to follow it : That it is false Doctrine, tending 'to the Reproach and Scandal of the Christian Religion,' p. 87.

Is it then come to this, that unless young Divines choose to serve *Mammon* as well as God, their Profession is a renouncing of *Grace* and *Sense*, and a *Reproach to Religion?* And must they that pretend to act in Christ's Name, as Successors in his Office, take Care that they renounce not the Politics of the Kingdom of this World? For my part, I thought it as safe, as Christian, as consistent with the Honour of the Gospel, to give this Advice thus to suppress all worldly Views, as to resist all the Temptations of the Devil.

Had *Martin Luther*, when he gave his Reasons and Motives for withdrawing from Communion with the *Pope*, been able to have added this : that the *Advice* here given, had been formally condemned by the *Pope* in a great Council, the Defenders of that Church would have found it as hard to have made such a *Decree* consistent with the Gospel, as the selling of Indulgencies: And it may well be supposed, that no Protestant writer, when setting forth the *Marks* of Antichrist, and the *Beast* in that Church, would have forgot to have made this *Condemnation* to be one of them.

For who can show it to be so contrary to the whole Spirit of the Gospel, to call in the *Assistance* of the Saints, or to deny the *Cup* to the Laity in the Manner the Church of *Rome* does, who can show this to put so entire a Stop to the Salvation by the Gospel, as to condemn the *Advice* here given to young Divines as a Scandal and Reproach to Christianity? For all the Ends and Designs of the Gospel may be pursued, and Men may arise out of the Corruption of their Nature, notwithstanding these two Mistakes: But to condemn it as an Error inconsistent with *Grace* and *Sense*, a Scandal and Reproach to Christianity, for young Divines to renounce worldly Views, and devote themselves wholly to God, is striking at the whole Root of all Holiness of Life, and no less than a Denial of the whole Spirit of the Gospel.

Our Church requires all its Candidates for Holy Orders, to make Profession of their being moved and called by the Holy Ghost to enter into the Service of the Church: This, I should think, is Proof enough, that the Spirit of this World ought not to be alive in them, when they make this Profession; and yet, if any young Persons should come to be ordained, thus dead to all worldly Views, thus wholly devoted to God, as I have here recommended, they ought, according to the Doctor, to be rejected by the Bishop, of being led by a Spirit that has lost all *Grace* and *Sense*, and is a *Scandal* and *Reproach* to the Christian Religion.

It is needless to quote particular Texts of Scripture, teaching the same that I have here taught; as, that our Saviour assures us, that we 'cannot serve God and Mammon': That St. *Paul* requires us, *having Food and Raiment, to be therewith content,* for this Reason, *because they that will be rich, fall into divers Temptations of the Devil:* That St. *John* forbids us to ' love the World, ' or the Things of the World,' for this Reason, because all that is in the World, the ' Lust of the Flesh, the Lust of the Eyes, and ' the Pride of Life, is not of the Father, but is of the World.' It is needless to have Recourse to particular Texts of this kind, because the whole Nature and Reason of our Redemption is a standing, plain Proof of the same Thing; for we want to be redeemed for no other Reason, but because we are born Children of this World, and have by Nature only the Life, Spirit and

Temper of this World in us: This is our Fall, our Curse, our Separation from God; and therefore we can have no Redemption, but by a Renunciation of all the Workings of the Life of this World in us, by a total dying to, and denying ourselves; because all that we are, as to our State, Spirit and Life in this World, is a Life that carries us from God, a Life that should not have been raised up in us; 'tis a Life begun by the Fall, a Life of Sin and Corruption, which cannot enter into Heaven. The Life that we have in this World, from the Fall of *Adam*, is not to be *naturally* destroyed or murdered, nor are the Necessaries and Conveniences of Life to be rejected, nor is anyone to renounce his Share in the Employments that are necessary and useful to Social Life: The Renunciation of this World reaches no further than the renouncing the Spirit, Temper, and Inclinations of this worldly Life: We may stand in our Stations, when we stand in them as the Servants of God, as Citizens of the new *Jerusalem*, who have amongst earthly Things, our Conversation in Heaven: We may keep our Possessions, when we possess them as the Things of God, and use them not as Nature, but as the Spirit directs us; when we do thus, we have the Poverty of Spirit, which the Gospel requires, and come up to the very Letter of that Command given to the young Man, ' to sell all that he 'had, and give to the Poor.'

But now, if our natural Life in this World, is a corrupt, impure, disorderly, bestial, diabolical Life brought forth by the *Fall*, if we want to be redeemed because we have this State of Life in and from this World, if we want to be born again of the Son of God, born again of the Holy Spirit, because our natural Birth is according to the Spirit of this World; if nothing of the Beast, or the Devil, no kind or degree of Selfishness, Envy, Pride and Vanity can enter into the Kingdom of God, then it is plain from the Nature of the Thing, that all religion which leaves this Nature alive and unrenounced, which lets Selfishness, Pride, Wrath, and Vanity subsist in us, which bring us to our Graves in the same Nature in which we were born, is not the Religion that can save us. If this Nature in all its most secret Workings is not renounced and denied, it matters not what we are, or what we have been doing, it signifies little in what Chair we have sat, whether in *Italy*, or *England*, how long we have been Preachers, how many heretics and Schismatics we have opposed, or how many Books we have written in Defence of Orthodoxy; it is as vain to appeal to this, as to our having preached and *prophesied* in the Name of Christ, in the Streets and Fields: For if this Nature is allowed to live in us, all our good Works have been governed by it, they have sprung from

Selfishness, are animated with Pride, and only serve to gratify our own natural Passions. When therefore the Doctor calls upon young Divines to have *more Grace* and *Sense* than to be driven from Thoughts of advancing themselves by *Preferments and rich Marriages*, he would do well to consider, how little short this is of calling them to break their very Baptismal Vow, of *renouncing the Pomps and Vanities of the World*. And if young Candidates for Holy Orders, looking only at their Baptismal Vow, should be led into this Degree of Self-denial and Detachment from the World, does the Doctor think, that the Apostles, from whom this Baptismal Vow is descended, will rise up in the Day of Judgment, and condemn such gross Ignorance and Abuse of it? Does he think, that there are any departed Saints that will join with him in saying, that such a Spirit is a *Scandal* and *Reproach* to the Gospel? What more favourable Disposition could the Adversary of Mankind wish to see, either in young or old Divines, than a wanting and desiring to have Figure in the World, either by Preferments or rich Marriages? Would he find it difficult to enter into those Hearts, where the Lust of the Flesh, the Lust of the Eyes, and the Pride of Life had thus entered? Or would he look upon such as but half fitted for him, in Comparison of those who entered into holy Orders in a Spirit of Self-denial, and Renunciation of the Pomps and Vanities of the World? Does the Doctor think that these gross Instances of worldly Ambition have no Affinity with those Pomps and Vanities, which must be renounced in Baptism?

John the *Baptist* was but the Preparer of the Way for evangelical Purity of Life; but does the Doctor think that if the *Baptist* was now to come amongst us, as some have thought he will come again before the End of the Church, that he would look at Things as the Doctor does, that he would see such Perfections and such Corruptions, such Orthodoxy and such Enthusiasm as the Doctor sees; that this *burning and shining Light* would see no *Generation of Vipers* but where the Doctor sees them; that he would preach nowhere but in Churches; that he would spare no Clergy, nor any Church, but that which is established in this Island; that he would complain of the Hardships of our Clergy, and the suffering Spirit which they are forced to practise, as the Doctor does; that he would plead for a priestly Liberty of coveting Preferments and rich Marriages, as the Doctor doth; that he would condemn the *Treatise upon Christian Perfection* amongst the *most pernicious Books* of the Age, that he would recommend *Wharton's Defence of Pluralities*, and the Doctor's Discourse of the *Folly, Sin, and Danger of being righteous over-much*, as the true Fruits of that Spirit which first preached the Gospel? He that can believe this, must believe that the Baptist was come to confess the Errors and Mistakes of his first Appearance in the World.

I shall therefore proceed to tell young Divines, that a total Renunciation of the Spirit, Temper, and Inclinations of this Life, is the one Thing necessary to consecrate them to their holy Office; that as sure as the Church of Christ is not a Kingdom of this World, as sure as Jesus Christ came to deliver us from this evil World, as sure as he requires us to be born again from above, to hate even our own Life in this World, and to forsake all and follow him, so sure is it that no one has the *Call* of the Holy Spirit to the Ministry of the Gospel, nor the least Ground of hoping to be led and governed by it in his Ministry, till he at least prays, desires, and heartily endeavours to have all that Disregard of worldly Prosperity, Figure, and Distinction, which the Spirit of Jesus Christ, the Maxims of the Gospel, and the Practice of the Apostles set before him. Till this Renunciation of the World is made, we cannot enter into the Ministry at its *own Door*, but, like Thieves and Robbers, climb over its Walls; and then it will be no Wonder if we do no more Good to the Church than Thieves do the House they break open and plunder. If a young Minister wants to act the Part, and have the Appearance of a fine Gentleman, to go on in the common Spirit of the World, to cover a secular Spirit with an ecclesiastic Garb, and make his Fortunes in the Church, he must be told, that it is much safer to be a *Publican* and a *Sinner*, than to be a *Trader* in spiritual Things; that he who with unsanctified Hands attends at the Altar, is further from the Kingdom of God, than he who has not yet made one Step towards it.

Covetousness is *Idolatry*; it is a heathenish, Anti-christian Vice, though only trafficking in worldly Matters; but when it takes Possession of the Altar, and makes a Trade of the Mysteries of Salvation, and turns Godliness into Gain, it has a Blackness of Vice and Depravity which much exceeds that of the worldly Miser. The Spirit of an Ecclesiastic should be the Spirit of Heaven, knowing nothing of this World, but how to escape its Snares and Temptations, burning in the Love of God, and holding out Life and Direction to all that aspire after every Perfection of the Christian Life.

'Tis too commonly thought, that when a young Student has taken his Degree, and shown some Signs of a Genius for Learning, that he is well prepared to enter into the Service of the Church. But alas! all the Accomplishments of human Learning are but the Ornaments of the *Old Man*, which leave the Soul in its Slavery to Sin, full of all the Disorders and

Corruptions of the fallen Nature, and under the Blindness and Perverseness of some of its Passions. If it were not thus, how could the Errors of all Churches have the *greatest* Scholars for their *Champions*? All the learned Catholic World is amazed at the Prejudice, the Blindness, the Perverseness, the Partiality, the Weakness, the Sophistry, the Unfairness of *Protestant Critics*. All the Protestant World is in the same Degree of Wonder at the same Disorders in *Catholic Disputants*. Is not this a Demonstration of the *Nature, Power,* and *Place* of human Learning? Of its great Usefulness and Benefit to Religion? Does not this enough show, that it is the Effect and Offspring of the old Man, has his Nature and Qualities, dwells in him, and is governed by him? Is not this a Demonstration, that the *greatest Degrees* of historical, verbal, critical Knowledge are no real Hindrance of spiritual Blindness? Is not this a Demonstration, that human Learning is as different from Divine Light as Heaven is from Earth, the new from the old Man; and that considered in itself, it leaves us in our first State of Slavery to blind and corrupt Passions? Now nothing can deliver a Man from this State, but a Spirit born into him from above, a Light from the Spirit of God derived into his Soul, which alone can bring forth a *new Man* created in Christ Jesus. Nothing can make way for this new Birth from above, but a total Renunciation and Dying to all that we are by our natural Birth in this World. 'Tis only *this Separation* from Things below, that can make us Partakers of the Truth and Light that comes from above. Take away *all Selfishness* from the Papist and the Protestant, or let them both be dead to the Workings of this Spirit, and then they will be as fully agreed about Gospel Truths, as they are in the Form of a *Square* and a *Circle*. For nothing stands in the way of Divine Truths, or hinders its plain and full Entrance into us, but this *Partiality* or *Selfishness*, which adheres to everyone who does not make it his first Maxim, Prayer, and Endeavour to die to, and deny himself in all the Tempers and Inclinations of our fallen Nature. This Self-denial is the continual Doctrine of our Lord; it is by him made the Beginning of all Conversion to God, and he that cannot, or will not begin there, can make no Beginning of that Life, Light, and Salvation to which he is called in Christ Jesus: Therefore he that offers himself for holy Orders, without this Spirit of Self-denial, is a miserable Intruder into the Mysteries of Salvation; he only hardens and fixes himself in the Corruptions of his own Nature, and instead of becoming an Instrument of saving others, his very Office makes his own Salvation more dangerous.

I doubt not but some will here charge me with pleading for

Poverty in the Ministry, and with Enmity to that Maintenance which they have both from the Law and the Gospel. But this is so far from being true, that I wish every good Minister, whom the Spirit of God has called to his Office, and governs in it, had much more of this World's Goods than are needful for his own reasonable subsistence; because it is certain, that such a one's Money would all be put into the *Poor's Bag*, and he would as gladly and liberally administer to their temporal as to their spiritual Necessities. I write against nothing but *Avarice*, *Selfishness*, *Pride*, and *Ambition*, and the making the Provisions of the Church *subservient* to these Tempers. A Provision arising from the Gospel, is *consecrated* by the Gospel, and is profaned by being touched and used by a worldly Spirit. And he who turns this Provision of the Gospel into a Support and Gratification of worldly Passions, sins against the Nature and Law of the Gospel more than he that pays his Tithes with Reluctance.

I can easily believe there are Clergy in this Land, who labour in the Gospel, without having a sufficient Subsistence from it; but if much of this Evil was to be charged upon *Pluralities*, *Commendams*, and such like spiritual Trading, there would be no Injustice in it. And if the inferior Clergy had their Labours only undervalued by the Laity, they would be in much better Condition than they are.

When it is complained by what shameful *Qualifications*, empty *Titles*, and unworthy Pretences, Numbers of Persons get *loaded* and *dignified* with Variety of Preferments; it is answered, in Excuse of this great Evil, That if Preferments might not be thus crowded together, great *Learning*, distinguished *Abilities*, and eminent *Labours* for the Service of Religion, must go unrewarded.

As this Answer is not fetched from the Gospel, or the Primitive Church, so I shall show, that it is a little supported by Reason. For if this great Learning is truly Gospel Learning, if this eminent Labour is truly pious Labour, what State of Life can so little want to be rewarded? How can Imagination itself place a Man more *above* the Thoughts and Desires of worldly Advancement? If such a one is full of the Light and Spirit of the Gospel, if his Labours have been like those of an Apostle, must he not like an Apostle be *dead* to the World? Can such a one look upon his Labour as a *Hardship*, because it has left him as *low*, and as far from the *Pomp* of the World as it found him? Can he repine because the Gospel has not proved a good *worldly Bargain* to him? If the Spirit of God has begun, and directed all his Labours, animated all his Studies and Designs, can such a one think it hard, that he has not by such Labours purchased to himself a Share in the State and Pride of Human Life?

If by a *great Divine*, is only meant a Person well skilled in *Critical Contention*, who can artfully, plausibly, scholastically defend a Set of Notions, amongst which he happened to be born, and bred, such a Divine, I own, may be very *impatient*, and *much cooled* in his Zeal, unless he finds himself well rewarded; but if an eminent Divine is to be understood in a Sense suitable to the Gospel, he is that *particular Person* that must needs have the greatest *Contempt* and *Dislike* of every Thing, that has but the *Appearance* of the Pomp and Vanity of this World in it. If therefore it was urged, that this Conjunction of Preferments and dignifying Rewards was necessary to bring *ambitious Scholars* into the Church, or to keep them in it, there would be some Sense, though no Gospel in the Pretence; but to talk of them as necessary to be the Rewards of eminent Piety and Apostolic Labour, is as absurd, as to say, that those who have truly put on Christ, who stand in the highest Degree of a renewed Nature, who best know and feel the Blessing of a mortified, heavenly Spirit, have less Reason to be *content with Food and Raiment*, than those who stand in a lower Degree of the Christian Life; 'tis saying, that a *Bishop*, because having most of the *Spirit* and *Office* of an Apostle in him, may well desire more of the *Pride* and *Figure* of this World, than the lower Clergy, who have less of the Apostolical Spirit and Perfection in them.

To want to stand in some Degree of worldly Figure, is the State of a *Babe* in the Christian Life, that hath hardly tasted the Milk of Evangelical Nourishment, and therefore can no way become those, who are to lead and compel others to the Perfection and Fulness of the Stature in Christ Jesus.

A *great Divine* is but a *cant* Expression, unless it signifies a Man *greatly advanced* in the Divine Life, whose Experience and Example is a Demonstration of the *Reality* of all the Graces and Virtues of the Gospel. No Divine has any more of the Gospel in him, than that which proves itself by the Spirit, Actions, and Form of his Life, the rest is but Hypocrisy, not Theology: If therefore Poverty of Spirit, a Disregard of worldly Figure, a total Self-denial is any Part of the Gospel, an eminent Divine, or one advanced in the Spirit and Life of Jesus, can have no Wish with regard to the Figure, Pride and Pomp of this Life, but to be placed out of every Appearance of it: And if the first and highest in Divine Knowledge are not the foremost in Poverty of Spirit, and the outward Humility of Christ and his Apostles; if eminent Divines want and desire to have a Dignity of worldly Figure, to have Respect by any other Means than by the Divine Virtues and Graces of an Evangelical Spirit and Conversation, and are not content with all the Contempt that such a Life can expose them to, they may be *great Scholars,* but they are *little Divines,* and must be thought to be much wanting in that which is the chief Part of the Ministers of Jesus Christ. But to proceed :

The next Thing I said to the young Clergy, was this ; 'Con-'sider yourselves *merely* as the Messengers of God, that are sent 'into the World *solely* on his Errand ; and think it Happiness 'enough that you are called to the same Business for which the 'Son of God was born into the World,' p. 81.

Now, I thought what I *here* said, was as unexceptionable, as pious, as unfit to be condemned by a Professor of Christian Theology, as if I had only recommended the loving of God with all our Heart and Soul, and Mind and Strength ; and that if any Clergyman disliked it, he would be forced to keep his Dislike to himself : But the Doctor is very open in his Indignation at it ; the same Answer, he says, is to be given here, as before, *viz.,* 'that it is false Doctrine, tending to the Scandal and 'Reproach of the Christian Religion.'

Our Blessed Lord, when he sent the first Preachers of the Gospel into the World, said unto them, 'As my Father hath sent 'me, so send I you——go ye and teach all Nations——and lo 'I am with you to the End of the World.' Now let it be supposed, that these first Preachers of the Gospel fully believed, that from the Time of their Appointment to this high Office, they *were to consider themselves merely as the Messengers of God, sent into the World solely on his Errand,* and that *it was Happiness enough for them to be called to that Business,* for which *the Son* of God was *born into the World;* if they had this Belief, what follows ? Why, according to the Doctor, it follows, that they set out from the very first in one of the greatest Errors, had mistaken the Nature and Intent of their Mission, and had gone into the World upon a Principle that *was false* in itself, and *scandalous* and *reproachful* to the Christian Religion.

But if this Belief is not to be condemned in the first Clergy, as a false Opinion of their Office, scandalous and reproachful to the Christian Religion, I desire to know why those Clergy, who claim their Succession from the first, and expect the Presence of Christ in and with their Ministry, are not to be called upon to be of the same Spirit and Belief with the first of their Order ; or how it can be a Scandal to the Gospel, for the modern Clergy to be as wholly devoted to the Service of God, as the Apostles were : Surely there is something so extravagant in the Doctor's Condemnation of the Advice here given to young Divines, as must shock even the common Reader; and if it could be supposed, that there are others amongst the learned Clergy, who are in this like minded with the Doctor, and glad to see this Advice condemned in this manner, if it could be supposed, that there are not Numbers amongst them of Rank and Eminence that want and desire to bear their Testimony against it, have we not too much Reason to fear that, which God threatened to the Angel of the Church at *Ephesus*, namely, *the Removal of our Candlestick out of its Place?*

The Doctor sets it out as an extraordinary Presumption in *such a Man* as I am, to pretend to give advice to young Divines, when it is so sufficiently done already by the 'Offices of our 'Church, the Charges, Instructions and Exhortations of our 'Bishops at their Visitation, and so many excellent Ordination 'and Visitation Sermons,' p. 87. Now, granting the Plenty and Excellency of all these, yet I have some hope, that my Presumption may be found to be only like that of the *poor Widow*, who after so many rich Oblations of great People, *presumed* to put her little *Mite* into the Treasury. And if it be true, that the Things here suggested by me, are only such as have been already fully set forth by so many great Bishops and excellent Preachers, how will the Doctor come off for condemning it, as false Doctrine, scandalous, and *reproachful* to the Christian Religion?

Dr. *Trapp* gives a Reason for his condemning this Advice, which is thus expressed: 'It is,' says he, 'false to say, that 'Clergymen ought to mind nothing, in any Degree, but their 'Profession and Duty, as Clergymen; they are Husbands, 'Parents, Men, as well as Clergymen, and must in some measure 'be concerned in the Affairs of the World,' p. 88.

Part of this I own to be very true, *viz.*, that they are Men, and have the Wants of Human Nature which must be supplied; and for a full Proof of this, the Doctor might have justly appealed to St. *Paul*, who, though miraculously called to be an Apostle, and separated from the World to be *merely* a Messenger and Apostle of Jesus Christ; yet, after this high Apostleship, worked at his *Trade*, and often spent some Part of the Day and the Night in making Tents: Therefore, if all those whom I have exhorted to consider themselves as so highly set apart for the sole Service of God, should show such a Degree of worldly Care as St. *Paul* did, when he worked at his Trade, they might yet justly be said to act suitably to their Station, as the Ministers of God, that are wholly devoted to his Service; for if they should refuse to live, how could it be their Desire to live wholly to the Service of God; or, who can say that St. *Paul* departed from his Character, as a Minister of God, when he laboured with his own Hands, that he might gloriously and freely preach the Gospel? For it was for the Sake of the Gospel, to promote and recommend the Gospel, to make his Preaching the more successful; it was to show that he had fully renounced the World, desired nothing from it, but for the Glory and Love of God, would preach Salvation *freely* to the World: And thus have all the Ministers of the Gospel an Example in St. *Paul*, how they may make their *Care* of a Livelihood a *Part* of their Service to God.

But when the Doctor says, that Clergymen are *Husbands* and *Parents*, I must object a little; because no Scripture, or Antiquity shows me, that these Characters must belong to a Preacher of the Gospel; and therefore, when a Clergyman excuses himself from any Heights of the Ministerial Service, by saying, *he has married a Wife*, and *therefore cannot come* up to them; it seems to be no better an Excuse, than if he had said, *he had hired a Farm*, or *bought five Yoke of Oxen*.

I know very well, that the *Reformation* has allowed Priests and Bishops not only to look out for Wives, but to have as many as they please, one after another: But this is only to be considered as a *bare Allowance*, and perhaps granted upon such a Motive, as *Moses* of old made one to the *Jews*, for *the Hardness of their Hearts*, though *from the Beginning it was not so;* and therefore when *Elogiums* are sometimes made from the *Pulpit* on this Matter, I think they had better been spared; an Allowance granted to Weakness, is but an indifferent Subject to be made a Matter of Glory.

The Doctor should also have observed, that my Address was made to the young Clergy, and such as are only upon entering into holy Orders, *nine* in ten of which, may be supposed to be neither *Husbands* nor *Fathers*. He should also have remembered that our *Universities* are full of Clergy, who are obliged to live *unmarried*, that they may have proper *Leisure* and *Freedom* to attend their Studies without Impediment from worldly Cares. And therefore if I pointed at such a Dedication of the Clergy to the Service of God, as *Husbands* and *Fathers* cannot enter into, yet the Matter is not blamable, because there are so many that have not yet entered into this State of Subjection to the World, but are at Liberty to devote themselves wholly to the Service of the Gospel. And therefore if to such as these, I can so represent the Weight, the Duties, the heavenly Nature of the Priesthood, as to prevent or extinguish in them all Thoughts and Desires of being thus married to the World, what hurt have I done them, or the married Clergy, or the Gospel of Jesus Christ?

Virginity or *Celibacy*, when entered into from a Principle of *divine* Love, from a Heart burning with the Desire of living *wholly* and *solely* to God, is a State that gives Wings to all our Endeavours, and truly fits the Soul for the highest Growth of every heavenly Virtue : And if he that is consecrated to the Service of the Altar, desires not to keep his Heart from carnal Love ; if he feels not such an Ascent of his Soul towards Heaven, as to have no Wish, but that his *whole Body*, *Soul*, and *Spirit*, may be presented to God in its utmost Degree of Purity, he must be said to have his Lamp *much less* kindled, than many of the Laity, both *Men* and *Women* have had, in all Ages of the Church. Custom and common Practice has too great a Power over our Judgments, and reconciles us to any Thing ; but if a Christian, who lived when Christianity was in its Glory, when the first *Apologists* for it, appealed to the Numbers of *both Sexes*, devoted to the Chastity of the single Life, as an *invincible Proof* of the Power, and Divinity of the Gospel ; if a Christian of those Days was now to come into the World, he must needs be much more shocked at Reverend Doctors in Sacerdotal Robes, *making Love* to Women, than at seeing a *Monk* in his *Cell*, *kissing* a wooden Crucifix.

The Knowledge and Love of the Virgin State began with Christianity, when the Nature of our Corruption, and the Nature of our Redemption were so fully discovered by the Light of the Gospel. Then it was, that a new Degree of heavenly Love was kindled in the human Nature, and brought forth a State of Life that had not been desired, till the Son of the Virgin came into the World. *John* the *Baptist* may be looked upon as the Beginner of the Gospel Dispensation ; this *burning and shining Light* was in his Person, the Figure of *Judaism* ending in Christianity. In his outward Birth and State he was a *Jew*, in his inward Spirit and Character he belonged to the Gospel. He came out of the Wilderness burning and shining, to preach the Kingdom of Heaven *at Hand*. This may show us that Heat and Light from above, kindled in a State of great Self-denial are necessary to make us able Ministers of the Gospel ; and that if we pretend to the Ministry with these Qualifications, and come only burning and shining with the Spirit of this World, we are only as well fitted to hinder, as the Baptist was to prepare the Way to the Kingdom of Heaven. Look at this great Saint, all ye that desire to preach the Gospel. He came forth in the highest Degrees of *Mortification* and *Chastity* of Life. But why did he so come ? It was to show the World that these two great Virtues must form the Spirit of every Preacher of the Gospel. His Character does not call you to a Wilderness beyond *Jordan*, or to be clothed with Camels' Hair, *&c.* Such

Circumstances are particular to himself; but it calls you to his inward Spirit of Self-denial, to stand in his State of Death to the World, and all carnal Love, if you would not only preach, but prove the Perfection of the Gospel: For if the *Baptist* was to be thus dead to the Flesh and the World, that he might only preach thus much, that the Kingdom of heaven *was at Hand ;* can a less Self-denial be required of those, who are to preach that which is much more, namely, that the Kingdom of Heaven *is come ?*

Now if this holy *Baptist*, when he came to *Jerusalem*, and had preached awhile upon Penitence, and the Kingdom of Heaven *at hand*, had made an Offering of his Heart to some fine *young Lady of great Accomplishments*, had not this put an End to all that was burning and shining in his Character? And if those Clergy who date their Mission from Jesus Christ himself, who claim being sent by him as he was by his Father, to stand as his *Representatives*, applying the *Means* and *Mysteries* of Salvation to all that desire to be *born again* from above, if they, whether they be *Vicars, Rectors, Arch-Deacons, Deans*, or *Bishops*, should look upon their Office to be as *sacred*, and their Station as *high*, in the Kingdom of God, as the *Baptist's* was; if they should look upon *Love-Addresses* to the Sex, as *unbecoming*, as *foreign*, as *opposite* to their Character, as to the *Baptist's ;* could anyone say, that they took too much upon them, or paid too great a Reverence to the Holiness and Purity of that Priesthood, which they derived from the very Person and Office of Jesus Christ ?

Our blessed Lord improved upon these two Articles of Mortification and Chastity, and sets them before every Preacher of the Gospel in a yet fuller Light. It is needless to show how much he speaks of the Nature and Necessity of a total Self-denial ; but what he says of the Virgin-Life, as to be chosen by those who are able to choose it, for the Kingdom of Heaven's sake, Matt. xix. 12, is more than a Volume of human Eloquence in Praise of it. What Wonder is it, if after this great Numbers both of Men and Women were found in the first Ages of the Church, that chose to know no Love, but that of God in a single Life?

St. *Paul* has done everything to hinder a Minister of Jesus Christ from entering into Marriage, except calling it a sinful State, when he says : ' He that is married, careth for the Things ' of the World, how he may please his Wife ;' and how could he more powerfully press the Virgin Life upon the Clergy, than when he says, ' He that is unmarried, careth for the Things that ' belong to the Lord, how he may please the Lord ' ? Now, who would imagine, that after this Determination of the Matter, by so great an Apostle, there should be any need of Church Authority to restrain anyone in Holy Orders, from seeking after a Wife? Yet it must be supposed, that even in the primitive Church there was some Fear at least, that such a Restraint would soon be needful; because the twenty-seventh *Apostolical Canon* orders, that none amongst the Clergy be permitted to *enter* into Wedlock, except those, who have no higher an Office in the Church, than that of mere *Singers* and *Readers*.

When our Blessed Lord sent the first Preachers of the Gospel into the World, he took them from amongst *married Men, Fishermen, Publicans,* and *Tentmakers ;* and there was no more Reason to look upon a Person as unfit to be an Apostle, because he had a Wife, than because he had a Trade: And therefore, St. *Paul* does not tell *Timothy* and *Titus* to ordain no married Person, for then no Elders could have been ordained in the Church, but he only enjoins them to lay Hands only on such as were in the most perfect Condition of the married Life, who had been the Husbands but of one Wife, and whose whole Family was a *Proof* of their Wisdom and Piety.

Hence it was, that the primitive Church made so great a Difference between a married Clergyman, and a Clergyman that married; the former was allowed for the Reasons above-mentioned, but the latter always censured as a thing *highly reproachful*, as a departing from that Self-denial, Devotion and Consecration to God, in which everyone in Holy Orders ought to live: But when Christianity had breathed a while in the World, there soon became less Occasion to ordain Persons that were married; for the *Apologists* appeal to the Numbers of both Sexes consecrated to God in a Virgin Life, as one great Proof of the Divinity of the Christian Religion. But when such Arguments as these were used, to set forth the Glory of the Gospel, need anyone be told, that it must have been *highly shameful* in those Days, for a Priest of such a Religion, to be *looking out* for a Wife? There is scarce a *Saint*, or *eminent* Father of the first Ages, who did not write set Discourses, and preach entire Homilies in Praise of this Virgin Perfection of Life; but surely this was enough telling the World, that *that Order* of Men who officiated in the Mysteries of this Divine Religion, and were Teachers of its Perfection, were Persons devoted to God in a Holy Virginity of Life: And if it be asked, why amongst all our modern fine Sermons, we have none upon the *Perfection and Advantage* of a holy Virginity; the Reason can be only this, because our Priests and Bishops marry as often, as the Common People of the World. In the Primitive Church, if a *Subdeacon* married a *Widow*, he was degraded from his Office; and the Reason was, because he who tempted a Woman to marry a *second Time*, was looked upon to be a Corrupter of Human Nature: These were the Sentiments of the Church, when it might be truly called the Spouse of Jesus Christ.

I shall conclude this Matter with a Passage taken from the 'Serious Call to a Devout and Holy Life'; it is a Quotation from the great and learned *Eusebius*, who lived at the time of the first *general Council*, when the Faith of our *Nicene Creed* was established: His Words are these, 'There hath been, *saith he*, 'instituted in the Church of Christ, *two ways* or *Manners* of 'Living; the *one* raised above the ordinary State of Nature, 'and *common Ways* of Living, rejects *Wedlock, Possessions*, and '*Worldly Goods*, and being wholly separated and removed from 'the ordinary Conversation of Common Life, is appropriated 'and devoted solely to the Worship and Service of God, through 'an *exceeding Degree* of *heavenly Love:* They who are of this 'Order of People, seem dead to the Life of this World, and 'having their *Bodies* only upon Earth, are in their *Minds* and '*Contemplations* dwelling in Heaven; from whence, like so many 'heavenly Inhabitants, they look down upon Human Life, 'making *Intercessions* and *Oblations* for the whole Race of Man-'kind; and this, not with the Blood of Beasts, or the Fat, or 'Smoke and burning of Bodies, but with the *highest Exercises* 'of true Piety, with cleansed and purified Hearts, and with a '*whole Form* of Life strictly devoted to Virtue: These are their 'Sacrifices, which they are continually offering unto God, and 'implore his Mercy and Favour for themselves and their fellow 'Creatures. Christianity receives *this* as the perfect Manner of 'Life.

'The *other* is of a *lower Form*, and suiting itself more to the 'Condition of Human Nature, admits of *chaste Wedlock*, the 'Care of Children and Families, of Trade and Business, and 'goes through all the Employments of Life, under a Sense of 'Piety and Fear of God: Now, they who have chosen this 'Manner of Life, have their set Times for *Retirement* and '*Spiritual Exercises*, and particular Days are set apart for their 'hearing and learning the Word of God: And *this Order* of 'People are considered as in the *second State* of Piety.'* Here you see the Perfection of the Christian Life plainly set out, and how it was, that Numbers of private Persons, Men and Women, who had no Share in the Ecclesiastical Office, yet, by this Perfection of Life, made themselves *holy and heavenly Intercessors*

---

* *Serious Call, &c.*, page 134.

for the whole Race of Mankind. Now, are we not here obliged to suppose, that in this Father's Days, the Clergy were in *this Number* of People, that were thus heavenly in the *whole Form* of their Life, thus *devoted* to God and the *Edification* of the Church, by embracing the perfect Life of Christianity? If they were not, do they not stand plainly condemned by the Religion of the Gospel, since this Father assures us, that *Christianity held this to be the perfect Manner of Life?* I shall only add thus much here, that till such *a Degree* of heavenly Love, such a *Sense* of the Purity, Holiness and heavenly Nature of the sacred Calling, till such a *Desire* of Perfection is awakened in the Clergy, as shuts out all *carnal* Love and *worldly* Tempers from their Hearts, they cannot be such *Priests* and *Intercessors* with God, such *Patterns* of Purity and Holiness, such *Kindlers* of Divine Love and heavenly Desires amongst Men, as the Nature of their Office both intends and requires of them.

If a *Candidate* for Holy Orders dares not make this *total Donation* of himself to God, to be an Instrument of his good Pleasure only in the Service of the Gospel, if it is not the real State of his Heart, to wish nothing for himself in this World, but the most *perfect* Purification of his Nature, the *highest* Advancement in all Divine Virtues; if he desires anything in and by his Office, but a *Concurrence* with Jesus Christ in the Salvation of Souls; if he has *any Reserves* of Self-seeking, or Self-advancement in the World, any fleshly Passions which he hopes to make consistent with the Duties of his Profession; if he is not separated in *Will* and *Desire* from all that is not God, and the Service of God, he must be said to want the best Proofs of his being called by the Holy Ghost.

Dr. *Trapp's* violent Condemnation of what I said to the young Clergy, and Candidates for Holy Orders, made it necessary for me to enter thus far into this subject. If anything that I have said to these Persons, concerning the Excellency, the Advantage, the Purity, the Necessity of a Virgin Life, in order to their own Perfection, and the full Edification of the Church, gives Offence to any of the married Clergy, it can only be to those, who don't wish to see the Church in a better State, than that, in which they found it; and to such there need no Apology be made.

But to turn to another Matter; I had said, that 'Salvation 'wholly consists in the Incarnation of the Son of God in the 'Soul or Life of Man; that that which was *done* and *born* in the 'Virgin *Mary*, must be done, and born in us: As our Sin and 'Death is *Adam in us*, so our Life and Salvation is *Christ in us*— 'As we are earthly, corrupt Men, by having the Nature and Life

'of *Adam* the first propagated in us, so we must become new and
'heavenly Men, by having the Life and Nature of *Adam* the
'second regenerated in us: But if we are to be like him in
'*Nature*, as we are like to *Adam* in Nature, then there is an
'*absolute Necessity*, that *that* which was *done* and *born* in the
'Virgin *Mary*, be also by the same Power of the Holy Ghost,
'*done* and *born* in us. The Mystery of Christ's Birth must be
'the Mystery of our Birth, we cannot be his Sons but by having
'the Birth of his Life derived into us: The new Paradisaical Man
'must be brought forth in the same Manner in every *individual*
'Person. That which brought forth this *Holy Birth* in the first
'*Adam* at his Creation, and in the second *Adam* in the Virgin
'*Mary, that alone* can bring it forth in any one of their Offspring.'*
Now, there seems to be nothing in all this, but what is easily to
be apprehended, and fully believed by everyone, that knows
anything of the Christian Life; but the Doctor makes *two
Replies* to this Doctrine: The first is this, 'Were such Words,'
says he, 'ever heard amongst Christians before?'† Yes, good
Sir, they have often been heard before, by such as *have Ears to
hear;* for they are the very Words which Christ, and his Apostles
have as plainly spoken, as they have spoken any one Article of
the Apostles' Creed: They are only as different from the Words
of Christ and his Apostles, as the *English* Words of the Bible,
are different from those *Greek* Words, in which the Gospels were
written. When the Scripture saith, that Christ must be *formed*
in us, doth it not say, that Christ must be born, or become
incarnate to us? When it saith, Christ was born of the Virgin
Mary, does it not say, that Christ was incarnate of the Virgin
Mary? Or is there anything to fright a learned Divine, who
has for forty Years been told, that Christ must be *formed in us,
revealed in us*, that he must *put on* Christ, to be told, that Christ
must *become incarnate* in us, that he must bring forth himself in
us, and have *such a Birth* in our Soul and Life, as he had in the
Virgin *Mary?* For wherever he is born, must he not be born
in the *same Manner?* Was it not the *Word* of God, that by the
Power of the Holy Ghost became Man in the Virgin *Mary?*
And is there any Thing in this Birth on this wise that is inconsistent with the Birth of our new Man in Christ Jesus? Must
not the *same Word* of God, by the *same Operation* of the Holy
Spirit, bring forth that in us, which is the new Man in Christ
Jesus, or Christ formed in us? When our Lord saith, that we
must be born again from Above, of the Word of God, is it more
or less than saying, that *that* Word which was born in the Virgin

---

* *Serious Answer*, page 41. † *Reply*, page 47.

Mary, and was incarnate in her, must be *born* and *incarnate* in us? When the Apostle saith, that we must be born again of the *incorruptible Seed of the Word*, is not this expressly saying, that *that must be done and born in us*, which was done and born in the Virgin *Mary?* If he says, that Christ must be formed in us, does he not say, that he must have such a Birth and Form in us, as he had in the Virgin *Mary;* only with this Difference, that in the Birth of Christ, the *Fulness* of the Deity, or eternal Word became Man, and dwelt personally in him; but in us, only a *Spark*, or *Seed* of the *Word* is formed and raised up into a new, heavenly Man. Is there now any Thing in all this, but the most comfortable, substantial Part of our Redemption set out in the plainest Words of Scripture? Reject this Doctrine, say that you cannot, you will not, you desire not to have Christ *thus born and formed* in you, and then you reject all that Salvation, which the *Word* of God, born of a Virgin, hath brought into the World. For the Scripture is absolutely plain in telling us, that lost Man cannot be made alive again unto God, but solely by this way, by being born again of the *Word* and holy *Spirit* of God; if therefore we desire not, but reject *such a Birth*, as was brought forth by the *Word* and holy *Spirit* of God in the Virgin *Mary;* do we not plainly reject *that Birth* in which all our Salvation consists? And therefore to say that *that* must be *done* and *born* in us, which was done and born in the Virgin *Mary*, is as plain, as scriptural, as to say, that we must be born again of the *Word* and holy *Spirit* of God. And on this Ground it is, that *Christ in us*, is said to be our *Hope of Glory.—And that the Kingdom of Heaven is within us*—that we must be in Christ new Creatures—that we must put on Christ—that he must be formed in us, revealed, manifested in us—that he is our Life—that he brings us forth out of himself, as the Vine does its Branches— that unless we eat his Flesh and drink his Blood we have no Life in us. These, and many other the like Sayings of Scripture, which are the strongest, deepest Expressions of the Nature and Manner of our Salvation, are all grounded on this Truth, *viz.*, That the Mystery of Christ's Birth is the Mystery of our New Birth; that *that* must be done and born in us, which was done and born in the Virgin *Mary*, namely a New Man brought forth in the Likeness of Christ, by a Birth from the Word, and holy Spirit of God.

But the Doctor has a *second Reply* to this Matter, which stands thus expressed. *Whether*, says he, *you consider the* Divinity, *or the* Sense *of this, could* George Fox *himself have outdone it?* p. 48. This Reply, considered in itself, might have its Place amongst those *algebraic Quantities*, that are some Degrees less than nothing; but with Regard to the Doctor's Purpose it has *something* in it, for it is an Appeal to *that* which is very powerful, which has suppressed many a good Truth; it is an Appeal to *vulgar Prejudice,* and shows that the Doctor is not without his Expectations from that Quarter. And thus it is, that the *Catholic Artist* in his Country, plays a *Martin Luther,* when he wants to reproach *that,* which he knows not how to confute. What Degree of Sense, or Divinity *George Fox* was possessed of, I cannot pretend to say, having never read any of his Writings; but if he has said any good and Divine Truths, I should be as well pleased in seeing them in his Books, as in any of the *Fathers* of the primitive Church. For as the Gospel requires me to be as glad to see, *Piety, Equity,* strict *Sobriety,* and extensive *Charity* in a *Jew,* or a *Gentile,* as in a Christian; as it obliges me to look with Pleasure upon their Virtues, and be thankful to God, that such Persons have *so much* of true and sound Christianity in them; so it cannot be an unchristian Spirit, to be as glad to see Truths in one Party of Christians, as in another; and to look with Pleasure upon any good Doctrines, that are held by any Sect of Christian People, and be thankful to God, that they have so much of the genuine, saving Truths of the Gospel amongst them. For if we have no Anger or Complaint against those that are divided from us, but what proceeds from a Christian Fear, that what they *hold* and *practise* will not be so *beneficial* to them, as our Religion will be to us, must we not have the utmost *Readiness* and *Willingness* to find, own, and rejoice in those good Doctrines and Practices which they still retain and profess? If a poor *Pilgrim,* under a Necessity of travelling a dangerous and difficult Road by himself, had through his *own Perverseness* lost the Use of a *Leg,* and the Sight of *one Eye,* could we be said to have any *charitable Concern* for his Perverseness and Misfortune, unless we were glad to see, that he had one good Leg, and one good Eye still left, and unless we hoped and desired they would bring him at last to his Journey's End. Now let every Part of the Church which takes itself to be *sound* and *good,* and is only angry at every other Part, because they have *lessened the Means* of their own Salvation; let her but have thus much Charity in her Anger, and then she will be glad to see, in every perverse Division, something like the one *good Leg,* and the one *good Eye* of the Pilgrim, and which she will hope and wish may do them the same Good.

Selfishness and *Partiality* are very inhuman and base Qualities, even in the Things of this World, but in the Doctrines of Religion they are of a baser Nature. Now this is the *greatest Evil* that the Division of the Church has brought forth; it raises in every Communion a *selfish, partial* Orthodoxy, which consists in courageously defending all that it has, and condemning all that it has not. And thus every Champion is trained up in Defence of their *own Truth*, their *own Learning*, and their *own Church*, and he has the most Merit, the most Honour, who likes every Thing, defends every Thing amongst themselves, and leaves nothing uncensured in those that are of a different Communion. Now how can Truth, and Goodness, and Union, and Religion be more *struck at*, than by such Defenders of it? If you ask why the great Bishop of *Meaux* wrote so many learned Books against all Parts of the *Reformation*, it is because he was born in *France*, and bred up in the Bosom of *Mother Church*. Had he been born in *England*, had *Oxford*, or *Cambridge* been his *Alma Mater*, he might have rivalled our great Bishop *Stillingfleet*, and would have wrote as many learned *Folios* against the Church of *Rome* as he has done. And yet I will venture to say, that if each Church could produce but one Man apiece that had the *Piety* of an Apostle, and the *impartial Love* of the first Christians, in the first Church at *Jerusalem*, that a Protestant and a *Papist* of this Stamp, would not want *half a Sheet* of Paper to hold their Articles of Union, nor be half an Hour before they were of one Religion. If therefore it should be said, that Churches are divided, estranged, and made unfriendly to one another, by a *Learning*, a *Logic*, a *History*, a *Criticism* in the Hands of *Partiality*, it would be saying that, which every particular Church too much proves to be true. Ask why even the best amongst the Catholics are very shy of owning the *Validity* of the Orders of our Church, it is because they are afraid of removing any *Odium* from the Reformation? Ask why no Protestants anywhere touch upon the Benefit or Necessity of Celibacy in those, who are separated from worldly Business to preach the Gospel, 'tis because that would be seeming to *lessen* the Romish Error of not suffering Marriage in her Clergy? Ask why even the most worthy and pious amongst the Clergy of the established Church, are afraid to assert the Sufficiency of the Divine Light, the Necessity of seeking only to the Guidance and Inspiration of the holy Spirit, 'tis because the *Quakers*, who have broken off from the Church, have made this Doctrine their Corner Stone.

If we loved Truth as such; if we sought it for its own Sake; if we loved our Neighbour as ourselves; if we desired nothing by our Religion but to be acceptable to God; if we equally desired the Salvation of all Men; if we were afraid of Error only because of its hurtful Nature to us, and our Fellow-Churches, then nothing of this Spirit could have any Place in us.

There is therefore a *Catholic* Spirit, a *Communion of Saints* in the Love of God and all Goodness, which no one can learn from that which is called *Orthodoxy* in particular Churches, but is only to be had by a *total Dying* to all worldly Views, by a *pure Love* of God, and by such an *Unction* from above, as delivers the Mind from all *Selfishness*, and makes it love Truth and Goodness with an Equality of Affection in every Man, whether he be *Christian, Jew,* or *Gentile.* He that would obtain this Divine and Catholic Spirit in this disordered, divided State of Things, and live in a divided Part of the Church without partaking of its Division, must have these *three Truths* deeply fixed in his Mind: *First*, that universal Love, which gives the whole Strength of the Heart to God, and make us love every Man as we love ourselves, is the Noblest, the most Divine, the God-like State of the Soul, and is the utmost Perfection to which the most perfect Religion can raise us; and that no Religion does any Man any Good, but so far as it brings this Perfection of Love into him. This Truth will show us, that *true Orthodoxy* can nowhere be found, but in a pure disinterested Love of God, and our Neighbour. *Secondly*, That in the *present divided* State of the Church, Truth itself is torn and *divided asunder;* and that therefore he can be the only *true Catholic*, who has more of Truth, and less of Error, than is hedged in by any divided Part. This Truth will enable us to live in a divided Part, *unhurt* by its Division, and keep us in a true Liberty and Fitness to be edified and assisted by all the Good that we hear or see in any other Part of the Church. And thus uniting in Heart and Spirit with all that is *holy* and *good* in all Churches, we enter into the true *Communion of Saints*, and become real Members of the holy Catholic Church, though we are confined to the outward Worship of only one particular Part of it. It is thus, that the Angels, as ministering Spirits, assist, join, unite, and co-operate with every Thing that is holy and good, in every Division of Mankind. *Thirdly*, he must always have in Mind this great Truth, that it is the Glory of the Divine Justice to have no Respect of *Parties* or *Persons*, but to stand equally disposed to that which is right and wrong, as well in the *Jew* as in the *Gentile.* He therefore that would like as God likes, and condemn as God condemns, must have neither the *Eyes* of the *Papist* nor the *Protestant;* he must like no Truth the less because *Ignatius Loyola*, or *John Bunyan* were very zealous for it; nor have the less Aversion to any Error, because Dr. *Trapp* or *George Fox* had brought it forth. Now if this universal Love, and impartial Justice, is the Spirit which will judge the World at the last Day, how can this Spirit be *too soon*, or *too much* in us; Or what can do us more Hurt than that which is an *Hindrance* of it? When I was a young Scholar of the *University*, I heard a great *Religionist* say in my *Father's* House, that if he could believe the late *King of France* to be in Heaven, he could not tell how to wish to go thither himself. This was exceeding shocking to all that heard it: Yet *something* of this kind of Temper must be supposed to be more or less in those, who have, as a Point of *Orthodoxy*, worked themselves up into a hearty *Contempt* and *Hatred* of those that are divided from them. He that has been all his Life long used to look with great Abhorrence upon those whom he has called *superstitious Bigots, dreaming Visionaries, false Saints, canting Enthusiasts, &c.*, must naturally expect they will be treated by God as they have been by him; and if he had the *Keys* of the Kingdom of Heaven, such People would find it hard to get a Place in it. But it stands us greatly in Hand to get rid of this Temper *before* we die; for if nothing but *universal Love* can enter into the Kingdom of God, what can be more necessary for us, than to be full of this Love before we die?

We often hear of People of great *Zeal* and *Orthodoxy*, declaring on their *Death-beds* their strict Attachment to the Church of *England*, and making *solemn Protestations* against all other Churches; but how much better would it be, if such a Person was to say, ' In this *divided State* of Christendom, I must con-
' form to some outwardly divided Part of it, and therefore I have
' chosen to live and die in outward Communion with the Church
' of *England;* fully believing, that if I worship God in *Spirit*
' *and in Truth* in this divided Part of the Church, I shall be as
' acceptable to him, as if I had been a faithful Member of the
' *one whole* Church, before it was broken into separate Parts.'
But ' as I am now going out of this disordered Division into a
' more *universal State* of Things, as I am now falling into the
' Hands of the great Creator and Lover of *all Souls;* as I am
' going to the God of *all Churches*, to a Kingdom of *universal*
' *Love*, which must have its Inhabitants from *all People, Nations,*
' *and Languages* of the Earth; so in this Spirit of universal
' Love, I desire to perform my last Act of Communion in this
' divided Church, uniting and joining in Heart and Spirit with
' all that is *Christian, Holy, Good,* and *Acceptable* to God in all
' other Churches; praying, from the Bottom of my Soul, that
' every Church may have *its Saints;* that God's Kingdom may
' come, his Will be done in every Division of Christians and
' Men, and that *every Thing that hath Breath may praise the*
' *Lord.*'

Need anyone now be told of the superior Excellency of this

Spirit, or its Fitness to be admitted into the Kingdom of universal Love? Need we any Proof that nothing but this *Catholic* Spirit will carry us *unhurt* by Schism, through all those Divisions which the Devil, the World, and fleshly Wisdom have brought into the Church? *Again,* We have often seen learned Protestants very zealous in pulling to Pieces the Lives of the Saints of the *Romish* Church, and casting all the Reproach and Ridicule they can, upon their wondrous Spirit; though the Lives of the Saints of the primitive Church, written by the Fathers of the greatest Name and Authority, are as fit for to be exposed in the same Manner. Now, whence does this proceed? Why, from a *secret Touch* of that Spirit which could not bear to have the late King of *France* in Heaven; it proceeds from a *partial, selfish* Orthodoxy, which cannot bear to hear, or own, that the Spirit and Blessing of God are so visible in a Church from which it is divided, and against which it has so much preached: But if a Person be of this Spirit, what does it signify *where* he has his outward Church? If a *Romish Priest* in the North of *England* could not bear the Splendour of a Life *so devoted* to God, so fruitful in all the Works of Piety and Goodness, as was that of the late Lady *Elizabeth Hastings,* if he should want to sully the Brightness of her Christian Graces, and prove her to have been no *Saint,* lest it should appear, that the Spirit of God was not *confined* to the *Romish* Church, would not such a Zeal show a worse Spirit, than that of *Superstition,* a greater Depravity of Heart, than the saying now and then an *Ave Mary.*

The more we believe, or know of the Corruptions and Hindrances of true Piety in the Church of *Rome,* the more we should rejoice to hear, that in every Age so many eminent Spirits, great Saints, have appeared in it, whom we should thankfully behold as so many *great Lights* hung out by God, to show the true Way to Heaven, as so many joyful Proofs that Christ is still present in that Church, as well as in other Churches, and that the Gates of Hell have not prevailed, or quite overcome it? Who that has the least Spark of Heaven in his Soul, can help thinking and rejoicing in this manner at the Appearance of a St. *Bernard,* a *Teresa,* a *Francis* de *Sales, &c.,* in that Church? Who can help praising God, that her *invented Devotions, superstitious* Use of Images, *Invocation* of Saints, *&c.,* have not so suppressed any of the Graces and Virtues of an Evangelical Perfection of Life, but that amongst *Cardinals, Jesuits, Priests, Friars, Monks* and *Nuns,* Numbers have been found, who seemed to live for no other End, but to give Glory to God and Edification to Men, and whose Writings have every Thing in them, that can guide the Soul out of the Corruption of this Life into the highest Union with God. And he who through a *partial Orthodoxy* is diverted from feeding in these green Pastures of Life, whose just Abhorrence of Jesuitical *Craft* and *worldly Policy* keeps him from knowing and reading the Works of an *Alvares du Pas*, a *Rodrigues*, a *Du Pont*, a *Guilloree*, a *Pere Surin*, and such like Jesuits, has a greater Loss than he can easily imagine: And if any Clergyman can read the Life of *Bartholomeus a Martyribis*, a *Spanish* Archbishop, who sat with great Influence at the very Council of *Trent*, without being edified by it, and desiring to read it again, I know not why he should like the Lives of the best of the Apostolical Fathers: And if any Protestant Bishop should read the *Stimulus Pastorum* wrote by this Popish Prelate, he must be forced to confess it to be a Book, that would have done Honour to the best Archbishop, that the Reformation has to boast of. O my God, how shall I unlock this Mystery of Things; in the Land of *Darkness*, overrun with *Superstition*, where Divine Worship seems to be all *Show* and *Ceremony*, there both amongst Priests and People, thou hast those, who are fired with the pure Love of thee, who renounce everything for thee, who are devoted wholly and solely to thee, who think of nothing, write of nothing, desire nothing but the Honour, and Praise, and Adoration that is due to thee, and who call all the World to the *Maxims* of the Gospel, the Holiness and Perfection of the Life of Christ. But in the Regions where *Light* is sprung up, whence *Superstition* is *fled*, where all that is outward in Religion seems to be *pruned, dressed*, and put in its *true Order;* there a cleansed *Shell*, a *whited Sepulchre*, seems too generally to cover a *dead* Christianity.

The Error of all Errors, and that which makes the blackest Charge against the *Romish* Church, is *Persecution*, a religious Sword drawn against the Liberty and Freedom of serving God according to our best Light, that is, against our *worshipping the Father in Spirit and in Truth:* This is the great *Whore*, the *Beast*, the *Dragon*, the *Antichrist*. Now, though this is the frightful Monster of that Church, yet, even here, who, except it be the Church of *England*, can throw the first Stone at her? Where must we look for a Church that has so renounced this *persecuting Beast*, as they have renounced the Use of *Incense*, the *Sprinklings* of Holy Water, or the *extreme Unction* of dying Persons? What Part of the Reformation abroad has not practised and defended Persecution? What Sect of Dissenters at home have not, in their Day of Power, dreadfully condemned *Toleration?*

When it shall please God to dispose the Hearts of all Princes in the Christian World entirely to destroy this *Antichristian*

Beast, and leave all their Subjects in that religious Freedom which they have from God; then the *Light* of the Gospel, the *Benefit* of its Faith, the *Power* of its Ministers, the *Usefulness* of its Rites, the *Benediction* of its Sacraments will have proper *Time* and *Place* to show themselves; and that Religion which has the most of a *Divine Power* in it, whose *Offices* and *Services* do most good to the Heart, whose Ministers are most of all *devoted* to God, and have the *most Proof* of the Power and Presence of Christ with them, will become, as it ought to be, the most universal; and by this Destruction of the *Beast*, nothing but the Errors, Delusions, Corruptions and Fictions of every Religion, will be left in a helpless State. All that I have said on this Matter, has been occasioned by the Doctor's Appeal to *vulgar Prejudice;* and all that I have said is only to intimate this much, that the *greatest Evil* which the Division of the Church brings forth, is a *Sectarian, selfish* Spirit, that with the Orthodoxy of the *Old Jews*, would have God to be *only their* God, and themselves only, *his chosen* People. If therefore we would be true Christians of the *Catholic Church*, we must put off this *Selfishness* and *Partiality* of the carnal *Jew*, we must enter into a Catholic Affection for all Men, love the Spirit of the Gospel wherever we see it; not work ourselves up into an Abhorrence of a *George Fox*, or an *Ignatius Loyola;* but be equally glad of the Light of the Gospel wherever it shines, or from what Quarter it comes; and give the same Thanks and Praise to God for an *eminent* Example of Piety, wherever it appears, either in *Papist* or *Protestant*.

To return. Dr. *Trapp* supposing the World running into a Charity that would ruin Wife and Family, asks his charitable *Half-thinker* thus: 'Did you never hear that *Charity begins* at 'home? Did you never read that of St. *Paul*, If any provide 'not for his own, and especially those of his own House, he hath 'denied the Faith, and is worse than an Infidel.' The Doctor's Proverb I meddled not with, but the Text of St. *Paul* I rescued from his gross Misapplication of it. That Text has no more Relation to an *excessive Charity*, the Sin the Doctor was opposing, than to an *excessive Fasting*. The Apostle neither thought of this Sin in this Place, nor in any other Part of his Writings; nor does he ever give the smallest *Hint* of the Danger of falling into it. The one Thing in Question was this, whether poor Widows, who had near Relations, that could supply their Wants, should be maintained by the Charity of the Church: The Apostle determines the Matter thus; that if such Persons, who were thus able, did not *thus provide* for, that is, *supply* the Wants of their poor Kindred, they were so far from having the *Faith* of Christians, that they wanted a *Goodness* that was to be found amongst Infidels : This is the whole of the Apostle's Doctrine in this Text. He speaks of *providing* for those of our own House or Family, in *no other* Sense, than as it signifies our *Charity* to them, when they fall into Distress : But the Doctor, either led away with, or *trusting* to the *Sound* of the *English* Word, *provide*, grafts all these following Errors upon this plain Text. When it is said, a Person has *provided* well for his Family, everyone supposes that he has *laid up well in Store*, or got an *Estate* to be divided amongst them for their future Subsistence, from *this Use* of the *English* Word, *provide*, in the Text, the Doctor would have it believed, that the Apostle teaches every Head of a Family to be carefully and continually laying up in Store, and making some fixed Provision for the future Maintenance of his Kindred. But the Apostle is as *infinitely distant* from this Thought or Direction, as from teaching them to get their *Cellars* well filled with strong Liquors: When he here says, *provide*, he says only this, Shut not your Eyes to the Wants of your poor Kindred, but provide them *with what* they have need of, and don't let them fall to the Charge of the Church. The Doctor's *second Error* is this; that, according to this Text, a Christian ought not to *hinder* himself from thus laying up in Store for his Family, or leave them to live by their Labour and Industry, through an *Extent* of Charity to his poor Neighbours. Though the Apostle has not one single Syllable about this Matter; and is as far from saying any Thing like it, as from saying, that a Christian, when he *makes a Feast*, should only invite his rich Kindred and Acquaintance. The one has as much of the Apostle and the Gospel for it, as the other. The Doctor's *third* Error is this; that, according to this Text, he, who by a *daily, continual* Charity, has incapacitated himself to lay up in Store, a fixed Provision for the future Maintenance of his Family, is condemned by the Apostle, as *denying the Faith*, and *worse than an Infidel:* Though the Apostle speaks no more here of *such a Person*, or any more condemns him, than he speaks in the *Praise* of *Ananias* and *Saphira*, who kept back Part of the Price of the Land they had sold.

The Person here condemned, is not he, who through a *continual* Charity, or loving his Neighbour as himself, is *hindered* from laying up in Store; not he, who, through a Christian Love of relieving the distressed Members of Christ, is content with helping his own Family to Food and Raiment, such a Person is not thought of, much less condemned by the Apostle; but it is that Christian, who being *able*, is yet unwilling to *support* his near Relations, that are fallen into Poverty, but through a sordid

Selfishness, leaves them to be maintained by the Church; this is the only Christian the Apostle here condemns, as having put off the Piety of the Gospel, and wanting even the Virtue of good-natured Infidels.

I said further, Had the Apostle known a *Parent* in his Days, who, through his *great Charity* for others, had reduced his own Family to a want of Relief, he would have been so far from rebuking him as an *half-thinking Fool,* or exposing him to others, as guilty of *Madness,* that he would have told them, that such a one had consecrated himself and Family to the Church, as the proper Objects of their Care. To which the Doctor gives this Answer, *This he affirms, and this I deny; and as he produces no other Proof, so I give no other Answer,* p. 69. Had the Doctor said, as his Affirmation has no Sense in it, so there need be no Sense in my Denial of it, he had answered as well as he has here done. What I affirmed, did not consist, as the Doctor's *Denial* doth, only of *two Words;* but was, a large Proposition that carried its *own Proof* along with it, because I said nothing of the Apostle, but what the Nature of the Thing obliged me to say of every sober Christian. For if any Christian could be supposed to want Compassion and Affection for such a Sufferer, from his *own Charity* to others, he must be such a one as the Apostle affirms to *have denied the Faith, and to be worse than an Infidel.* But to show the Doctor what I said, has its Proof from the common Voice of Christianity in the Apostle's Days, may sufficiently appear from the following Passage of St. *Clement,* who was a Companion and Fellow-labourer of the Apostle, and Bishop of no less a Church than that of *Rome.* 'We have 'known *many* amongst us, (says St. *Clement*) who have delivered 'themselves into Bonds and Slavery, that they might restore 'others to their Liberty; *many* who have hired out themselves 'Servants unto others, that by their Wages they might feed and 'sustain them that wanted.'*

Will the Doctor now say, that this is no Proof of that which I affirmed of the Apostle, that he would have had a Love for those who were become Sufferers by their own Charity to others? Does not this Apostolical Bishop make it his Boast, and the Glory of Christianity; not that they had some, but *many* such amongst them?

It was not only in the first Church at *Jerusalem,* that the Christians had all things common. For St. *Barnabas* writing to some converted *Jews,* teaches them to have all Things common, to call nothing their own in this World, because they were called

---

* 1 Epist. ad Cor.

to the common Enjoyment of the Things of Eternity. 'Com-
'municabis in omnibus rebus proximo tuo ; nihil dices quicquam
'tibi proprium, si enim Communicatis in Vicem, in bonis, incor-
'ruptibilibus, quanto magis in corruptibilibus.'*

An Age after this, *Justin Martyr* thus glories of the Power of
the Gospel-Faith ; 'We,' says he, 'who before were become
'Christians, loved our Wealth and Possessions above all Things,
'now give up all Property in them, that they may be in common
'for all that want them. Qui Pecuniarum & Possessionum
'Fructus ac Proventus præ rebus omnibus adamabamus, nunc
'etiam quæ habemus in Commune conferimus, & cum indi-
'gentibus quibuscunque communicamus.'† What a *lean,
heathenish* Figure must the Doctor's Proverb of *Charity beginning at home*, have made in the Days of St. *Barnabas, Clement*,
or *Justin Martyr ?* Or who durst then have made such a Use of
the Text of St. *Paul*, as the Doctor has done, or coupled it with
such a Proverb ? Were any of these first Saints to judge of this
Matter, the Doctor might, for aught I know, have a worse
Reprimand from them for so doing, than if he had only coupled
Cardinals with Pluralists.

In order to show the Doctor that he was very unseasonably
preaching against the *Sin* and *Folly* of an excessive Charity,
when yet every Part of the Church wanted to be shown how
they were fallen from the Gospel-degree of it, I set before him
an *imaginary* Bishop of *Winchester*, yet drawn according to the
Model of the Holy Bishops of the first Ages. I supposed this
Bishop so born again from Above, so filled with the Spirit of Jesus
Christ, that he looked upon all the *Revenues* of his *See*, with no
other Eyes, than as our Saviour looked at that *Bag* that was
carried along with him by his Disciples, as *so much* for his own
Necessities, and the Necessities of others. I supposed that in
this Spirit, he so expended his yearly Income, that he chose to
bring up his Children as much *Strangers* to all worldly Figure,
and in as *low a State* of Labour as that to which our Lord and
his Apostles had been used. I supposed, that by a Piety of Life
and Conversation, equal to this exalted Charity, he had *instilled*
such a heavenly Spirit into his Wife and Children, as made
them *highly thankful* for their Condition, and full of Praise to
God for the Blessing of such a *Relation*. Dr. *Trapp*, though an
ancient Divine, seems to start back with Fright, at the *Sight* of
this Apostolical Bishop, and supposes, that if such a Monster of
a Man was now to get into a Bishopric, he must needs make his
Children extraordinary wicked, fill them with Abhorrence of his

---

* Epist. Bar. N. 10.   † 2 Apol.

Memory, and spread Infidelity in the World, by making Christianity a Jest to Infidels, p. 71.

'I say,' says the Doctor, *very clearly and plainly*, that ' such a 'Bishop must be a Madman,' p. 70. Now, if the Doctor will prove from the Scriptures this Bishop to be a *Madman*, it must be for the following Reasons ; *First*, because he had so *mean a Spirit*, as to suffer the Son of a *Bishop* to work under a *Carpenter*, as the Redeemer of Mankind had done. *Secondly*, because he taught himself and his Family to believe *that* which St. *Paul* believed, that 'having Food and Raiment, we ought to be there-'with content.' *Thirdly*, because he came up to the very Letter of the great Commandment, of 'loving our Neighbour as our-'selves.' *Fourthly*, because he seemed to imitate the Spirit of the first Christians at *Jerusalem*, who accounted 'nothing to be 'their own that they possessed.' *Fifthly*, because he had turned himself and Family from all the Vanity of this World, the *Lust* of the *Flesh*, the *Lust* of the *Eyes*, and the *Pride of Life*. *Sixthly*, because he seemed to have *this* of the Apostle *fixed* in his mind. ' He that saith, he abideth in Christ, ought so to walk, 'as he walked.' *Seventhly*, because his Life was fashioned according to this Doctrine of the Holy Jesus, ' Learn of me, for 'I am meek, and lowly of Heart : I am among you, as he that 'serveth : Whosoever will be great among you, let him be your ' Minister ; even as the Son of Man came not to be ministered 'unto, but to minister.' For it may be said with the greatest Certainty, that if the Doctor will have *any Proof* from the Scripture of the Madness of this Bishop, it must be as absurd as the Reasons here alleged.

Come we now to consider this Bishop according to the Spirit, Practice and Laws of the Church in all Ages. Anyone versed ever so little in the History of the Church, must see at the first Sight, that this *supposed* Bishop is a *true Copy* of the first Apostolical Fathers. And if this Bishop was to be accounted a Madman, because of the *Manner* of his Life, we must come down several Ages after *Constantine*, to the *Mitre* and *Triple Crown*, before we could find a Bishop in *his Senses*. The *Clements*, the *Polycarps*, the *Ignatius's*, the *Irenæus's*, the *Cyprians*, the *Gregorys*, the *Basils*, the *Ambroses*, the *Chrysostoms*, the *Hillarys*, the *Augustins*, and a Number that have long graced our *Calendars*, as Saints, must take their Place among *Bedlamites ;* for they were all of them to a *Tittle*, the very Man I have supposed at *Winchester*. They considered every *Penny* that was brought in by the Gospel, as a *Provision for the Poor*, and themselves as only entitled to their common Share out of it. They durst no more raise any of their Relations into a *Splendour* of Life, or give them any *Figure* from the Revenues of the Church, than commit *Sacrilege*. They gloried as much in their own *strict* Poverty and Want of worldly Figure, as in their having *totally* renounced Idols.

But we have much more than primitive Example for our Bishop of *Winchester;* the Doctrine and Laws of the Church have unanimously from Age to Age, to the very Council of *Trent*, required every Bishop to be of the same Spirit of which we have supposed him. The Church, both by the Doctrine of Fathers, and the Canons of Councils constantly maintains ; *First*, that the Clergy are not *Proprietors*, but barely *Stewards* of the Benefices they enjoy ; having them for no other End, but for their own necessary, frugal Subsistence, and the Relief of the Poor. *Secondly*, that a Clergyman using his Benefice for his *own Indulgence*, or the enriching his *own Family*, is guilty of Sacrilege, and is a Robber and Murderer of the Poor. *Thirdly*, that if a Clergyman has a reasonable Subsistence of his own, and is not in the *State* of the Poor, that then, let his Benefice be what it will, he has no Right to use any Part of it for himself, nor for *his Kindred*, unless they be fit to be considered amongst those Poor that are to be relieved by the Church. *Fourthly*, that every Bishop and Clergyman is to live in an humble, lowly, frugal, outward State of Life, seeking for no Honour or Dignity in the World, but that which arises from the Distinction and Lustre of his Virtues. *Fifthly*, that a *Beneficed* Clergyman using the Goods of the Church for his own Indulgence, or raising Fortunes for his Children, or their expensive Education, is sacrilegious, and a Robber of the Poor. *Sixthly*, that every Clergyman is to die out of the Church as *poor* as he entered into it. *Seventhly*, that a Clergyman *dying*, cannot *leave* or *bequeath* any Thing to his Children or Friends, but *barely that* which he had *independently* of the Church.*

---

* (*a*) Nihil ecclesia nisi Fidem possidet—Possessio ecclesia est Egenorum sumptus, *Amb. Ep.* 31. (*b*) Si Pauperum Compauperes sumus, & *nostra* sunt, & *illorum*. Si autem privatim quæ nobis sufficiunt, possidemus, non sunt illa *nostrum*, sed Pauperum *Procurationem* gerimus, non Proprietatem nobis Usurpatione damnabili vindicamus, *Augus. Ep.* 50, *ad Bonif.* (*c*) Quoniam quicquid habent Clerici, Pauperum est—Qui bonis Parentum & opibus sustentari possent, si quod Pauperum est, accipiunt *Sacrilegium profectò* committunt, & per Abusionem Talium, Judicium sibi manducant, & bibunt, *Hieron. Ep. ad Damas.* (*d*) Episcopus vilem *Suppellectilem*, & *Mensam*, ac *Victum Pauperem* habeat, & Dignitatis sua Authoritatem Fide & Vitæ meritis quærat, *Concil. Carthag.* 4. (*e*) Memento quod *Pauperem Vitam* Sacerdos gerere debet, & ideo si superbiam habet, si magno gaudet Beneficio, præter Victum & Vestitum *quod superest*, Pauperibus dare non differat, quia omnia *Pauperum* sunt. *Aug. Serm.* 37. *ad Fratres.* (*f*) Hujus tu e vicino sectare Vestigia, & cæterorum, qui Virtutum illius similies sunt, quos

May it not therefore well be wondered what could provoke Dr. *Trapp* to censure our Bishop as a Madman, whose *whole Form* of Life, and *Use* of his Bishopric, is not only after the Model of the first and greatest Saints that ever were Bishops, but also such as the whole Church from the Beginning, both in Council and out of Council, from Age to Age, hath *absolutely* required of every beneficed Clergyman, who would not be condemned by her, as sacrilegious, and a Robber of the Poor? They who would see the whole of this Matter set in a clear Light, may read an excellent Treatise of the learned *Dupin*, wrote near the End of his Life, where this Truth is by him asserted and incontestably proved, *viz.*, That whatever Changes have been made in the *Nature* and *Tenure* of the Goods and Revenues of the Church, or however they have been variously divided amongst Ecclesiastics, yet this has remained *always unchangeable and undeniable,* That a Clergyman was no Proprietor of his Benefice; that he could only take so much of it to his own Use, as was *necessary* to his Subsistence, and then the Remainder, be it what it would, belonged to the Poor. This, says he, is strictly maintained by the Canons of Councils,

---

Sacerdotium & *humiliores* facit, & *pauperes.* *Hieron. Ep.* 4. *ad Rustic.* (*g*) Præcipimus ut in potestate sua Episcopus Ecclesiæ Res habeat—ex iis autem quibus indiget, (si tamen indiget) ad suas necessitates percipiat. *Canon. Apost.* 40.—eas veluti Deo contemplante dispenset ; nec ei liceat ex iis aliquid contingere, aut Parentibus propriis (quæ Dei sunt) condonare. Quod si Pauperes sunt, tanquam Pauperibus subministret, ne eorum occasione Ecclesiæ Res depredantur, *Can. Apost.* 39. (*h*) Manifesta sint quæ pertinere videntur ad Ecclesiam cum Notitia Presbiterorum & Diaconorum, ut si contigerit Episcopo migrare de Seculo, nec *Res Ecclesiæ* depereant, nec quæ *propria* probantur Episcopi, sub Occasione Rerum Ecclesiæ pervadantur : justum enim est ut sua Episcopus quibus voluerit, derelinquat, & quæ Ecclesiæ sunt, eidem conservantur Ecclesia. *Concil. Antioch,* chap. 24. (*i*) Quicunque Clerici, qui nihil habentes ordinantur, & *tempore Episcopatus,* vel *Clericatus sui,* agros, vel quæcunque predia nomine suo comparant, tanquam Rerum dominicarum *Invasionis Crimine* teneantur obnoxii, nisi admoniti, Ecclesia eadem ipsa contulerint. (*N.B.*) Si autem ipsis proprie aliquid *liberalitate* alicujus, vel *Successione* Cognationis obvenerit, faciant inde quod ipsorum Proposito congruit. (*k*) Sacerdotes ipsis quoque Filiis suis, quibus paterna debetur Hæreditas, nihil debent derelinquere, nisi quod sibi a Parentibus derelictum est : *Ergo* qui *ditior est* Sacerdos, quam venit ad Sacerdotium, quicquid plus habuerit, *non filiis debet dare,* sed Pauperibus, & Sanctis fratribus, ut reddat ea quæ Domini sunt, Domino suo. *Hieron. in Ezech.,* chap. 46. (*l*) Timeant Clerici, timeant Ministri Ecclesiâ, qui *in terris Sanctorum* quas possident, tam iniqua gerunt, ut Stipendiis quæ sufficere debeant, minime contenti, Superflua quibus egeni sustendandi forent, impiè, sacrilege, sibi retineant, & in usus suæ Superbiæ atque Luxuriæ victum Pauperum consumere non vereantur, duplici profectò Iniquitate peccantes, quod & *aliena* diripiunt, and *Sacris* in suis vinitatibus abutuntur. St. *Bernard, Serm.* 23, *in Cantic.* Vide, lege, & relege. S. *Prosperum* de Vitâ contemplativâ.

both before and after the Division of ecclesiastical Revenues. '*C'est ce que portent precisement les Canons, & avant, & apres la Partition des Biens ecclesiastiques.*'*

But now if this be the Case, if this be an incontestable Doctrine, supported by every Authority that can be brought for any one Doctrine of the Gospel, have we not here an *utter Condemnation* of Pluralities? Is it not an Affront to the Gospel, to the plainest Maxims of Right and Wrong, the whole Authority of the Church, to offer one single Word in Defence of them? Logical, scholastic Distinctions and Definitions of the Nature of *Parishes* and *Residence,* can signify no more here, where the *whole Nature* of the Thing is to be avoided, than the *same Art* of Words, when used by *Jesuitical Casuists,* can justify the Violation of moral Duties. And if Dr. *Trapp* was only to look at this one Doctrine, he would have no reason to think it so sad a Thing, to see *Pluralists* coupled with *Cardinals.* 'See,' says the learned Dupin, 'Rules which appear hard to many of 'the beneficed Clergy, but yet,' says he, 'they are true, con- 'formable to natural Equity, the Laws, Custom, and Tradition 'of the Church, and the Practice of the most holy Bishops; and 'woe be to those that observe them not.' Malheur a Ceux qui ne les suivent pas.† And therefore he concludes thus, 'There 'may be many amongst the beneficed Clergy who err in this 'Matter, through an Ignorance of that which is required of 'them; therefore what I have said ought to be taken in good 'Part, as proceeding from Charity, and a sincere Love of Truth.'

I come now to that which the Doctor says of Enthusiasm and Enthusiasts. Speaking to the younger Clergy of the Means of attaining Divine Knowledge, I had these Words, 'The Book of 'all Books is your own Heart, in which are written the deepest 'Lessons of Divine Instruction; learn therefore to be deeply 'attentive to the *Presence* of God in your Hearts, who is always 'speaking, always instructing, always illuminating that Heart 'that is attentive to him.' Now can any Thing be conceived more scriptural, or more inoffensive than all this? Is there anything to suppress or hurt the Piety and Devotion of that Heart, which would place its all in God? Which desires to be moved and guided in all Things by his holy Spirit. How can we worship God in Spirit and in Truth, how can we pray unto him, turn to him, how can we raise any Act of Faith or Hope in him, Resignation unto him, or Dependence upon him, but by thus thinking of him? Take any Thing from God that I have

---

* Traite Philos. & Theolog. sur l'amour de Dieu, page 415.
† *Ibid.,* page 442.

here ascribed to him, suppose him not to be thus inwardly speaking, instructing, illuminating, and then tell me why my Heart should seek him, or how it can find him? A Page or two after this, to show the deep and intimate Union the Soul has with its Creator, I said, 'God is an *all-speaking, all-working, all-illuminating* Essence, possessing the Depth, and bringing forth 'the Life of every Creature according to its Nature. Our Life is '*out of* this Divine Essence, and is itself a *creaturely Similitude* 'of it; and when we turn from *all Impediments*, this Divine 'Essence becomes as certainly the true Light of our Minds *here*, 'as it will be *hereafter*.' Now is there any Thing here to shock, or fright, or delude the Piety of any Christian? Is it a monstrous Thing to be told, that the Light of Heaven reaches us in this World, that we have this Communion with God; that when we turn rightly to him, he dwells in us and we in him; that we receive his Operation and Light upon us in this Life, as we shall do in the next, only with this Difference, that now what is done *in Faith* will then be in *open Vision?* How can we believe anything that is said of the Light and holy Spirit of God in the Scripture, without believing this? If this be not true, how can we believe that Jesus Christ is the Light which lighteth every Man that cometh into the World? Or is there any Thing here more said of God, than when the Apostle saith, that 'in him we live, move, and have our Being'? If the *Word* of God was not an *ever-speaking* Word, how could Nature and Creature *speak forth* any Thing? If God was *ever* silent could any Thing else speak? Again, if Nature is *constantly* at Work; if there could be no Nature but because there is a *continual stirring* and *working* which cannot cease; is not this a sufficient Proof that there is an *all-working Deity?* And if we are told, that, in the Kingdom of Heaven, there shall be no Sun, nor Moon, but the *Lamb shall be the Light thereof*, is not this telling us, that God himself is the uncreated Light, always in the same State of Infinity, and therefore an *all-illuminating* Being? And if there is *always* Light *in Nature*, a Light that cannot be extinguished, must it not come from the *all-illuminating* Being? Yet Dr. *Trapp* says, all this 'is Enthusiasm, if ever there was any 'in the World'; that they are the 'Words of Falsehood and 'Frenzy.'* If the Doctor had been clear in this Matter, it had been very easy for him to have shown his Reader wherein this Enthusiasm and Frenzy lay; and it was also very necessary for him to have here said something very plain and clear concerning the Nature and Ground of Enthusiasm: For if his Reader,

---

* Page 86.

without any clear and distinct Notion of Enthusiasm, is taught to cry out against a Doctrine, which only teaches, that God is always speaking, instructing, and illuminating that Heart that is in great *Purity* turned to him; if he is taught boldly and blindly to condemn *this* as Enthusiasm and Frenzy, how shall such a one be able to defend himself, when he is told by others, that two Thirds of the New Testament is Enthusiasm? As where it is said, 'I am the Light and Life of the World: The King-'dom of Heaven is within you: Except ye eat my Flesh and 'drink my Blood, ye have no Life in you: If any Man love me, 'my Father will love him, and we will come unto him, and make 'our Abode with him: No Man can come unto me, except the 'Father draweth him: The natural Man cannot receive and know 'the Things of the Spirit of God: He breathed on them, and 'said, Receive ye the Holy Ghost: The Spirit of Truth, he 'dwelleth in you, and shall be with you: No Man can say, *Abba* 'Father, or that Jesus is the Lord, but by the Holy Ghost: As 'many as are led by the Spirit of God, they are the Sons of 'God.' *In our Liturgy* we pray that God would prevent us in *all our* Doings, and further us with his *continual Help:* That we may obey the godly Motions of the Spirit in Righteousness and true Holiness: That by his holy Inspiration we may *think* those Things that be good, and by his merciful Guiding may perform the same: That his holy Spirit may in all Things direct and rule our Hearts, *&c*. Now what must the unlearned Reader, or the learned Doctor himself do with these and the like Places of Scripture, and Prayers of the Church, if it be *Enthusiasm*, *False-hood*, and *Frenzy* to say, that God is intimately present in the Depth of our Souls, always speaking, instructing, enlightening that Heart, which is truly turned to him? Or how can these Scriptures and Prayers have the *least Truth* or *Reasonableness* in them, but upon this Supposition, that God is an all-speaking, all-knowing, all-illuminating Being, out of whom we are born, and in whom we live, and move, and have our Being. But I shall here speak a Word or two of the true Ground, and Nature of Enthusiasm.

In *Will, Imagination,* and *Desire*, consists the Life, or fiery Driving of every intelligent Creature. And as every intelligent Creature is its own *Self-mover*, so every intelligent Creature has Power of *kindling* and *inflaming* its Will, Imagination and Desire as it pleases, with Shadows, Fictions, or Realities; with Things carnal or spiritual, temporal or eternal. And *this kindling* of the Will, Imagination, and Desire, when raised into a *ruling Degree* of Life, is properly that which is to be understood by Enthusiasm: And therefore Enthusiasm is, and must be of as *many Kinds* as those Objects are, which can kindle and inflame the Wills, Imaginations, and Desires of Men. And to appropriate Enthusiasm to Religion, is the same Ignorance of Nature, as to appropriate *Love* to Religion ; for Enthusiasm, a kindled, inflamed Spirit of Life, is as *common*, as *universal*, as *essential* to human Nature, as *Love* is ; it goes into *every Kind* of Life as Love does, and has only such a Variety of Degrees in Mankind as Love hath. And here we may see the Reason, why no People are so angry at Religious Enthusiasts, as those that are the *deepest* in some Enthusiasm of *another Kind*.

He whose Fire is kindled from the Divinity of *Tully's* Rhetoric, who travels over high Mountains to salute the dear Ground that *Marcus Tullius Cicero* walked upon ; whose *noble Soul* would be ready to break out of his Body, if he could see a *Desk*, a *Rostrum* from whence *Cicero* had poured forth his Thunder of Words, may well be unable to bear the *Dulness* of those, who go on *Pilgrimages* only to visit the *Sepulchre*, whence the *Redeemer of the World* rose from the dead, or who grow devout at the Sight of a *Crucifix*, because the Son of God hung as a Sacrifice thereon.

He whose heated Brain is all over painted with the *ancient Hieroglyphics ;* who knows *how* and *why* they were *this* and *that*, better than he can find out the Customs and Usages of his *own Parish ;* who can clear up every Thing that is *doubtful* in Antiquity, and yet be forced to live in Doubt about that which passes in his own Neighbourhood ; who has found out the Sentiments of the *first Philosophers* with such Certainty, as he cannot find out the *real Opinion* of any of his Contemporaries ; he that has gone thus high into the *Clouds*, and dug thus deep into the *Dark* for these *glorious Discoveries*, may well despise those Christians, as *brain-sick Visionaries*, who are sometimes finding a *moral* and *spiritual* Sense in the bare Letter and History of Scripture-Facts.

It matters not what our Wills and Imaginations are employed about ; wherever they *fall* and love to *dwell*, there they *kindle* a Fire, and that becomes the *Flame of Life*, to which every Thing else appears as *dead*, and *insipid*, and *unworthy* of Regard. Hence it is that even the poor Species of *Fops* and *Beaux* have a right to be placed among Enthusiasts, though capable of no other Flame than that, which is kindled by *Tailors* and *Peruke-Makers*. All *refined Speculatists*, as such, are great Enthusiasts ; for being devoted to the Exercise of their Imaginations, they are so *heated* into a Love of their *own Ideas*, that they seek no other *summum bonum*. The *Grammarian*, the *Critic*, the *Poet*, the *Connoisseur*, the *Antiquary*, the *Philosopher*, the *Politician*, are all violent Enthusiasts, though their Heat is only a Flame from *Straw*, and therefore they all agree in *appropriating* Enthusiasm to Religion. All *ambitious, proud, self-conceited* Persons, especially if they are *Scholars*, are violent Enthusiasts, and their Enthusiasm is an *inflamed* Self-Love, Self-Esteem, and Self-Seeking. This Fire is so kindled in them, that every Thing is nauseous and disgustful to them, that does not offer Incense to that Idol, which their Imagination has set up in themselves. All *Atheists* are dark Enthusiasts; their Fire is kindled by a Will and Imagination turned from God into a gloomy Depth of *Nothingness*, and therefore their Enthusiasm is a *dull burning* Fire, that goes in and out, through *Hopes* and *Fears* of they know not what that is to come. All *professed Infidels* are remarkable Enthusiasts, they have kindled a *bold* Fire from a *few faint Ideas*, and therefore they are all Zeal, and Courage, and Industry to be *constantly blowing* it up. A *Tyndal* and a *Collins* are as inflamed with the Notions of Infidelity, as a St. *Bennet* and St. *Francis* with the Doctrines of the Gospel.

Enthusiasts therefore we all are, as certainly as we are Men; and consequently, Enthusiasm is not a Thing blamable in *itself*, but is the common Condition of human Life in *all its States;* and every Man that lives either *well* or *ill*, is that which he is, from that *prevailing Fire* of Life, or *driving* of our Wills and Desires, which is properly called Enthusiasm. You need not then go to a *Cloister*, the *Cell* of a *Monk*, or to a *Field Preacher*, to see Enthusiasts, they are everywhere, at *Balls* and *Masquerades*, at *Court* and the *Exchange:* They sit in all *Coffeehouses*, and *cant* in all Assemblies. The *Beau* and the *Coquette* have no *Magic*, but where they meet Enthusiasts. The *Mercer*, the *Tailor*, the *Bookseller* have all their Wealth from them; the Works of a *Bayle*, a *Shaftesbury*, and *Cicero*, would lose *four Fifths* of their astonishing Beauties, had they not *keen Enthusiasts* for their Readers.

That which concerns us therefore, is only to see with what Materials our *prevailing Fire* of Life is kindled, and in what *Species* of Enthusiasts it truly places us. For either the *Flesh* or the *Spirit;* either the Wisdom from *above*, or the Wisdom of *this World*, will have *its Fire* in us; and we must have a *Life* that governs us either according to the Sensuality of the *Beast*, the Subtlety of the *Serpent*, or the Holiness of the *Angel*. Enthusiasm is not blamable in Religion, when it is true Religion that kindles it. We are created with *Wills* and *Desires* for no other End, but to love, adore, desire, serve, and co-operate with God; and therefore the more we are inflamed in *this Motion* of our Wills and Desires, the more we have of a God-like, Divine Nature, and Perfection in us. Religious Enthusiasm is not blamable, when it is a *strong Persuasion*, a *firm Belief* of a continual Operation, Impression, and Influence from above, when it is a total Resignation to, and Dependence upon the *immediate Inspiration*, and *Guidance* of the holy Spirit in the whole Course of our Lives; this is as sober, and rational a Belief, as to believe that we *always* live, and move, and have our Being in God. Both Nature and Scripture demonstrate this to be the true Spirit of a Religious Man. Nature tells everyone, that we can only be heavenly by a Spirit derived from Heaven, as plainly as it tells us, that we can only be earthly, by having the Spirit of this World breathing in us. The Gospel teaches no Truth so *constantly*, so *universally* as this, that every good Thought and good Desire is the Work of the holy Spirit. And therefore both Nature and Scripture demonstrate, that the *one only* Way to Piety, Virtue and Holiness, is to *prepare*, *expect*, and *resign* ourselves up wholly to the Influence and Guidance of the holy Spirit, in every Thing that we think, or say, or do. The moment anyone departs from *this Faith*, or loses *this Direction* of his Will and Desire, so far, and so long he goes out of the one only Element of all Holiness of Life. There is nothing that so sanctifies the Heart of Man, that keeps us in such habitual Love, Prayer, and Delight in God; nothing that so kills all the Roots of Evil in our Nature, that so renews and perfects all our Virtues, that fills us with so much Love, Goodness, and good Wishes to every Creature, as *this Faith*, That God is always *present* in us with his *Light* and *Holy Spirit*. When the Heart has once learnt thus to find God, and knows how to live everywhere, and in all Things in this immediate Intercourse with him, seeing him, loving him, and adoring him in every Thing, trusting in him, depending upon him for his continual Light and holy Spirit; when it knows that *this Faith* is infallible; that by thus believing, it thus possesses all that it believes of God; then it begins to have the Nature of God in it, and can do nothing but flow forth in Love, Benevolence, and good Will towards every Creature; it can have no Wish towards any Man, but that he might thus know, and love, and find God in himself, as the true Beginning of Heaven, and the heavenly Life in the Soul.

On the other hand, no Error so hurtful to the Soul, so destructive of all the Ends of the Gospel, as to be led from this Faith and *entire Dependence* upon the holy Spirit of God, or to place our Recovery in any Thing else, but in the Operation of the Light and holy Spirit of God upon the Soul. It is withdrawing Men not only from the earliest, the most natural, the most fruitful, but the only possible Source of all Light and Life. For every Man, as such, has an open Gate to God in his Soul, he is always in that Temple, where he can worship God in Spirit and Truth: Every Christian, as such, has the *first Fruits* of the Spirit, a *Seed* of Life, which is his *Call* and *Qualification* to be always in a State of inward Prayer, Faith, and holy Intercourse with God. All the *Ordinances* of the Gospel, the daily *sacramental* Service of the Church, is to keep up, and exercise, and strengthen *this Faith;* to raise us to such an habitual Faith and Dependence upon the Light and holy Spirit of God, that by thus seeking and finding God in the *Institutions* of the Church, we may be habituated to seek him and find him; to live in his Light, and walk by his Spirit in all the Actions of our ordinary Life. This is the Enthusiasm in which every good Christian ought to endeavour to live and die.

I come now to an *Enthusiast*, which the Doctor has accidentally met with, from whom, it seems, ' I have borrowed some ' of my strange Notions, and would put them off as my own,' p. 119. The Doctor has this Intelligence from his *trusty Assistant*, who says, 'what else can be expected from those, Who ' read Jacob Behmen, Dr. Pordage, and Mrs. Lead, with almost ' the same Veneration and implicit Faith, that other People read ' the Scripture,' *ibid.* Two of these Writers I know very little of, yet as much as I desire to know; but *J. Behmen*, called the *Teutonic Theosopher*, I have read much, and much esteem: But the Design of putting off some of his strange Notions, as *my own*, is as well grounded, as if the Doctor had charged me with a Design of picking his Pocket.

The illustrious Sir *Isaac Newton*, when he wrote his *Principia*, and published to the World his great Doctrine of *Attraction*, and those *Laws of Nature* by which the *Planets* began, and continue to move in their Orbits, could have told the World, that the *true and infallible* Ground of what he there advanced, was to be found in the *Teutonic Theosopher*, in his *three first Properties of Eternal Nature;* he could have told them, that he had been a *diligent Reader* of that wonderful Author, that he had made large Extracts out of him, and could have referred to him for the Ground of what he had observed of the Number *Seven*. Now why did not this great Man do thus? Must we suppose that he was *loth* to have it thought, that he had been *helped* by any Thing that he had read? No: It is an unworthy Thought. But Sir *Isaac* well knew, that *Prejudice* and *Partiality* had such Power over many People's Judgments, that Doctrines, though ever so deeply founded in, and proved by all the Appearances of Nature, would be suspected by some as dangerous, and condemned by others, even as *false* and *Wicked*, had he made any *References* to an Author that was *only called* an Enthusiast.

Dr. *Trapp* may take himself for an *eminent* Example and Proof of this. He has here shown with what *Speed* Matters may be determined by Prejudice. For here a *Stranger*, a *Layman*, not so much as known to the Doctor by Name, who, for aught he can tell, may be some *small Retailer* of Infidelity, or *Snuff-Candle* in the Playhouse, who has gained upon the Doctor by no other *Marks* of Ability and Judgment, but his *Compliments* to him, and his *Scurrility* upon me; from the *Authority* of this Informer, the Doctor immediately puts *J. B.* into his *List* of Enthusiasts. Is not this a Proof of what Sir *Isaac Newton* must have met with from some great Scholars, and to what a *speedy Confutation* he must have exposed himself, and the plainest Appearances of Nature, had he ever referred to the *Teutonic Theosopher?* Now am I here to suppose, that this Censure of the Doctor's relating to *J. B.* is a *Rashness* that has here *first* seized upon him by *Chance*, that he never *before* in his Life allowed himself to treat any *Man*, or any *Book* in this manner; that if he took the Judgment of another, it was of somebody that he knew; if he condemned an Author, he always *stayed* till he had read *something* of him, at least an *Index*, or a *Title Page* or two of his Works? Or am I to suppose, that this has been the Doctor's Method *upwards of thirty-seven Years;* calling one Man an Enthusiast, another a Fanatic, this a monstrous, that the *most pernicious Book of the Age*, as rashly, as hastily, regarding no more of Right or Wrong in that which he affirms of these Matters, than he has here done with regard to *J. B.?* But I hope the Doctor is singular in this Spirit; for if it could be supposed, that it was common amongst learned Men, to get their Knowledge of ancient and modern, foreign and domestic Enthusiasts, as hastily and slightly as the Doctor here doth; must it not be very dangerous for the *Unlearned* to take any Opinions of this kind from them? Must it not be said, that *one Grain* of Equity, good Sense, and real Knowledge, is more to be desired, than an *hundred Weight* of such Learning?

When I considered the *fallen* Soul, as a *Fire-Spirit*, deprived of its *proper Light*, and therefore become of a Diabolical Nature, I could have directed to *J. B.* for the deep and infallible Ground of it; but what need was there for that, when I could make the plainest Principles of *Nature*, the plainest Doctrines of *Scripture*, everything that was said of the *Fall*, of *Heaven*, of *Hell*, and the like, to be undeniable Proofs of it? What I said in the *Second Proposition* of the Discourse upon *Regeneration*, concerning the Holy Triunity of God *in Man*, stands not in *that Form* of

Expression anywhere that I know of; but for the true Ground and Certainty of it, I could have referred to the *Teutonic Theosopher*, to many ancient and modern Writers of the greatest Name, and to a *venerable Record* of Antiquity, ascribed even to St. *Peter* himself; where he asserts, even upon the *same Ground* as I have done, that because we were created in the Image and Likeness of God, therefore the triune Life arises in us, as it does in God, and we have *in us*, the *Father, Son*, and *Holy Spirit*.*

But what Occasion was there for these References, when I had so much better Proof, when I could show, that all which the Scriptures say of the whole *Nature* and *Manner* of our Redemption, of the whole *Nature* and *Form* of Baptism, all that they say of the *Necessity* of the *Word*, and Holy Spirit of God having again a *Birth in us*, are absolute, decisive Proofs of it?† I knew also very well, that the most essential, fundamental, and joyful Doctrines of the Gospel would be *questioned*, or received with *Difficulty*, had I referred to a *poor Shoemaker* for any Proof of them: And it may well be believed, that the Doctor would have been amongst the *first* and *loudest* of those, who would have cried out at my Folly and Presumption in directing to an Author, whom all the World knew to be an *illiterate Enthusiast;* and yet, if all the World knows it as the Doctor knows it, all the World may be said to know nothing about it.

Dr. *Trapp* has a Fling at my Want of Taste for his *Virgil's*, *Horace's*, and *Terence's:* I own, when I was about *Eighteen*, I was as fond of these Books as the Doctor can well be *now*, and should then have been glad to have translated the *Sublime Milton*, if I had found myself able; but this *Ardour* soon went off, and I think it as good a Proof of the *Sublime*, to desire the Death of all that is Diabolical and *Serpentine* in my own Nature, as to be *charmed* with those *Speeches* which the *Devils* make in *Milton*. Had the Doctor been more conversant in the Writings of a Set of Men called *Mystical Divines*, than he appears to have been, he had been better able to have charged me with *humble Plagiary* than he is at present, and might have done more Service to what he calls the *Noble Science of Theology*, than by all that *Light* which he has got from his *Poets*, which he acknowledges to have *somewhat of Wantonness in them*, p. 38. Of these Mystical Divines, I thank God, I have been a

---

* Rationalis Homo, factus ad Imaginem, & Similitudinem Dei, fert in se Symbolicè Factoris sui *Imitationem*. Habet enim in se Patrem, Filium & Spiritum. Mens quidem *locum* Patris obtinet, Filii vero, qui ex mente gignitur, Sermo *Interior*, at quæ auditur Vox *Prolationis*, Spiritum repræsentat, &c., *Coteler, S. S. Patr.*, pages 595—1719.

† *See* Regeneration, pages 22-33.

diligent Reader, through all Ages of the Church, from the Apostolical *Dionisius the Areopagite*, down to the great *Fenelon* Archbishop of *Cambray*, the illuminated *Guion*, and M. *Bertot*. Had the Doctor read St. *Cassian*, a Recorder of the Lives, Spirit and Doctrine of the Holy Fathers of the *Desarts*, as often as he had read the *Story* of *Æneas* and *Dido*, he had been less astonished at many Things in my Writings: But I apprehend the Doctor to be as great a Stranger to the Writers of this kind, with which every Age of the Church has been blessed, and to know no more of the Divine *Rusbrochius, Thaulerus, Suso, Harphius, Johannes de Cruce, &c.*, than he does of *J. B.* For had he known any Thing of them, he had known that I am as chargeable with the Sentiments of all of them, as with those of *J. Behmen*. For though I never wrote upon any Subject till I could call it *my own*, till I was so fully possessed of the Truth of it, that I could sufficiently prove it in my *own Way*, without borrowed Arguments; yet, Doctrines of Religion I have none, but what the Scriptures and the *first-rate* Saints of the Church are my Vouchers for.

Writers, like those I have mentioned, there have been in all Ages of the Church, but as they served not the Ends of *Popular Learning*, as they helped no People to *Figure* and *Preferment* in the World, and were useless to *scholastic, controversial* Writers, so they dropped out of public Use, and were only known, or rather *unknown*, under the Name of *Mystical Writers*, till at last some People have hardly heard of that very Name. Though if a Man was to be told what is meant by a Mystical Divine, he must be told of something as *heavenly*, as *great*, as *desirable*, as if he was told, what is meant by a real, *regenerate, living* Member of the *Mystical* Body of Christ. For they were thus called, for no other Reason, than as *Moses* and the Prophets, and the Saints of the Old Testament may be called the *Spiritual Israel*, or the true *Mystical Jews*. These Writers began their Office of Teaching, as *John* the *Baptist* did, after they had passed through every kind of Mortification and Self-denial, every kind of Trial and Purification, both inward and outward. They were deeply learned in all the Mysteries of the Kingdom of God, not through the Use of *Lexicons*, or meditating upon *Critics*, but because they had *passed from Death unto Life*. They highly reverence and excellently direct the true Use of everything that is *outward* in Religion, but like the Psalmist's *King's Daughter*, they are *all glorious within:* They are truly Sons of *Thunder*, and Sons of *Consolation;* they break open the *whited Sepulchres;* they awaken the Heart, and show it its *Filth* and *Rottenness* of Death, but they leave it not, till the Kingdom of

Heaven is raised up within it. If a Man have no Desire but to be of the Spirit of the Gospel, to obtain all that Renovation of Life and Spirit, which alone can make him to be in Christ a new Creature, it is a great Unhappiness to him to be unacquainted with these Writers, or to pass a Day without reading something of what they have written. For though the Scriptures are an inexhaustible Source of Spiritual Instruction, leading the Heart to the deepest Knowledge of all the Mysteries of the inward, new Life in God, with the greatest Plainness and Openness of Expression, yet a *worldly Spirit*, the *Schools*, *Criticism*, and *Controversy* have so dried, and deadened every Thing into an outward Letter and figurative Expression, that much of their Use is lost, till these Holy Writers, who interpret them by the same Spirit which wrote them, guide us to the true Use and Understanding of them; for in these Writers, the Spirit of God speaks a second Time, and every Thing that can awaken, convert, instruct and inflame the Heart with the Love of God, and all Holiness and Purity of Life, is to be found in the most irresistible Degree of Conviction. You will perhaps say, Do I then call all the World to these Spiritual Books? No, by no means. But I call all those, whom our Saviour called to himself in these Words: 'Come unto me all ye that labour, and 'are heavy laden, and I will refresh you.'

But to return to the Doctor's Enthusiast.

Jacob Behmen, in his natural Capacity and outward Condition of Life, was as *mean* and illiterate as anyone that our Lord called to be an Apostle, but as a *chosen Servant* of God, he may be placed amongst those who had received the highest Measures of Light, Wisdom and Knowledge *from Above*. He was no more a *human Writer*, spoke no more from *Opinion*, *Conjecture*, or *Reason*, in what he published to the World, than St. *John* did, when he put his *Revelation* into Writing. He has no Right to be placed amongst the inspired *Penmen* of the New Testament, he was no Messenger from God of any Thing *new* in Religion, but the Mystery of all that was *old* and *true* both in Religion and Nature was *opened* in him. This is the *Particularity* of his Character, by which he stands fully distinguished from all the Prophets, Apostles, and extraordinary Messengers of God. They were sent with occasional Messages, or to make such Alterations in the Economy of Religion as pleased God; but this Man came on no particular Errand, he had nothing to alter, or add, either in the *Form*, or Doctrine of Religion; he had no new Truths of Religion to propose to the World, but all that lay in Religion and Nature, as a Mystery unsearchable, was in its deepest Ground opened in this Instrument of God. And all his Works are nothing else but a deep Manifestation of the Grounds and Reasons of that which is *done*, that which is *doing*, and is to *be done*, both in the Kingdom of Nature, and the Kingdom of Grace, from the Beginning to the End of Time. His Works therefore, though immediately from God, have not at all the *Nature* of the Holy Scriptures, they are not offered to the World, as *necessary* to be received, or as a Rule of Faith and Manners? and therefore no one has any Right to complain, either of the *Depths* of his Matter, or the *Peculiarity* of his Style: They are just as they should be, for those that are fit for them; and he that likes them not, or finds himself unqualified for them, has no Obligation to read them.

The whole System of Christianity has generally been looked upon as a Mystery of Salvation, solely founded in the Divine Pleasure; and to be such a Scheme of Redemption, as is wholly to be resolved into the Contrivance of the *Will* and Wisdom of God; and therefore Men can think as differently of it, can fall into as many Opinions about it, as they can of the Will and Wisdom of God. Hence has arisen all the *speculative Opposition* to the Gospel: It is because Reason, human Speculation, and Conjecture, is always imagining it can form a Religion more worthy of the Wisdom and Designs of the Supreme Being than the Christian is; and would be thought to oppose the Gospel only for the Honour of God, and the Divine Attributes. This is the great, prevailing *Idolatry* of the present *Heathen World*, or *that* Part of Mankind who are Infidels, or Deists. Hence also is risen another Species of Idolatry, even amongst Christians of *all Denominations;* who, though receiving and professing the Religion of the Gospel, yet worship God not in Spirit and in Truth, but either in the Deadness of an outward Form, or in a *Pharisaical*, carnal Trust and Confidence in their own Opinions and Doctrines. This Body of People, whether they be *Clergy* or *Laity*, are but *nominal Christians ;* because they have little more than the *Name* of every Mystery of the Gospel: *Historical Christians*, because satisfied with the *History* of Gospel-Salvation: *Literal Christians*, because looking only to, and contending only for, the *Letter* of the Institutions and Mysteries of Jesus Christ. For the Letter, for the federal Rite, and the *figurative* Expression of Regeneration, they are all Zeal and Industry; but the *Reality* of it, the *true Life* of the New Birth, they *oppose* and *reject* as heartily as the *Deist* does the outward Form and Letter. Now this *twofold Idolatry* of the present Heathen and Christian World has its full Discovery and Confutation in the Mystery opened in *J. B.* which, when understood, leaves no Room for any Man either to disbelieve the Gospel, or to content himself with the *Letter* of it. For, in the Revelation made to this Man, the first *Beginning* of all Things is opened, the *whole State*, the *Rise*, the *Workings*, and the *Progress* of all Nature is revealed, and every Doctrine, Mystery, and Precept of the Gospel is found, not to have sprung from any *arbitrary Appointment*, but to have its *eternal, unalterable* Ground and Reason in Nature ; and God appears to save us by the Methods of the Gospel, because there was *no other* possible Way to save us in all the Possibility of Nature. And therefore the *idolatrous* Confidence of the Deist in his *own Reason*, and of the nominal Christian in the *outward Letter* of their Religion, have equally their full Confutation.

To those who confine Idolatry to the Worship of *such Idols* as the old Heathens and *Jews* worshipped, it may seem a Paradox, to talk of the Idolatry of the *present World*, either amongst *Deists* or *Christians*. But if we consider Things more than Words, we shall find, that Idolatry is nowhere, but where the Heart has *set up* Something in the *Place* of God ; and therefore is everywhere, and in every Thing, where the Heart places that *Repose, Trust,* and *Delight*, which should be placed in God alone. For God is only owned, and confessed to be *our God*, by these Acknowledgments and Dispositions of our Hearts towards Him. It is an infallible Truth, That all Sin has its Beginning and Continuance in and from Idolatry : This alone debauched the former and the later Ages of the World, and is the one Source of all the Corruption of Manners, from the Beginning to the End of Time. You don't make a *Golden Calf*, as the *Jews* did, to worship it ; but if *Mammon* is your God, if your Life is devoted to Pride, Ambition, and Sensuality, your Idolatry is not so *sensible*, but it is as *real* as theirs, who danced about a Golden Calf. You fancy that *Venus* is not your *Goddess*, because you are not worshipping a *figured Image* of her, in a Temple called by her Name ; but if you look at the *Odes*, the *Hymns*, the *Songs*, which you love, which Lust has inspired, then you may know that *Venus* is the Goddess of your Heart. It is thus with every Object, and in every Course of Life, that which possesses and governs our Heart, has usurped the *Right* and *Place* of God in it, and has that *Worship, Trust,* and *Devotion* of the Heart, which is due to God alone : And therefore the Idolatry of the present World, is only of a different Kind from that of the ancient, it is less seen, and less confessed, but not less real, than when carved Images, and figured Idols were adored.

Deism, or the Religion of *human Reason*, set up in Opposition to the Gospel, is *direct Idolatry*, and has every Grossness and

Vanity of Image Worship. For to put our Trust in our own Reason, to be content with its Light, to resign ourselves up to it, and depend upon it as our Guide, is a Mistake that has every Grossness and Vanity of the Adoration of an Idol. Now this Kind of Idolatry has overrun all the last Ages of the World; it is the last Effort of human Vanity; it is the utmost that Idolatry can do, both to hide and propagate itself, and is the Devil under the Appearance of an Angel *of Light*. The Gospel has no Enemy but this Idolatry, and it is as visible in the Church, as out of it: Hence it is, that the State of the Church is so sadly described in the *Revelation* of St. *John*, for so many Ages, as a spiritual Whoredom. When the old *Jews* left off the *Idols* of the Heathens, they fell into an Idolatry of another kind, which was this, they *idolized* the Rites and Ceremonies of their own true Religion; they placed that *Confidence* in the outward Letter, and expected that Good from their outward Rites, which they should have placed, sought, expected from God alone. This is the Idolatry of the rational Deist, and the nominal Christian. But when the Mystery of all Nature and Grace, which by the Mercy of God has opened itself in the Writings of *J. B.* shall find its Children, every Idolatry, both within and without the Church, will be ashamed to show itself.

But it may be asked by some, what warrant I have for all that I have said of *J. B.* or how I can prove to the World, that his Writings are the Work of the holy Spirit? It is answered, I neither intend, nor desire to prove this to the World. And if anyone will dispute or deny every Thing that I have said of him, he will meet with no Opposition from me. I have given notice of a *Pearl*, if anyone takes it to be otherwise, or has neither Skill or Value for Pearls, he is at Liberty to trample it under his Feet. Nothing passes with the World for Proof of a divinely inspired Writer, but Miracles; if People can see no other Proof but this, it is not in my Power to give them better Eyes. I suppose the Gospel, and all the Writings of the New Testament, have *internal Characters* of their Divine Original, for those that can see them; but if they had been left to those internal Characters, I am apt to think, that the Sons of *Cicero*, the Disciples of a *Bayle*, or those who stand the highest in such like Literature, would, of all Men, be the most indisposed and unwilling to see and own them.

Had we no Miracles for Proof of the Inspiration of the Scriptures, they would be still what they are, the *true Word*, and *Wisdom* of God, and there would be the same Benefit in believing and receiving them as such. But to *whom* could they be proved to come from the Spirit of God? Not to a *Ciceronian*, because it is the Character, the *Genius*, the *Greatness* of *Cicero*, to *dissemble* and *personate;* and as an *Orator*, a *Statesman*, and a *Philosopher*, to affirm or deny as he pleases, without any Regard to his own Sentiments. And therefore to the Sons of *Cicero* nothing can be proved, because they depart from his Character, if they discover their own Sentiments, and don't either, as *Philosophers, Orators*, or *Statesmen*, affirm and deny as they please, or as suits the Character which they choose to act under.

Again; It cannot be proved to a Disciple of *Bayle;* because, though he was a Man, 'whose Strength and Clearness of 'Reasoning can be equalled only by the Gaiety, Easiness, and 'Delicacy of his Wit; who, pervading human Nature with a 'Glance, struck into the Province of *Paradox*, ——— and had 'not enough of real Greatness, to overcome the last Foible of 'superior Geniuses, the Temptation of Honour, which the '*Academic Exercise of Wit* is supposed to bring to its Pro-'fessors.'*

And therefore to a true Disciple of *Bayle*, nothing that is just, sober, or true, can be sufficiently proved; because it is his Genius, his Honour, his Ambition, to maintain the *Paradox*.

The next Question is, *How* this can be proved, *viz.*, That the Scriptures have internal Characters of their Divinity. Now this can only be, by an honest Simplicity, and Love of Truth, by Humility and Prayer, and Conversion of the Heart to God in the reading of them. These are the only Dispositions that could possibly bring any Man into a Sense and Belief of their Divine Original: and therefore, all those critical Scholars, and rationally wise Men, whose Enquiries are animated with a Love of Glory and personal Distinction, and who looked into those Writings for such Ends, and with such Views as they read other Books, would be of all Men the most unable to see, and unwilling to own the very *best Truths* of the Holy Scriptures; because it is the very Nature and End of the Scriptures, to discover the Vanity and Falseness of that Light and Knowledge, which is got from human Reasoning, and to subdue that Self-sufficiency, which is so inseparable from certain *Kinds* and *Degrees* of human Learning.

FINIS.

---

* *Divine Legation of Moses*, B. I., page 33.

www.ingramcontent.com/pod-product-compliance
Lightning Source LLC
Chambersburg PA
CBHW070741160426
43192CB00009B/1528